Hardeman County Tennessee

COUNTY COURT MINUTES

Volume 2

1827–1829

WPA RECORDS

Heritage Books
2024

HERITAGE BOOKS

AN IMPRINT OF HERITAGE BOOKS, INC.

Books, CDs, and more—Worldwide

For our listing of thousands of titles see our website
at
www.HeritageBooks.com

A Facsimile Reprint
Published 2024 by
HERITAGE BOOKS, INC.
Publishing Division
5810 Ruatan Street
Berwyn Heights, MD 20740

June 1936

International Standard Book Number
Paperbound: 978-0-7884-9073-6

WPA RECORDS

The WPA Records are, for the most part, carbon copies of the original that was typed on onion skin paper during the Depression. Since these records were typed on poor machines by people who did not type well either and read by persons not always sure of the older handwritten material, the results are often less that perfect.

We have made every attempt to make as good a copy as can be made from these older papers. Sometimes there are water stains and burned edges around the paper.. This is the results of a fire at the home of one of the workers, Mrs. Penelope Allen, who was over most of the project.

The WPA Records are now very scattered between the State Archives, various Public and Private Libraries and other collections. Some day, there is a hope that all of these can be collected and stored in one place. In spite of their many mistakes and problems, these are still the most complete collection of Tennessee records found anywhere.

TENNESSEE

RECORDS OF HARDEMAN COUNTY

MINUTES COUNTY COURT - VOL. II

1827-1829

HISTORICAL RECORDS PROJECT

Official Project No. 65-44-1457

COPIED UNDER WORKS PROGRESS ADMINISTRATION

MRS. JOHN TROTWOOD MOORE

STATE LIBRARIAN & ARCHIVIST, SPONSOR

MRS. ELIZABETH D. COPPEDGE

STATE DIRECTOR OF WOMEN'S & PROFESSIONAL PROJECTS

MRS. PENELOPE JOHNSON ALLEN

STATE SUPERVISOR

MRS. KATHLEEN W. CARADINE

SUPERVISOR, FIFTH DISTRICT

ELIZABETH WHITE

TYPIST & COPYIST

JUNE 26, 1936

INDEX

Note: Page numbers in this index refer to those of the original Volume from which this copy was made. These numbers are inserted within parentheses throughout the text, as (p 124).

A

B

N

Nabers, Benjamin, 465
Nabers, Perry G., 366
Nabers, Samuel, 438,439
Nabor, Benjamin, 365
Nabors, Saul A., 73
Nail, A., 418
Nail, Archer, 261
Nail, Nicholas, 334,418,470
Nail, Nichols, 287,292
Nail, Rebecca, 268
Nails, (Widow),416,418
N. Carolina, 170
Neal, E.P., 452
Neal, John A., 390,398,399,400
Neal, John N., 442
Nears, John A., 397
Needham, Alexander, 471
Needham, B., 73
Needham, Bailey, 465
Needham, Burley, 418
Neely, John, 84,418
Neely, John M., 87,184
Neely, Rufus P., 306,446,447,452
Neely, Ruphus P., 348
Neely, Samuel, 84
Neely, Thomas A., 265
Neighbers, Samuel A., 69
Neilly, Rufus P., 384
Neilson, A. G., 25,343
Neilson, Alex G., 420
Neilson, Alexander G., 24,413,418
Nelson, Basil, 33
Nelson, James L., 31,32,47,56,119,
    120,158
Nelson, Wm., 348
Neuland, Thomas, 52
New, M., 471
New Orleans, 143
Newland, Thomas, 126,127,130,132,133
    134,135,136,137,138,139,140,141
    142,143,287,299,301,302,303,315
    316,319,324,330,333,334
Newland, Thos., 300,335
Newsom, Eaton R., 307
Newsom, Samuel, 270
Newsum, Herbert, 120
Newton, Ebenezer, 17
Nicholas, Isaac, 44,49,50
Nicholas, Nathaniel, 53
Nichols, Hardeman, 173
Nicholson, 311
Norden, Alec, 440,444
Norden, Alexander, 426,441

Norman, Thomas W., 136,140
Norman, Thos. W., 64,164
Norment, Nathaniel E., 29,88
Norment, N. E., 15
Norment, Nath E., 80,312,417
Norton, 443
Norton, Jacob, 369,421,424,425,427
    428,429,430,431,433,442,449,451
    455,456,463
Nuehles, Sterling, 457
Nucholls Mill, 270
Nuckolls, John, 182,199,444
Nuckols, John, 57,197,198

O

O'Brien, John, 161
Old, J. E., 375
Old, Jacky, 71,73,321,375
Old, Joan E., 71
Old, John C., 121,267
Old, John E., 75,297,320,321,375,376
Oliver, Roderick, 196,345
Oliver, T. J., 2
Oliver, Thomas I., 136
Oliver, Thomas J., 1,2,3,6,127,130,
    132,134,135,136,137,138,139,
    140,141,142,193,255,297,298
    332,335,348,392, *195
Oliver, Thomas L., 113,135
Oliver, Thos. J., 325, 326,328,331
Oswald, Edward, 405
Outlaw, Medicos R. T., 167
Overall, William, 103,104,110,114,
    116,118,120,122,179,232,233,234,235
    236,237,239,240,410
Overall, Wm., 23
Owen, David F., 189
Owen, E., 81
Owen, Shadrack, 61
Owen, William, 279
Owen, William, 177 (marked out)
Owen, Wm., 278
Owens, David F., 52,53,112,113,115
Owens, Edward, 8,9,65,75,168,183,259
    275,342
Owens, Ezekiel, 9,27,29,70,73,358
Owens, Samuel, 373,456
Owens, Shadarock, 445
Owens, Shaderick, 127
Owens, Shadrock, 411,444
Owens, Wm., 29,177
Owens, Zekial, 172

P

Russell

HARDEMAN COUNTY
MINUTES COUNTY COURT
1827-1829
Vol. 11

Saturday October 6, 1827

Pg
1   Court met according to adjournment. Present- West Harriss, Nath Steele &
John Y. Cockeran, Esquires, Justices of the Quorum.
Tho. J. Hardeman Clk   .   ------- J. C. W. Robertson, Shff.

John Lea & James Leafain) Present West Harriss Nath Steele & John Y. Cock-
John Lea & Co.   ) eran Esquires.
        vs.) Debt   )
Enoch Carter   )

          This day came the parties by their attorneys and thereupon came a jury of
good and lawful men To Wit John Cole William Warren Oney Harvey Richard Dabby
Josiah C. Hale, William Rust, James Barclay, Robt. C. Moore, John Foster, Benjamin Gay, Powhatan Gray, Thomas J. Oliver who being elected empannelled and
sworn the truth to speak upon the issues joined upon their oath do say they find
the issues joined in favor of the plaintiffs and that the defendants hath not paid
the debt of one hundred and twenty dollars in the plaintiffs declaration mentioned and they assess the plaintiffs damage by reason of the detention thereof to
four dollars and twenty cents. Therefore it is considered by the Court that the
Plaintiffs recover of the defendant his debt aforesaid together with the damages
aforesaid in form aforesaid assessed by the Jury aforesaid and their costs about
their suit in this behalf expended and that they have execution etc.

          The Sheriff returned into Court a list of salable property for the year 1827
not before listed and it was ordered to be received and recorded.

October Term Saturday the 6th of October, 1827

Pg
2 C. T. & W. Howard   )   Present West Harriss Nath Steele & John Cock-
        vs.   ) Case   )   eran Esquires.
Robert Rivers   )

          This day came the parties by the attornies and thereupon camea jury of good
and lawful men To Wit Wm. Warren, John Cole, Oney Harvey, Richard Dabby, Josiah C. Hale, James Barclay, Robt. C. Moore, John Foster, Benjamin Gay, Powhatan Gray, T. J. Oliver William Todd who being elected impannelled and sworn, the
truth to speak upon issue joined upon this do say they find the issues joined
in favor of the plaintiff and assess his damage by reason of the non performance
of the promises on the declaration mentioned sixty nine dollars and eighty five
cents.

          Thereupon it is considered by the Court that the Plaintiff recover against
the defendant the said sum of sixty nine dollars damages together with their
costs by them about their part in this behalf expended and etc.

Benjamin Bowers for the   ) Present the worshipful West Harris, John Y. Cock-
use of Chesterfield Bowers) eran and Nathaniel Steele Esquires Justices.
        vs.   ) Assumpact)
John A. McKinnie   )

          This day came the parties by their attorneys and thereupon came a jury of
good and lawful men to wit Wm. Warren, John Cole, Oney Harvey, Richard Dobbs,
Josiah C. Hale, James Barkly, Robert C. Moore, John Foster, Benjamin Gay, Powhatan Gray, Thomas J. Oliver & William Todd who being elected impanalled and
sworn the truth to speak upon the issue joined upon their oath do say they find
the same in favour of the plaintiff & assess his damages by reason of the non
performance of the undertaking in the declaration to one hundred and forty five
Pg dollars. Thereupon it is considered by the Court that the plaintiff recover of
3 the said defendant the said sum of one hundred and fifty five dollars

Pg his damages aforesaid by the jury aforesaid in form aforesaid assessed also his
3 costs about this suit in this behalf expended etc.

Thomas McNeal) Present the worshipful West Harris, John Y. Cockeran
vs.) Debt) Nathaniel Steele, Espuires Justices.
Archabald S. Lockman)

  This day came the parties by their attorneys and thereupon came a jury of
good and lawful men to wit William Warren, John Cole, Oney J. Harvey, Richard
Dabby, Josiah C. Hale, James Barkley, R obert C. Moore, John Foster Benjamin
Gay, Powhatan Gray, Thomas J. Oliver and William T odd who being elected impannelled and sworn to the truth to speak upon the issue joined upon their
oath do say they find the same in favour of the plaintiff and that the defendant hath not paid the debt of four hundred and fifty nine dollars and fifty
cents in the plaintiff declaration mentioned and they do assess his damages by
reason of the detention thereof to eleven dollars and fifty cents.

  Thereof it is considered by the Court here that the plaintiff recover of
the defendant the said sum of four hundred and fifty nine dollars and fifty
cents his debt aforesaid and together with the damages aforesaid also his costs
about his suit this behalf expended etc.

Pg
4 Daniel Billumps)
vs.) Case)
Chancery Davenport)

  This day came the plaintiff by his attorney and says he will no further
prosecute his suit therefore it is considered by the that defendant recover
up the plaintiff his costs about his defence in this behalf expended & that
the defendant go hence etc.

David Wood))
  vs.) Appeal from a Justice of the peace
J. Haniss)
Samuel B. Harris)

  This day came the defendants by their attorney and the plaintiff being solemnly called to come into court and prosecute his suit came not. Therefore it is
considered that the defendant go hence without day & recover of the plaintiff
their costs about this suit about their defense expended etc.

Hugh Blackwood) Present the worshipful West Harris, John Y. Cockeran
vs.) Debt) and Nathaniel Steele.
Samuel Bond)

  This day came the plaintiff justices by his attorney and the defendant being solemnly called came not but made default therefore it is considered by the
Court that the plaintiff recover of the defendant the sum of one hundred and
eight dollars and fifty three cents his debt in his declaration mentioned to-
Pg gether with the further sum of sixteen dollars damages by reason of the deten-
5 tion thereof also his costs about this suit in this behalf expended etc.

William Paskel)
  vs.) Same Justices as before
John Jones)

  The plaintiff being solemnly called to come into Court and prosecute his
suit came not therefore it is considered that the defenant go hence without
day and recover of the plaintiff his costs about this suit expended etc.

John McKinnie)
  vs.) Certiovari
William Cone)

  This day came the plaintiff his attorney and the defendant being solemnly
called to come into court came not but made default . Therefore it is considered
by the Court that the plaintiff recover of the defendant his costs about his
suit in this behalf expended etc.

Pg
5

Charles Slater)
vs Trover)
Mark R. Roberts)

This day came the defendant by atty. and payed and obtained an appeal to the next Circuit Court which is granted he having given Ezekial P. McNeal and Austin Miller security thereto etc.

Thomas J. Hardeman)   Present the worshipful West Harris John Y. Cockeran and
vs.)   Gabriel Bumpass, Esquires Justices.
William Rust and)
Nathaniel Steele)

This day came the parties by their attorneys and thereupon came a jury of good and lawful men to wit William Warren, John Cole, Oney I. Harvey, Richard Dabby, Josiah C. Gale.

Pg
6

Robert Moore, John Foster, Benjamin Gray, James Barkley Thomas J. Oliver and William Todd who being elected and impanneled and sworn the truth to speak upon the issues joined upon their oath do say they find for the plaintiff and that the defendants have not paid the debt of sixty five dollars debt in the plaintiff declaration mentioned and assess his damages by reason of the detention thereof to three dollars therefore it is considered by the Court that the plaintiff recover of the defendant the sum of sixty five dollars his debt aforesaid together with his damages aforesaid also his costs about this suit in the behalf expended etc.

John Foster)   Debt on a writ issued at this term the plaintiff comes
vs.)   into Court and testifies his suit therefore it is con-
Thomas J. Oliver)   sidered that the defendant recover his costs about this
)   suit.

John W. Patterick)   Present West Harris Nath Steele and Jno. Y. Cockeran,
vs.)   Justices.
William W. Crisp)

This day came the parties by their attornies and thereupon came a jury of good and lawful men to wit John Cole Robert C. Moore William Warren Oney

Pg
7

K. Harvey Josiah C. Hale, Richard Dabby John Foster, Benjamin Gay, Powhatan Gray, James Barclay, Thomas J. Oliver and William Todd who being elected impannelled and sworn their oaths do say they find the issues joined in favor of the plaintiff and that the defendant has not paid the debt of ninety nine dollars in the plaintiffs declaration mentioned and assess his damages by reason of the detention thereof to four dollars and forty five cents. Therefore it is considered by the Court that the plaintiff recover of the defendant the debt aforesaid in form aforesaid assessed by the jury and that he have execution.

Ordered by the Court that Enoch Carter be released from the payment of the tax on one block poll improperly charged him.
A
A deed of mortgage from Duguid Mims to David W. Wood and Pitser Miller was produced in open Court and the execution thereof acknowledged by said Duguid to be his act and deed and so ordered to be certified for registration.
                    And the Court adjourned to term of in
                    course.
                    N. Steele B P
                    John Y. Cockeran J. P.
                    West Harris J P

Pg
8

January Term Monday 7th of January 1828

At a Court of pleas and quarter sessions begun and helf for the county of Hardeman at the Court House in the town of Bolivar on the 1st Monday in January A. D. 1828. Present the worshipful West Harris John Y. Cockeran, Nathaniel Steele John Pitchford Thomas Deen Elizah Gossett Elijah W. Boyte Gabriel Bum-

Pg pass Drew Champion Thornton Irons, John Rosson, Wm. L. Duncan Wm. B. Robinson
8 Joseph W. McKean and Edward Owens.
Tho. J. Hardeman Clk--V. D. Barry Sol Just.--+--- J. C. N. Robertson Shff.

This day came into open Court Martin Taylor James Bougard, Alexander
McKenzie, Lazarris Stewart Walter Scott Daniel Hughes Edmund D. Tarver, Francis
Shoemake and Thomas James and presented their commissions from the Governor
of the State of Tennessee appointing them a conformity to a resolution of the
General Assembly of the State of Tennessee Justices of the Peace for the County
of Hardeman and state aforesaid and took the oath severally as prescribed by
law and then seats upon the bench of said court.

T   This day came into open C ourt Thomas Patten and produced to the Court
one wolf scalp adjudged to be over 4 months old and ordered that he have his
certificate.

Pg   This day came into C ourt J esse W. Cocke and produced one wolf scalp
9 adjudged over 4 months old. Ordered that he have a certificate.

This day came into open Court Lazarus Stewart and produced one wolf scalp
adjudged over 4 months old, ordered that he have a certificate.

This day came into open C ourt James Marlin and produced one wolf scalp
adjudged over 4 months old. Ordered that he have a certificate.

This day came into open Court William Duncan and produced four wolf scalps
adjudged over 4 months old. Ordered that he have a certificate.

Ordered by the Court that Thomas Boyte be allowed to establish a ferry on
Hatchie River on his occupant claim.

Ordered by the Court that Joseph W. McKean and Samuel Lambert be appointed
Commissioners to settle with the administration of Jefferson Key decd. relative
to said Keys guardianship of Ann L. Key and make report to this Court and which
said report was made and ordered to be recorded.

Ordered by the Court that Trustee pay John Rosson Coroner, the sum of six
dollars 25 cents for holding inquest over the body of Mrs. Mochen decd.

Pg   V. D. Gossett came into open Court and tendered his resignation as con-
10 stable by the Court and ordered to be recorded.

Ordered by the Court that Edward Owens, Isaac Rocks and Isam Smith be
appointed Commissioners to settle with Ezekial Owens administrator and Rachene
Warren administrator on the estate of David Warren deceased and make report to
next Court.

On motion the Court proceeded to elect for Constable to supply vacancies
in the County. Whereupon in balloting Andrew T homas was duly elected in Cap.
Chisums Company, Hiram Williams in Capt. Crans Company and John C. Cherry in
Capt. Crawfords Company and who came forward gave bond and security according to
law and were qualified in accordance with the statute on such cases made and
provided.

On motion the Court proceeded to elect a quorum Court out their whole number
to serve for the ensuing year and thereupon balloting it appeared that Edmund
D. Tarver James Ruffin and John Y. Cockeran, Esquires were duly elected to that
office.

Ordered by the Court that John H. Bills or his assignee shall have leave to

Pg alter the Brownsville road about 4 miles North West of Bolivar at his own ex-
10 pense. So as not to interfere with a new ground field he is about clearing on
274 acres of land owned by him.

A transfer of an occupant claim from Moses Bumpass to William Hicks and
Joseph Hicks was produced in open Court and the execution thereof was duly acknowledged by said Moses Bumpass and so ordered to be certified.

A deed of conveyance from the Commissioners of Bolivar to Thompson D.
White for one town lot was produced in open Court and the execution thereof
duly proven by the oaths of A. Kirkpatrick and E . R Belcher subscribing witnesses thereto and ordered to be certified for registration.

A deed of conveyance from the Commissioners of Bolivar to Thomas J. Hardeman for one town lot was produced in open Court and the execution thereof duly
proven by the oaths of A. Kirkpatrick and E. R. Belcher subscribing witness
thereto and ordered to be certified for registration. ,

Two deeds of conveyance from Ezekial P. McNeal to Thomas J. Hardeman, one for
Pg 15 acres of land and the other for 129½ acres of land were produced in open
12 Court and duly acknowledged by said McNeal to be his acts and deed and so ordered to be certified for registration.

A deed of conveyance from William Posten to John A llison for 100 acres of
land was produced in open Court and duly acknowledged by said by Posten to be
his act and deed and ordered to be certified for registration.

A deed of conveyance from William Posten to Thomas Cox for 30 acres of land
was exhibited in open C ourt and duly acknowledged by said Posten to be his act
and deed and ordered to be certified for registration.

A deed of conveyance from Solomon Willoughby to Isaac S mith for 200 acres
of land was exhibited in open Court and duly acknowledged by said Willoughby
to be his act and deed, and ordered to be certified for registration.

A deed of conveyance from James Burlison to Isaac Ricks for two tracts of
land amounting to 219 acres was produced in open Court and duly acknowledged by
said Burleson to be his act and deed and ordered to be certified for registration.

Pg.   A power of attorney from Thomas G. Williams to T homas J. Hardeman was ex-
13 hibited in open Court and the execution thereof duly proven by the oath of Joseph W. McKean & Henry Stevens subscribing witnesses thereto and the same was
ordered to be certified for registration.

An inventory of the property of Samuel F. Steele deceased was returned into
open Court by Ninia Steele administrator and the same was ordered to be recorded.

An account of sales of the personal property of Sam F. Steele decd. was
returned into open Court by Ninian Steele admn. and the same was ordered to be
recorded.

This day came into open Court David Brooks and prayed the Court to be admitted as Administrator on the estate of Osburn Gregory deceased and it appearing to the satisfaction of the Court that said Gregory died without making a
will, it is ordered that said Brooks have letters of administration and thereupon came the said David Brooks and was gratified according to law, and gave
bond in the sum of two hundred dollars with Thornton Irons and Jacob Davis as
his securities.

A deed of conveyance from Jacob Bartholomew to Edmund D. Tarver & Geo. M.

Pg Pirtle for 640 acres of land was exhibited in open court and the execution there-
13 of duly proven by the oath of Edward L. Peters and John A. Pirtle subscribing wit-
Pg nesses thereto and it was so ordered to be certified for registration.
14

An inventory of the personal estate of William Barnett deceased was returned into open Court by Samuel Lambert and Robt. W. Barnett executor of the
last will and testament of said decedant and ordered to be recorded.

A deed of conveyance from Robt. Thompson to William Bougard for 120 acres
of land was exhibited in open Court and the execution thereof duly acknowledged
by said Thompson to be his act and deed and it was ordered to be certified for
registration.

A deed of conveyance from John Brantley to Joseph Hicks for nine acres of
land was produced in open court and the execution thereof duly acknowledged by
said Brantley to be act and deed and it was so ordered to be certified for
registration.

A deed of conveyance from John Brantley to Joseph Hicks for 50 acres of
land was produced in open Court and the execution thereof duly acknowledged by
said Brantley to be his act and deed and it was ordered to be certified for
registration.

Pg A   An inventory and account sales of the personal property of Jefferson Key
15 decd. was returned into Court by Chesley D. Key administrator on said estate
and ordered to be recorded.

Ordered by the Court that George M. Pirtle be appointed overseer to keep
in repair that part of the Covington Road from the East bank of Clear Creek
as far as the western boundary of said County and all the hands work under his
directions that formerly worked under N. E . Norment as overseer of the same
part of said road, and that said road be of the first class.

O   Ordered by the Court that Peter Rogers be appointed overseer to keep in
repair that part of the Covington road from the Branch west of Peeler's field
to the East bank of Clear Creek and all the hands that formerly worked under
the directions of Larkin T. Smyth work under his directions and that said road
be of the first class.

Ordered by the Court that John Rossan, Thomas L. Duncan, Barney Chambers,
Obadiah Townsend, Mark Lea & Lincian Rosson be appointed a jury of view to
commence at Linsey's on the Simpson ferry road and run to the County line by
way of Crossland ferry.

Pg
16   Ordered by the Court that Daniel Minner be appointed overseer of and keep
in repair that part of the road leading from Bolivar to Brownsville beginning at
the north bank of Short Creek from thence to the north bank of Clear Creek and
to have all the land north of Short Creek that formerly worked under J. Moore
to work under his directions.

The report of the Commissioners for laying off one years provision for the
widow Chinault was returned into Court and ordered to be certified for registration.

The Sheriff returned into Court a list of taxable property and polls to
be listed for taxation for the year 1827, which was ordered to be received in
payment of fees.

Ordered by the Court that Julius C. N. Robertson Sheriff and collector
of the public taxes for the said County of Hardeman for the year 1824, 1825,
&1826 be released from the payment of the state & county taxes for said

Pg year on the following quantity of land (to wit) for the year 1824 5500 acres
16 for the year 1825 2222 acres and for the year 1826 5782 acres as the same
would not sell for the taxes cost and charges for said year.

Pg   Ordered by the Court that Robert Box and A lsey Deen, Russel Cain, Bennet
17 Heighfield, Wm. G__age, John P. Bordstone and Thomas Boyte, be appointed a
jury of view to lay out a road leading from Fowlers ferry to the County
line of Madison County the nearest and best route to Jackson.

       Ordered by the Court that Wm. Kennedy be appointed overseer of the road
in the place of Andrew Jones and work the hands as usual at Samuel Johns and work
to the county line of McNairy County.

       Ordered by the Court that a road lately opened by Stephen Pruett be kept
up in lieu of the former road.

       Ordered by the Court that the following rates of ferrage be established
during the prevalence of high waters on the ferry on the road to Jackson.
       From highland to highland going up, man & horse)--- $1.00
       "   "   "   "   4 wheeled carriage ----   3.00
       "   "   "   "   2 "   "   ----   2.00
       2   "   "   "   going down, horse & man----   .75
       "   "   "   "   4 wheeled carriage   2.50
       "   "   "   "   2 "   "   1.50

       Ordered by the Court that Ebenezer Newton John N. Jenkins, Robert Cagle
Walter Jacobs, Wm. L. D uncan, John Rosson, Isiah Davis and Wm. B. Robinson
Pg be a jury of view to review the route from Michial Reed to the County line in a
18 direction for Purdy by the way of Lionel and report to next term of this Court.
                              And the Court adjourned till tomorrow
                              morning 9 O'clock
                              Edmund D. Tarver
                              West Harris J. P.
                              Lazarus Stewart
                              Wm. L. Duncan J. P.

Pg   Tuesday January 8th, 1828
19
       Court met according to adjournment present the worshipful West Harris, John
Y. Cockeran, Edmon D. Tarver, Joseph W. McKean, Nathaniel Steel, John Pitchford
Thomas Dean, John R ossan, William B. Robertson, Elisha W. Boyt, Drew Champion
James Ruffin, Caleb Brook Thornton Jones, Elijah Gossett Gabriel Bumpass , Mar-
tin Taylor James Boguard, Alexander McKenzie Lazarus Stewart, Walter Scott
Daniel Hughs Francis Shoemake & Thomas Tarver Esquires Justices Thomas J. Harde-
man Clerk & J. C. N. Robertson Sheriff, V. D. B arry Solicitor.

       The Court adopted the following resolutions for the government of (Court)
(vis)Rule 1st- It shall be the duty of the County Court to attend to the 1st
applicant and shall not attend to any other until it is disposed of and made
known by the chairman, no motion can be made to the Court only from the Bar on
an equal distance with the bar. To meet at 9 O'clock.
2nd-The space between the Bar and the Court to be kept clear of the crowd during
the hours of business, 3'd- The clerk shall not record any order unless signed
by the chairman. 4th- If the chairman is absent it shall be the duty of the
Court to appoint a chairman protem. 5th- There shall be no spirituous liquors
brought into the Courthouse during the hours of business.

       John Slaughter came into open Court and presented a Commission from the
Governor appointing him a Justice of the Peace & was qualified accordingly.
Pg
20   This day came into open Court Jacob Pirtle and moved the Court to permit
him to administer on the Estate of Samuel Lewis Decd. ordered by the Court

Pg that he have letters testamentory who gave bond of two hundred dollars with
20 George W. Pirtle or his security and was qualified according to law.

This day came into open Court Green C arter and prayed the Court that he
might administer on the estate of Hampton Hosskins decd. ordered by the
Court that he be bound in the sum of one hundred dollars, qualified.

Ordered by the Court that Walden Fuller be appointed an overseer of
the Jackson Road in the place of A len Hill resigned and that he have all
the hands worked under Allen Hill.

This day came into Court Edmond Richmond and produced his license as an
attorney who was qualified accordingly.

Ordered by the Court that Wm. Polk, Austin Miller and George W. Pirtle
be appointed commissioners to settle with the county Trustee of said County
and Clerks of the Circuit on County Courts from the present year according
to acts of assembly of 1827.

Ordered that Richmond Baker oversee the clearing out and keeping in repair that part of the road leading from Bolivar to Purdy from the east end
of the part under Robt. Hays to Wades Creek and that all the hands on Wades
Creek N. W. of the same and the hands on Hays Creek and all on sd. part of
the road work thereon under his direction 1st class.

Ordered that Edward R. Belcher David W. Wood James K. Lutch be appointed
Pg commissioners to settle with the present County Trustee for the last four
21 years and report to next court.

Wm. B. Robinson presented in open C ourt an inventory of the Est. of
Tho. B. Hughs decd. the same was ordered to be recorded.

A deed of conveyance from Wm. Love to West Harris for twenty acres of
land was produced in open court and the execution thereof was duly acknowledged by John H. Bills, Tho. J. Hardeman and West Harris. Three of the
assignees thereto to be their act and deed the same was ordered to be certified for registration.

A deed of conveyance from Thos J. Hardeman to Dave W. Love for one
town lot was produced in open Court and the execution thereof was duly
acknowledged and ordered to be certified for registration.

A transfer on an occupant claim from Wade C olverd to Wiatt W. Hester
was produced in open Court and the execution thereof was duly acknowledged
and the same was ordered to be so certified.

A division of the personal estate of E. Polk decd. was returned into
open Court by the Commissioners that was appointed to assist in dividing the
same and the same was ordered to be recorded.

Pg   Ordered by the Court that Isaac Jones, E lijah Rudolph, John Garrison,
22 Benjamin Rook, Jason Cloud Wm. B. Duncan & Henry T. Rucker be fined the
sum of twenty five dollars each for their non attendance as jurors to this
Court and that sirafacias issue accordingly.

Ordered that Nathnl Steel John Y. Cockran Jno. H. Bills ThosJ.Hardeman
and West Harris be allowed the sum of twenty five dollars each for their
services as commissioners for the town of Bolivar.

Pg   John Pitchford Esqs. comes into Court and tenders his resignation as a
22 Justice of the Peace for this County which was received by the Court.

        Ordered by the Court that the following magistrates be appointed to
take tests of taxable property and poles in this County for the present year
(viz) W. B. Robinson in Cap. Boyt's Company Martin Taylor in Capt. Burleson's
Com. West Harris in Capt. Smith's Com. Walter Scott in Capt Chisolm's Com.
L. Stewart in Capt. Mahondro's Com. James Ruffian in Capt. G. Smith's Com.
Jno. Slaughter in Capt. Canes Com. C. Brock in Capt. Bond's Com. Alex Mc-
Kenzie's in Capt. Ichols Com. R. R. Gossett in Capt. Crawford's Com. W.
Duncan in Capt. Duncan Com. I. C. Hensley in Capt. Hides Com. F. Shoemake in
Capt. Hazlewoods Com. Thos. Dean in Rainey's Co.

        Ordered that the County trustee pay to West Harris Esq. fifty dollars
of the poll tax collected for this county and that said Harris contract & pay
for the support and maintenance of the two infant children of John Meacham
in this County until sd. amt. is exhausted in that way.

        Ordered that Wm. Boguard be appointed overseer of the road in place
of Thos. Alsap, decd. and that he have the hands in the same bounds etc.

Pg   Ordered that Josiah Hatley Adm. on the lot of Lewis Dillahunty decd.
23 be authorized to make sale of such negroes belonging to the estate of L.
Dillahunty decd. as he may select on a credit of twelve months on the purpose of raising the sum of one thousand dollars to meet the claims against
sd. estate which the personal property is insufficient to discharge.

        Ordered that John Crane oversee the clearing out and keeping in repair
the road leading from Bolivar to Memphis from town to the seven mile post
and that Soloman Tuttle Benj. Gay & Wm. Overall be appointed to allot the
hands to work thereon by his direction.

        Ordered that Moore Hendley be appointed overseer for the purpose of
clearing out and keeping in repair the road from the fork of the Brownsville
and Jackson road to Clover Creek and all the hands formerly worked on sd.
road by S. Tisdall and H. Stockton the hands on the plantation where Vincent
Willoby lives the hands on Henley plantation John Crawley and all west of
sd. road as far as to include Jacob Pirtles work thereon by his direction.

        Ordered by the Court that the County Trustee pay Jeremiah Williams the
sum of fifty three dollars and one half cents for furnishing clothing and
boarding for the orphan children of widdow Satawhite.

Pg   Ordered that the Sheriff pay to the Commissioners of the town af Bolivar
24 the sum of seventy five dollars and sd. Commissioners to pay the same over to
William Ramsey for a public grave yard purchased from him by sd. Commissioners
and their receipt shall be a sufficient voucher on settlement with the County

        The Court rate of taxes for the present year (viz) County tax on each
hundred acres of land 19 cts. Poor tax 6 cents jury tax 18 3/4 cts. river tax
12½ cts. Court House tax 25 cts. total 84¼ cts. On each town lot County tax
25 cts. poor 6 cts. jury 19 cts. C ourt House 25 cts. T otal 75 cts. on each
slave county 25 ¢ poor 6 cts. jury 19 cts. Court House 25 cts. Total 75 cts.
Free poll county 12½ cts. jury 12½ Court House 12½ cts Total 37½ cts on each
retail store $7.50 on each 4 wheel carriage of pleasure $5.00 on each wheel
carriage of pleasure $2.50 on each stud horse or Jack the price of the season
of the mare.

Pg
24
    Ordered that Matt Hester John H. McKennie Wm. S. Landom John U. Davis Charles Hunt, W. I. Riddle, N. Steele W. I. Hunt & R. W. Grove or any five of them be appointed a jury of view to lay out and mark a road or alter the road running from Middleburg to Spring Creek where it runs through Wilkins I. Hunts farming land to the best advantage with the least prejudice to sd. Hunt and make report to next term.

    An inventory and an account of sale of the Est. of David P. Hannis decd. and also one of the estate of Sam Hannis decd. Returned into open Court by the Est. the same was ordered to be recorded.

    Alexander G. Neilson came into open Court and on motion he was appointed Guardean to Charles P. Polk Benigna Polk and Edwin Polk minor orphans of W. Polk decd. who gave bond of sixty thousand dollars, with Green Pryor Dan.

Pg.
25
U. Gwinn John H. McKinnie Thompson D. White and Thos McNeal as his securities.

    On petition ordered that the County Trustee pay Julius N. Burton the sum of sixty nine dollars 12½ cents for the support of sd. Burtons two & keep up children.

    The Court proceeded to elect a Coroner for this County on counting the votes it appeared that Thompson D. White was duly elected who came forward and gave bond of two thousand dollars with A. G. Neilson and Thos. McNeal as his securities & qualified accordingly.

    The Court proceeded to ballot for County Trustee on counting the votes Joseph W. McKean was duly elected who gave bond of three thousand dollars with D. W. Wood A. Kirkpatrick W. R. Belcher and V. D. Barry as his securities and was qualified accordingly.

    Then proceed to ballot for Sheriff & collector on counting the votes J. C. N. Robertson was duly elected who came forward and gave bond of ten thousand dollars as Sheriff and three thousand dollars as collector of the public taxes with J. H. Shepperd B. Bowers Wm. B. Robinson and Wm. Ramsey as his securities and was qualified according to law.

    Ordered that Green Pryor oversee clear out and keep in repair that part of the Covington Road from the West Bank of Pleasant Run as far west as the branch West of Peelers field and that he have all the hands including Green Pryors Wm. Johnson Richd. Lamb Anthony Foster and Joseph Gray Edward Crawford and that theyz all work under his directions Road of the first class.

    This day came into open Court Elizabeth Barnett widow of Wm. Barnett decd. by her attorney and dissents from the will of said William decd. the same is continued until next court.

Pg
26
    The Clerk of the Court presented his receipts in open Court for one thousand & thirty seven dollars 25 cents public taxes paid into the public treasure.

    Ordered by the Court that Alexander Kirkpatrick be permitted to take William Satterwhite and keep him until next court at which time he can take him as an apprentice and that Jeremiah Williams take care of Drucilla Satta white and have her at our next Court and that said Williams put Martha Satta white to some good place to some good place until next cout at which time they are all to be brought forward and bound out according to law.

    Stephen Prewitt E. P. McNeal Thos. Joiner and James K. Leech who were summoned to attend at this term as jurors to be released therefrom

Pg   Elisha W. Boyte
26   O. S. Harvey
     John Y. Cockeran
     Isaac Jones
          vs.
     David P. Hannis
     E. P. Hannis admn.
     On motion and it appearing to the satisfaction of the Court that an ex-
ecution had issued against the defendants which had come to the hands of a
Constable of this county and by him in defect of personal property had levied
on one town lot in the town of Bolivar known as the plan of said town by Lot
No. 2 in Square No. 10. Therefore it is ordered adjudged and decreed by the
Court that said town lot be exposed to sale as required by law to satisfy the
debt of seventy one dollars sixty two and a half cents and costs accruing on
said execution together with all costs accruing upon this judgment.

Pg
27   Ordered by the Court that the petition of Ezekial Owens administrator and
Rachael Warren administrix be granted and that they sell the negro (Henkley)
as prayed for in said petition in twelve months credit on giving twenty days
notice of time and place.

Mons P. Estes)   Present James Ruffin Edmund D. Tarwer & John Y. Cockeran
     vs.) Case)   Esq. Justices.
Joel Estes   )
          This day came into open court Bignal Crook attorney in fact for Joel Estes
the defendant and after producing to the Court his said letter of attorney
confessed judgment in behalf of said defendant for the sum of eleven hundred and
eighteen dollars. Therefore it is considered by the Court that the plaintiff
recover of the defendant the said sum of eleven hundred and eighteen dollars also
his costs about his suit in this behalf expended.

Pg 2
28 Albert M. Estes)   Present same Justices as before.
        vs.   )
Joel Estes   )
          This day came into open Court Bignal Crook attorney in fact for the defend-
ant and after producing to the Court his said letter of attorney confessed the
judgment for sum of three hundred dollars debt and sixty six dollars damages.
Therefore it is considered by the Court this the plaintiff recover of the defendant the said sum of three hundred dollars debt and damages aforesaid also his costs
about his suit in this behalf expended.

Albert M. Estes)   Present same justices as before.
     vs.) Debt)
Joel Estes   )
          This day came into open Court Begnal Crook attorney in fact for the defendant
Pg   and after producing to the Court his said letter of attorney confessed judgment
29   for the sum of eighty two dollars debt and damages. Therefore it is considered
by the Court that the plaintiff recover of the defendant the said sum of eighty
two dollars debt etc. also his costs about his suit in their behalf expended.

          Ordered that the following persons be commanded to attend at our next County
Court as jurors James McDonald Randolph Matt Aguella Combs Russell Cane Alec Dean
Vivian Steel Edmond Kirkland William Love Edward Burless Champion Blythe Richmond
Carroll Stephen Jones Thos. Crossland Andrew Blackwood Moore Henly Jonathan Lind-
ley Elisha W. Harris Thomas Gilliam Tarver Tippet William Mayfield Tarver Lane
Enoch Carter Henry Ragan Tarver Davis Josiah Chandler & Nathaniel E. Norment also
Andrew Thomas & Henry Brown as constables and a sirafacias five accordingly

          Ordered by the Court that Thomas Shaw David B. Carnes, Ezekial Owens Wm.
Owens Samuel Duncan David Lane Robert Justice Isum Smith and Kennison Shutts

Pg
29   be a jury of view to review the Brownsville Road from Wm. Dotsons house on to
the County line and to turn said road if practicable without injury so not to
interfere with individuals ferry and report to next term.

Pg
30   Proclamation having been made in due form of law the Sheriff returned into
Court the following Venni Facias in the words and figures following to wit:
State of Tennessee)
Hardeman County   )   Court of Quarter Sessions October Term 1827
    Ordered that the following persons be summoned to attend at our next County
Court to be held for this County to serve as jurors viz; William B. Duncan, Isaac
Jones, Elizah Rudolph, Henry T. Fucker William Ramsay Ezekial P. McNeal, Francis
Shoemake, John Lea, James K. Leitch, George Martin, Daniel Hguhy, John Garrison,
Benjamin Rook, James Merlin, Stephen Pruett, William Chapman, Thomas Snead,
John Hensen, Johnson Hill, Robert Taylor, William H. Tisdale, William McCallister,
Shirly Tisdale, Hughes Pipkin, Thomas Joyner & Jason Cloud also Charles Jones
and Isaac Johnson to serve as Constables. You are therefore commanded to execute
the same. Witness my hand Thomas J. Hardeman Clerk of our said Court of pleas
Quarter Session at office the 1st Monday in October A. D. 1827 and in the 52nd
year of American Independence.   Tho. J. Hardeman Clerk

    To the Sheriff of Hardeman County Greeting. On the back of which said writ
is the following indorsements Venni Facias to County Court to January term Issd
Oct. 13, 1827. Came to hand the same day issd and I hereby certify that I have
summoned all of the within named jury except R. Taylor and that they were all
bondholders or free holders over the assess twenty one years and inhabitants of
Hardeman County. Given under my hand this 8th day of January 1827.
                                    J. G. N. Robertson, Shff
                                    James Ruffin
                                    E. D. Tarver
                                    John Y. Cockeran, J. P.

Pg
31   Wednesday January Term 1828
_____

    Court met pursuant to adjournment. Present the worshipful James Ruffin, West
Harris, John Y. Cockeran, Edmund D. Tarver, Esquires Justices of the Peace for
Hardeman County.

    A deed of conveyance from Edmund Jones to Peter G. Rives for two tracts of
land containing in the whole 374 acres was produced in open Court and the execution thereof duly proven by the oaths of Tho. J. Hardeman and Wm. Ramsay subscribing witnesses thereto and the same was ordered to be certified for registration.

    A plot & certificate with the transfer thereon from Edward Burlison to
Champion Blythe for 200 acres of land was produced in open Court and the execution thereof duly acknowledged by said Burlison to be his act and deed and ordered to be so certified.

Duguid Mims   )   Present James Ruffin, Edmund D. Tarver and John Y.
    vs.) Trespass)   Cockeran Esq.
James L. Nelson   )
    This day came the partiesx attornies and it being made known to the Court
Pg that the defendant has departed this life. Therefore it is considered by the
32 Court that the law finally abate and that the plaintiff pay the costs etc.

James L. Nelson   )
    vs.) Covenent)   Present same Justicesas before.
Duguid Mims   )
    This day came the plaintiffs attorney and suggested the death of the said
plaintiff and it is thereupon considered by the Court that said suit be revived

Pg
32

and that Sci Facias issue against the administrators on said decedants estate when he shall qualify etc.

Robert Carlton) Present same Justices as before
    vs) Case)
Buckner Jones)

    This day came the parties by their attornies and thereupon came a jury of good and lawful men To Wit Thomas Snead Shirley Tisdale, Wm. H. Tisdale, Johnson Hill, George Martin Wm. Chapman, James Marlin, John Henson, William Ramsay, Henry T. Rucker, Hughes Pipkin & Allen Hill who being elected impannelled and sworn the truth to speak upon the issue joined and thereupon the plaintiff withdraws a juor and a nonsuit is taken. Therefore it is considered by the Court

Pg
33

that the defendant recover of the plaintiff his costs by him about his suit in this behalf expended and that he have his execution etc.

Basil Nelson) Present same Justices as before.
    vs.) Debt)
Carter C. Collier)

    This day came the parties by their attornies and thereupon came a Jury of good and lawful men To Wit Thomas Snead, Shirley Tisdale Wm. H. Tisdale, Johnson Hill, George Martin, William Chapman, James Marlin, John Henson, Wm. Ramsay, Henry T. Rucker, Hughes Pipkin & Allen Hill, who being elected empannelled and sworn the truth to speak upon the issues joined upon their oath do say they find the issues joined in favor of the defendant.

    Therefore it is considered by the Court that the said defendant depart hence without day and recover of the plaintiff and Rober Barton his security his costs by him about his suit in their behalf expended and that he have execution etc.

Cox & Thos. Jameson) Present same Justices as before.
    vs.) Case)
Smith,Williams &CO.)

    This day came the plaintiffs by their attorney and suggested the death of

Pg
34

Dan Williams one of the defendents in this case and it is thereupon considered by the Court that said suit be revived against the administrator of said Williams deod. and that Scive Facias issue accordingly.

Nathaniel Steele for) Present same Justices as before.
the case of Ichabod Wadkins &)
Walter Shinault)
    vs.)
Joshua Hazlewood, Thomas Hazlewood &)
Wm. T. Land)

    This day came the parties by their attornies and thereupon came a jury of good and lawful men to wit Thomas Snead, Shirly Tisdale, William H. Tisdale, Johnson Hill, George Martin, William Chapman, James Marlin, John Henson, Wm. Ramsey, Henry T. Rucker, Hughes Pipkin & Allen Hill, who being elected impannelled and sworn will & truly to inquire of the damages the said plaintiff has sustained by reason of the breach of covenant in the plaintiff mentioned upon their oath do say that the said plaintiff has sustained damages by reason of the breaches aforesaid to the amount of ninety dollars and ten cents . Therefore it is considered by the Court that the plaintiff recover of said defendants for the use of said Watkins & Shinault the sd. sum of Ninety dollars & ten cents damages aforesaid by the jury aforesaid in form aforesaid assessed also his costs about this suit in this behalf expended etc.

Benjamin Arnold)
    vs.) Case No. 11) Present same justices as before.
John Johnson &)
Benjamin Gay)

Pg
35
This day came the parties by their attornies and thereupon came a jury of
good and lawful menk to wit Thomas Sneed, Shirley Tisdale, William H. Tisdale
Johnson Hill, George Martin, Wm. Coffman, James Marlin, John Henson, Wm. Ramsey, Henry T. Rucker, Hughes Pipkin and Allen Hill who being elected impannelled and sworn the truth to speak upon the issue joined , whereupon the said
jury not agreeing upon a verdict by consent of parties it is ordered that the
jury be discharged and that a mistrial be entered in this case, and that the
cause be continued until next term for another trial.

James Young and)
George Snider) Assumpset) Present same Justices as above.
        vs.) No. 13)
Abner Piller)

This day came the parties by their attorneys and thereupon came a jury of
good and lawful menk to wit Thomas Sneed, Portan Gray, John Ruffin Nathan Ragon,
Blackstone Hardeman, Andrew Taylor, Benjamin Gay, Thomas Highdon, Andrew Cavett,
James Pirtle, Peter Minner and Jesse Cockeran who being elected impannelled and
sworn the truth to speak upon the issue joined upon their oath do say that they
find for the plaintiffs and assess his damages to sixty three dollars. Thereupon it is considered by the Court here that the plaintiffs recover of the said
defendant the said sum of sixty three dollars damages aforesaid by the jury
aforesaid in form aforesaid assessed also their costs about their suit in this
behalf expended etc.

William Smith)
        Vs.) Debt No. 26) Present the same Justices as above.
Valentine Callahan))
Andrew M. Callahan))

This day came the parties by their attorneys and thereupon came on this cause
Pg   to be tried by the Court here and upon inspection and examination of the record
36   it doth appear to the said Court that there is such a record as the plaintiff
in pleading bath alledged. Therefore it is considered by the Court that the
plaintiff recover of the said defendants his debt of two hundred and seventy four
dollars debt in his declaration mentioned together with the further sum of
twelve dollars damages by reason of the detention thereof also his costs about
this suit in this behalf expended etc. From which said judgment the defendants
prayed and obtained an appeal to the next circuit court and give William U. Crxisp
and James Lane security etc.

Daniel Hughes)
        vs.) Covenant No. 28) Present same justices as before .
John H. Arnold) Demurrer to the declaration.

This day came the parties by their attorneys and thereupon all the matters
of law arising upon the said demurrer being argued by counsel and by the court
here fully understood. It is considered by the Court here that the said demurer be aveneted and because it doth not appease to the court what damages
the said plaintiff has sustained by reason of the breach in his declaration
mentioned it is ordered that a jury come at next term of this court to enquire
of the same etc.

Ordered by the Court that William Ramsay be fined the sum of twenty five
dollars for non attendance as a juror.

Pg   William Polk)
37   vs.) Covenant No. 14) Present same Justices as before.
Robert Rivers) Writ of Enquiry.

This day came the parties by their attornies and thereupon came a jury
of good and lawful men To Wit Thomas Ricad Partan Gray, John Ruffin, Nathan
Ragon, Blackstone Hardeman, Andrew Taylor, Benjamin Gay, Thomas Higdon, Andrew
Cavett, James Pirtle, Peter Minner and Jesse Cockeran who being elected empan-

Pg nelled and sworn well and truly to enquire of the damages the said plaintiff
37 has sustained by reason of the breach of covenant in the plaintiffs declaration mentioned upon their oath do say, that the said plaintiff has sustained
damages by reason of the breaches aforesaid to the amount of three thousand
one hundred and twenty dollars. Therefore it is considered by the Court that
the said Plaintiff has sustained by reason of the breach of covenant in the
Plaintiffs declaration mentioned upon their oath do say, that the said plaintiff has sustained damages by reason of the breaches aforesaid to the amount
of three thousand and one hundred and twenty dollars. Therefore it is considered by the Court that the plaintiff recover of said defendant the said
sum of three thousand one hundred and twenty dollars damages aforesaid by
the Jury aforesaid in form aforesaid assessed also his costs about this suit
in this behalf expended, etc.

Capt. Mat Morton
     vs.) No. 15 Debt) Present same Justices as before.
James Bond
    This day came the parties by their attorney and thereupon came a Jury
of good and lawful men To Wit James Lane, Poatan Gray, John Ruffin, Nathan
Pg Ragon, Blackstone Hardeman, Andrew Taylor, Benjamin Gay, Thomas Higdon,
38 Andrew Cavett, James Pirtle, Peter Minner, Jesse Cockeran who being elected empannelled and sworn the truth to speak upon the issue joined upon
their oath do say they find the issue joined in favor of the plaintiff and
that the defendant hath not paid the debt of one hundred dollars in the
plaintiffs declaration mentioned and they assess the plaintiffs damages by
reason of the detention thereof to nineteen dollars.
    Therefore it is considered by the Court that the plaintiff recover of
the defendant his debt aforesaid together with him damages aforesaid in
form aforesaid assessed by the Jury and this costs about his suit in this
behalf expended for which said judgment the defendant payed and obtained
an appeal to the next Circuit Court and gave Wm. M. Crisp and John M. Davis
as his security.

Capt. Mat Morton   )   Present same Justices as before.
     vs.) Debt   )
James Bond   )
    This day came the parties by their attorneys and thereupon came a Jury
of good and lawful men to wit James L ane, Poatan Gray, John Ruffin, Nathan
Ragan, Blackstone Hardeman, Andrew Taylor, Benjamin Gay, Thomas Higdon, An-
Pg drew Cavett, James Pirtle, Peter Minner and Jesse Cockeran who being elect-
39 ed empannelled and sworn the truth to speak upon the issue joined upon their
oath do say they find the issue joined in favor of the plaintiff and that
the defendant hath not paid the debt of one hundred and twenty nine dollars
and forty seven cents in the plaintiffs declaration mentioned, and they
assess the plaintiff damages by reason of the detention thereof to twenty
three dollars.

    Therefore it is considered by the Court that the plaintiff recover of
the defendant his debt aforesaid together with him damages aforesaid in
form aforesaid assessed by the Jury and his costs about his suit in this
behalf expended from which said judgment the defendant prayed and obtained
an appeal to the next Circuit Court and gave Wm. M. Crisp and John M.
Davis as his security.

Josiah Hodges
     vs.   No. 21) Debt) Present same Justices as before.
Peter Minner
    This day came the parties by their attornies and thereupon came a Jury
of good and lawful men To Wit Thomas Snead, Shirley T isdale, W. H. Tisdale,
Johnson Hill, George Martin, William Chapenan, James Marlin, John Henson,
Wm. Ramsay, Henry T. Rucker, Hughes Pipkin and Allen Hill who having elect-

Pg
39
Pg
40
ed empannelled and sworn the truth to speak upon the issues joined upon their oath do say they find the issue joined in favor of the plaintiffs and that the defendant hath not paid the debt of ninety dollars in the plaintiffs declaration mentioned and they assess the plaintiff damages by reason of the detention thereof to five dollars and forty cents.

Thereupon it is considered by the Court that the plaintiff recover of the defendant his debt aforesaid together with his damages aforesaid in form aforesaid assessed by the Jury and his costs about his suit in this behalf expended from which said judgment the defendant prayed and obtained an appeal to the next Circuit Court and gave Jesse Cockeran as his security.

John Chism for)   Present same Justices as before.
use of David Jarrett)
       vs.) No. 25 Debt)
Thomas J. Hardeman)

This day came the parties by their attornies and thereupon came a jury of good and lawful men To Wit, Thomas Snead, Shirley Tisdale, Wm. H. Tisdale, Johnson Hill, George Martin, Wm. Chapman, James Marlin, Wm. Chapman, James Marlin, John Henson, Wm. Ramsay, Henry T. Rucker, Hughes Pipkin & Allen Hill who being elected impannelled and sworn the truth to speak upon the issues

Pg
41
joined upon their oath do say the defendant has not paid the whole of the debt in the declaration mentioned but that there remains a balance of two hundred and forty eight dollars and fifty cents thereof unpaid, and they assess his damages by reason of the detention thereof to twenty one dollars and seventy four cents. Therefore it is considered by the Court that the plaintiff recover against the defendant the balance of debt aforesaid and the damages in form aforesaid assessed together with his costs by him about his suit in this behalf expended and that he have his execution etc.

Thomas O. Parran)   Same Justices as before.
       vs.) No. 27 Debt)
John McKinniex)

This day came the parties by their attornies and thereupon came a Jury of good and lawful men To Wit Thomas Snead, Shirley Tisdale, Wm. H. Tisdale, Johnson Hill, George Martin, William Chapman, James Marlin, John Henson, Wm. Ramsay, Henry T. Rucker, Hugh Pipkin & Allen Hill who being elected empannelled and sworn the truth to speak upon the issues joined upon these oaths do say they find the issues joined in favor of the plaintiff and that the defendant hath not paid the debt of eighty five dollars and seventy six cents in the plaintiffs declaration mentioned and they assess the plaintiff damages by reason of the detention thereof to two dollars and seventy nine cents. Therefore it is considered by the Court that the plaintiff recover against the de-

Pg
42
fendant the debt aforesaid assessed and his costs by him about his suit in this behalf expended & that he have his execution.

Alexander McDaniel)   Present same Justices as before.
       vs.) No. 31 Debt)
Daniel Davis)

This day came the parties by their attornies and thereupon came a Jury of good and lawful men To Wit Thomas Snead, Shirley Tisdale, Wm. H. Tisdale, Johnson Hill, George Martin, Wm. Chapman, James Marlin, John Henson, Wm. Ramsay, Henry T. Rucker, Hughes Pipkin and Allen Hill who being elected empannelled and sworn the truth to speak upon the issues joined upon their oaths do say they find the issues joined in favor of the plaintiff and that the defendant hath not paid the debt of two hundred dollars in the plaintiffs declaration mentioned and they assess the plaintiff damages by reason of the detention thereof to eight dollars. Therefore it is considered by the Court that the plaintiff recover of the defendant his debt aforesaid and the damages in form aforesaid assessed and his costs by him about his suit in this behalf expended etc.

Pg
43 John H. McKenzie   ) Present the same Justices as before.
              vs.) No. 33 Debt   )
Edmund R. Anderson   )

This day came the parties by their attornies and thereupon came a jury
of good & lawful men To Wit Thomas Snead, Shirley Tisdale, Wm. H. Tisdale,
Johnson Hill, George Martin, Wm. Chapman, James Marlin, John Henson, Wm.
Ramsay, Henry T. Rucker, Hughes Pipkin and Allen Hill who being elected tried
and sworn the truth to speak upon the issues joined on their oath do say they
find the issues joined in favor of the plaintiffs and they assess his damages
by reason of the detention of the debt of one hundred and forty six dollars,
nineteen cents in the Plaintiffs declaration mentioned to seven dollars and
thirty cents. Therefore it is considered by the Court that the Plaintiff recover against the defendant the debt aforesaid and the damages form aforesaid assessed and by costs by him about his suit in this behalf expended
that he have his execution etc.

Benjamin Arnold   )   Present as before
              vs.) Case   )
Benjamin Gay   )
John Johnson   )

On motion by the Plaintiff Council it is ordered by the Court that the
plaintiff have leave to take the deposition of John Henson a' Alabama in
giving defendants 20 days notice and that of John Ganten in State of Tenn-
Pg essee or giving 10 days notice.
44

Nathan Ragan   )
              vs.   )   Case
Isaac Nicholes   )

Upon motion the plaintiff has leave to amend his declaration by adding
a new count when paying the costs of the amendment the defendant to plead
to the amendment at this term is the cause to be continued and stand for
trial at the next term.

Of the Venira called over yesterday the following good and lawful men
were this day elected impannelled sworn and charged to inquire into the
body of the County, to Wit John Lea, Foreman, James Marlin Shirley Tisdale, John Henson, Thomas Snead, Henry T. Rucker, Hughes Pipkin Johnson Hill, William H. Tisdale, George Martin, William Chapman and William
Ramsay and they thereupon returned under the charge of Martin A. Ramsay
a sworn constable for that duty to consider of Presentments etc.

Pg
45 Lewis Bolt   )
              vs.   )   Case
David W. Wood   )

This day came the plaintiff by his attorney and says he will no further
prosecute his suit. Therefore it is considered by the Court that the defendant recover of the plaintiff his costs by him about his defence expended
and that he go hence without day etc.

David W. Wood & Co.   )
              vs.) Case   )
Lewis Bolt   ))

This day came the Plaintiffs by their attorney and says they will no
further prosecute their suit. Therefore it is considered by the Court that
the defendant recover of the plaintiffs his costs by him about his defence
expended and that he go hence without day etc.

Ordered by the Court that the fine of twenty five dollars entered against Isaac Jones for non attendance in yesterday as a Juror be remitted.

Pg
45

                                        John C. Cockeran J. P.
                                        Edmund D. Tarver
                                        F. Shoemake

Pg
46   Thursday Jany. 10, 1828
        Court met according to adjournment. Present the worshipful James Ruffin
Edmund D. Tarver & John Y. Cockeran Esquires Justices of the Quorum.
Tho. J. Hardeman Clk   ----------   J. C. N. Robertson Shff.

        The Solicitor General being indisposed and unable to attend to bus-
iness it is ordered by the Court that Roger Barton Esq. be appointed Solicitor General, Pro Tem.

        Ordered by the Court that the fine of twenty five dollars entered again-
st Wm. Ramsay on yesterday be remitted.

        A deed of conveyance from Nathaniel Steele to Thomas A. Smith for 325
acres of land was produced in open Court and acknowledged by said Steele to
be his act and deed and so ordered to be certified for registration.

        An inventory and account sales of the estate of Thomas Alsup decd. was
returned into open Court by the administrator and ordered to be recorded.

        This day came into open Court Robert C. Moore and prayed the Court to
be admitted to administer on the Estate of Drusilla Satterwhite decd. and it
Pg appearing to the satisfaction of the Court that said Drucilla died Intestate
47 it is ordered that said Moore be allowed letters of administration on giving
bond and security as required by the acts of Assembly in such case made and
provided and thereupon came the said Robert C. Moore and gave bond in the
sum of two hundred dollars with Joseph W. McKean and Thomas James as his security was qualified according to law and received letter of administration.

        This day came into open Court Thomas James and prays the Court to be
admitted to administer on the Estate of Dan W illiams decd. and it appearing to the satisfaction of the Court that Dan Williams died Intestate it is
ordered by the Court that said James be allowed to administer on said Estate, on his giving bond and security as required by the act of Assembly
in such case made and provided and thereupon came the said Thomas James and
gave bond in the sum of one thousand dollars with Joseph W. McKean and
Robert C. Moore as his security and was qualified according to law and received letters of administration.

        This day came into open Court Thomas James and prays the Court to be
admitted to administer on the estate of James L. Nelson deceased and it
Pg appearing to the satisfaction of the Court that said Nelson died Intestate,
48 it is considered and ordered by the Court that said James be allowed to administer on said estate by giving bond and security as required by the acts
of Assembly in such cases made and provided and thereupon came the said
Thomas James and gave bond in the sum of five hundred dollars with Joseph
W. McKean and Robert C. Moore as his securities and qualified according to
law and received letters of administration.

James Smith   )
        vs.) Debt Attachment))   Present the Quorum
Andrew M. Ramsay   )
        This day came the Plaintiff by his attorney and the defendant being
solemnly called to come into Court and defend the said action of plaintiff
came not but made default. Therefore it is considered by the Court that

Pg
48 the plaintiff recover of the defendant the debt of two hundred and forty one
dollars and fifty cents in the Plaintiffs declaration mentioned and because
it appears on said note that this has been paid by the defendant the sum of
one hundred & three dollars sixty cents, it is considered by the Court that
judgment be released for that amount.

It is also considered and adjudged by the Court that the plaintiff recover of the defendant the sum of twenty eight dollars damages also his costs
by him about his suit in this behalf expended etc. & that he have execution etc.

Pg
49 State   )
       vs.   )   Presentment as overseer) Present James Ruffin Edmand D.
    Isaac Johnson)   Tarver & Jno Y. Cockeran Esqs.
        This day came the Solicitor General on the part of the State and the
defendant in proper person who being arraigned and charged on the Bill of
Presentment plead not guilty and for his trial puts himself upon the country
and the Solicitor General likewise and thereupon came a Jury of good and lawful
men To Wit John Foster Thomas Clift Poatan Gray, Isaac Nicholas, Andrew Cavett, Allen Hill, John E. Mayfield Robert O. Moore, Nathan Reagan, Matthias
Wright, Amos Johnson & Thomas Davis, who being elected empannelled and sworn
the truth to speak upon the issue of Traverse upon their oath do say they find
the defendant Not Guilty in manner and form as charged in the Bill of Presentment. Therefore it is considered by the Court that the defendant go hence
without day, and the County pay the costs of this prosecution.

        Pitser Miller appeared in open Court and was qualified as Deputy Ranger
for the County of Hardeman according to law.

    State
       vs.   ) Peace Warrant) Present as before same Justices.
    John Ruffin
        Ordered by the Court that John Ruffin the defendant in this cause be
Pg discharged from the custody of the Law on his paying the costs of this pros-
50 ecution.

    State
       vs.   ) Presentment Overseer etc.) Present same Justices as before.
    Andrew Jones
        This day came the Solicitor General on the part of the state and the
defendant in proper person and who being arraigned and charged on the Bill
of Presentment Plea of Not Guilty and for his trial puts himself on the
County and the Solicitor General likewise and thereupon came a jury of good
and lawful men (To W it) John Foster, Thomas Clifft, Poatan Gray, Isaac
Nicholas, Andrew Cavett, Allen Hill, John E. Mayfield, Robt. O. Moore, Nathan
Reagan, Matthias Wright, Amos Johnson & Thomas Davis who being elected empannelled and sworn the truth to speak upon the issue of Traverse joined upon
their oaths do say they find the defendant guilty in manner and form as charged
in the Bill of Presentment. Therefore it is considered by the Court that the
defendant be fined the sum of five dollars, and pay the costs of this prosecution and he be taken etc. From which judgment the defendant prayed and
obtained an appeal to the next Circuit Court to be held for this County and
Pg gave bond with Richard Powell and John Jones in his security etc.
51
    State
       vs   ) Presentment etc.)
    Andrew Jones
        This day came into open Court Robert C. Farriss and Nathan Ragan, who
acknowledged themselves severally to be indebted to the State of Tennessee in
the sum of one hundred and twenty five dollars each, to be levied of goods and

Pg chattels, lands and tenements, but to be void on condition that they do make
51 the personal appearance at the next term of the Circuit Court to be held for
the County of Hardeman and give evidence on behalf of the State in a certain
matter of controversy depending wherein the said state is plaintiff and Andrew Jones defendant.

```
State              )  Indictment for obstructing road).  Present same Justices as
   vs.             )                                     before.
Enoch P. Hanniss   )
```

Pg   This day came the Solicitor General on the part of the state and the de-
51 fendant in proper person and who being arraigned and charged on the Bill of
Indictment pleads Not Guilty and for his trial puts himself on the Country
and the Solicitor General likewise and thereupon came a jury of good and lawful men (To Wit) Elijah C. Hull, Solomon Tuttle, John H. Arnold, Wm. P.
Haden, Lechaniah Chandler, Blackstone Hardeman, Benjamin Alexander Charles L.
Howard, Benjamin Gay, David F. Owens, Andrew Taylor and John Mills who being
elected empannelled and sworn the truth to speak upon the issue of traverse
joined upon their oath do say they find the defendant not guilty in manner
Pg and form as charged in the Bill of Indictment. Therefore it is considered
52 by the Court that the defendant go hence without day and the County pay the
cost s of this prosecution.

```
State              )
   vs  ) Sci Facias )  Present same Justices as before.
Thomas Neuland     )
```

This day came the Solicitor General on the part of the State and the
defendant being solemnly called to come into Court and plead to the Sci
Facias served on him came not but made default. Therefore it is considered
by the Court that the state have execution final for the sum of one hundred
and twenty five dollars penalty, and that the sum issue accordingly.

```
State              )
   vs.   ) Sci Fa   )
Thomas Neuland     )
```

This day came the Solicitor General on the part of the state and the
defendant in proper person and who thereupon moved the Court to set aside the
Pg judgment rendered against him, and filed his affadavit setting forth ground
53 upon which he applied for said Rule. Whereupon it was considered by the
Court that said judgment and Scie Facias be set aside on said defendants paying on costs according thereon.

```
State              )
   vs.             )  Presentment overseer  of Road.)  Present same Justices as before.
Amos Johnson
```

This day came the Solicitor General on the part of the State, and the
defendant in proper person who being arraigned and charged on the Bill of
Presentment plead Not Guilty and for his trial puts himself on the County and
the Solicitor General likewise and thereupon came a Jury of good and lawful men
To Wit Nathaniel Nicholas, Elijah C. Hull, Solomon Tuttle, Wm. P. Hayden,
53 Lochanah Chandler, Blackstone Hardeman, Benjamin Alexander, Charles L. Howard, Benjamin Gay, David F. Owens, Andrew Taylor and John Mills who being
elected empannelled and sworn the truth to speak upon the issue of Traverse
upon their oath do say they the defendant Not Guilty in manner and form as
charged in the Bill of Presentment.

This day it is considered by the Court that the defendant depart hence
without day and that the County pay the costs of this prosecution etc.

Pg
54

John H. McKinnie   )
  vs.)Debt   )   Present as before.
Edmund R. Anderson)

  This day came the defendant and prayed and obtained an appeal to the next Circuit Court upon the Judgment of this Court and gave bond with James H. Sheppard as his security.

Andrew Taylor Rangne)
  vs.) Appeal   ) Present as before.
Michial McKennie   )2

  On motion it is ordered by the Court that the defendant in this case have leave to take deposition of Enoch Carter on giving 10 days notice to the opposite party.

State   )
  vs.) A & B.) Present same justices as above.
Garner Duncan   )

  This day came the Solicitor General on the part of the State and on motion and by the assent of the Court a Nolli Provegeni is entered in this cause and the county pays the costs.

Nathaniel Henderson
     vs.) Debt) Present as Before.
Samuel Dickens

  This day came the defendant by his attorney and confesses judgment for
Pg
55
the sum of one hundred and thirty four dollars forty cents debt and eight dollars and four cents damages.

  Therefore it is considered by the Court that the Plaintiff recover of the defendant the said sum of one hundred and thirty four dollars forty cents debt and eight dollars and four cents damages aforesaid, also his costs by him about his suit in this behalf expended etc.

Samuel Dickens)
  vs.) Debt   )
Thomas Bunt   )

  It appearing to the satisfaction of the Court that a Judgment has been obtained against the Plaintiff for the sum of one hundred and thirty four dollars and four cents damages thereon as security for defendant. It is on motion considered by the Court that the plaintiff recover of the defendant according to the Statute the said sum of one hundred and thirty four dollars, forty cents debt and eight dollars and four cents damages together with his costs about his motion in this behalf expended etc.

Pg
56

  This day came into open Court Elizabeth Barnett and declares to the Court here her dissent from the will of her deceased husband William Barnett and by consent of the executors and said Elizabeth it is ordered by the Court that James Ruffin James Wood Isiah Hatley William Whitaker and Peter G. River be commissioners to lay off to the said Elizabeth her lawful dower of said Estate & also a childs part of the personal Estate after the payment of all jims debts and also that Caleb Brock, Henry Reagan and James H. McReynolds be Commissioners to lay off to said Elizabeth one years provisions for herself and family and that this be a final arrangement of her claims in this behalf.

George Steele)
  vs.   ) Debt
James L. Nelson)

  The death of the defendant hereof being heretofore suggested and Thomas James having qualified as administrator of said defendants Estate now comes into Court & acknowledges the service of a Scirefacias to make him an administrator as aforesaid defendant in plea of said Nelson.Cout adjourns until

Pg
56
                                                    Edmund D. Tarver
                                                    F. Shoemake
                                                    James Ruffin Chairman

_____ Friday January 11, 1828 _____ —

Pg
57
        Court met according to adjournment present the worhipful James Ruffin, Ed-
mund T. Tarver & Francis Shoemake Thomas J. Hardeman Clerk.
V. D. Barry, Solicitor   -------   J. C. N. Robertson Sheriff

State   )
   vs.   )   Presentment) Justices as above.
William M. Bee)
        This day came the Solicitor General on the part of the state and the de-
fendant in proper person who being charged in the Bill of Indictment-pleads re
Not Guilty & for his trial puts himself on his country & the solicitor likewise where upon came a Jury of good & lawful menk to wit Mathias Wright, Andrew Cavett, Robert Cagle, Oney S. Harvey, Allen Hill, Powtan Gray, Thomas
Clift, William Bell, John Nuckols, Thomas M. Patrick Ichabod Wadkins & Enoch Carter who being elected empanneled charged & sworn the truth to speak upon the
issue of Traverse upon their oaths do say the defendant is not guilty in
manner & form as charged in the bill of indictment, therefore it is considered
by the Court that the defendant go hence without day and that the county pay
the costs of this prosecution.

        A deed of conveyance from Ezekial P. McNeal to Austin Miller for seven
acres of land was produced in open court & the execution thereof was duly acknowledged by said McNeal & the same was ordered to be certified for registration.

State   )
   vs.   )   Prest. for obstructing a road.
Mathias Wright)
        This day came the Solicitor General on the part of the state and says with
Pg the assent of the Court that he will no further prosecute in this behalf. It
58 is therefore considered by the Court that the defendants depart hence without
day and that the county pay the costs of this prosecution.

State   )
   vs.   )   Prest. for obstructing a road.
John Foster   )
        This day came the solicitor general on the part of the state and with the
assent of the Court says he will no further prosecute in this behalf. It is
therefore considered by the Court that the defendant report here without day
& that the County pay the costs of this prosecution.

        A deed of conveyance from John Murray to James M. Warner for twenty six acres
of land was duly proven in open court by the oaths of John H. McKennie & James
Warner and ordered to be certified for registration.

William Polk   )
   vs.   )   C ovenant
Robert Rivers)
        This day comes the defendant and prays an appeal to the next term of the
Circuit Court for this County which is granted him he having bond and security
as required by law.

        This day came into open Court James Hubbard and being appointed Guardian
for Benjamin A. Harris a minor orphan entered into bond with security as re-

Pg quired by law in the sum of five hundred dollars.
58

A plot and certificate with the transfer thereon from Barney Chambers to Walter Jacobs was exhibited in open Court and duly acknowledged by said Chambers and ordered to be certified.

Pg
59

A transfer for an occupant claim from Will Hester to Wilkins L. Hunt was exhibited in open court & the execution thereof only acknowledged by said Hester & the same was ordered to be so certified.

A transfer on an occupant claim from Will Hester to Wilkins L. Hunt was exhibited in open court & the execution thereof was duly acknowledged by said Hester & the same was ordered to be so certified.

Peter Bertrand)
vs.) Debt appeal from a J. P.
Josiah Hatley)
Adm. of Lewis Dittahunty Decd)

This day came the parties by their attornies, and thereupon came a jury of good and lawful men of Hardeman County to wit James Hubbard, Samuel Lambert Garnett Fitzgerald, Wyate Hester, Solomon Tuttle, Barney C hambers, Charles Stewart, Matthews Wright, Andrew Cavitt, Robert Cagle, Oney L. Hervey, and Allen Hill, who being elected impannelled sworn & charged well and truly to try the matters in dispute upon their oath do say that the judgment of the justice of the peace is in all things correct.

It is therefore considered by the Court that the plaintiff recover against the defendant, the sum of twenty two dollars the amount of the judgment of the justice below, with interest from the 27 th day of October last, the date

Pg thereof and also his costs by him about his said land in this behalf ex-
60 pended to be levied of the good and chattels lands and tenements of said Lewis Dittahunty decd. in his hand. And on motion, if not, then of proper good and chattels of said defendant and of Richard Hatley his security in appeale, and that he have his execution etc. etc.

A power of attorney from Benjamin Arnold to John M. Davis was produced in open Court and the execution thereof duly acknowledged and the same order-ed to be certified for gegistration.

Robert Hays)
advs.) Certiovari
Anderson & Sheppard) Motion to dismiss.

This day came the parties by their attornies and thereupon all the matters and things arising on said defendants motion to dismiss the same being heard and by the court here fully understood, whereupon after Solomn argument had thereon. It is considered by the court that said defendants take nothing by their said motions that the same be overruled and said suit set for trial at the next term of this court.

Grand jury discharged 4th day.

John Martin&)
Pg Robert P. Baits) Covenants
61 vs.)
George Martin)

This day came the parties by their attornies and thereupon by leave of the Court files his plea puis darvein continuance to which the plaintiffs demur. And therefore all matters of law arising upon the said demurrer being heard and by the Court here fully understood it is considered by the Court that the de-murrer be overruled and that the defendant depart hence without day & recover against the plaintiffs his costs about his defence in this behalf expended etc.

Pg   A transfer on an occupant claim from Samuel Duncan to James Murray
61 exhibited in open Court & the execution duly acknowledged by said Duncan
    ordered that the same be so certified.

    The Grand Jury returned into open Court under the charge of their
sworn officer a bill of presentment State of Tennessee agst. Thomas
Deen & F. Booby indorsed by of said Jury also a Bill of Presentment. The
State of Tennessee agt. Walden Fuller & Shadrack Owen for an affray indor-
sed & subscribed by all said Grand Jury. A lso a bill of Indictment of the
State vs. Levi Todd indorsed a True bill John Lea foreman of the Grand
Jury.

    Ordered that Benjamin Bowers be appointed overseer of the Memphis
Road from the west bank of Spring Creek to Alsups Prairie and that the
hands of James Ruffin Robert A. Dandridge Luria Johnson L. Rod together
Pg with his own be given him.
62

    Ordered by the Court that Arthur Morrow oversee that part of the
Somerville from sd. Morrows West to Spring Creek and work the hands herein named six of Robert Rivers hands and all the hands in one mile and a
half north and east of said road and also Elijah Bennett work on sd. road.

    Ordered that Thomas Wood, oversee the Memphis road from the fork near
Arthur Morrows west to Spring Creek and work all the hands south of sd. roa d
to the first section line.

Alexander McDaniel   )
        vs.) Debt.   )   Present James Ruffin Edmund D. Tarver
Daniel Davis   )   and F. Shoemake Esq.
Fxx Shoemake Esqx   )
    This day came the defendant and prays and obtains an appeal to the
next Circuit Court and gave bond with John H. McKinnie as his security.

Hiriam Casey for the use of)   Present James Ruffin Edmund D. Tarver &
Nevil W. Crane   )   Francis Shoemake Esq. Justices.
        vs.) Debt   )
James Wright   ))
    This day came the parties by their attornies and thereupon the
matters of law arising on the plaintiffs demand coming on to be argued
Pg and the same being solemnly argued by council, it is the opinion of the Court
63 that the plaintiff denaner to the defendants plea be sustained. Whereupon
    it is considered by the Court that the defendant answer over to the declar-
    ation at this term.

    Ordered by the Court that Elijah Rudolphs be released from the five
entered against him.

Hardin S. Adams)
    _____)   Certoveri Motion to dismiss.
James N. Fleming)
    This day came the parties by their attornies, and thereupon the matter
and things arising on the defendants motion that the execution brought up by
the Constable under Supercedias be returned to the Magistrate to be renewed
being heard and here fully understood by the Court after argument. It is
considered by the Court that the defendant take nothing by his motion.

    Ordered that Cem B. Carter be permitted to give security as administra-
tor Hampton Hopkins decd. to the clerk out of term.

Pg Jesse Burnett   )
64   vs.) Certiovari   )
Lionel P. Smith   )

This day came the plaintiff by his attorney and the defendant being solemnly called to come into Court came not but made default.

Therefore it is considered by the Court that the plaintiff recover of the defendant his costs about his suit in this behalf expended etc.

A power of attorney from Joshua Hazlewood, Thomas Hazlewood, Warwick Hazlewood, and Randolph Hazlewood to George Hazlewood was produced in open Court and acknowledged by said Hazlewood to be their act and deed and so ordered to be certified.

Tho. W. Norman   )
     vs.) Demeaner   )
J. N. Pulliam   )

This day came the plaintiff by his attorney and moves this Court that he amend his declaration which was granted whereupon came Austin Miller his security and assumes costs on account of said amendment.

Walter Robinson came into open Court and was appointed Deputy Sheriff of this County by J. C. N. Robertson, Sheriff of said County, whereupon the said Walter took the oath prescribed by law and was then duly sworn as deputy sheriff etc. There being no further business before the said Court adjourned with Court in course.

Pg
65
                                        E. D. Tarver
                                        John Y. Cockeran
                                        F. Shoemake

Pg
66   Monday April 7, 1828

At a Court of pleas and quarter session began and held at the Court House in the town of Bolivar on the first Monday in April A. D. 1828 present the worshipful James Ruffin Nathaniel Steel Edmand D. Tarver Elijah Gossett, John Rossan, Dan Champion, Martin Taylor, Edward Owens, Alexander McKenzie John S. Slaughter & T. C. Hensley, Esquire Justices Thomas Hardeman Clerk, J. C. N. Robertson Sheriff V. D. Barry, solicitor.

On motion and it appearing to the satisfaction of the Court that Joseph Haynes Cole of said County died and has made no will therefore ordered that James Haynes be permitted to administer on said estate & have letters testamentory who gave bond in the sum of fifteen hundred dollars with Oney S. Harvey as his security.

Ordered by the Court that Elizabeth Murphy & William Caldwell be permitted to administer on the estate of Joseph Murphy decd. by her comeing in open Court and giving bond of one thousand dollars with good sufficient security.

Ranedon Gray produced in open court the scalp of one wolf adjudged to be over four months old ordered that he have his certificate for the same.

Robert W. Barnett came into open Court and by their consent was appointed guardean to John C. Barnett minor orphan of William Barnett decd. who
Pg 67 gave bond of three thousand dollars with James Ruffin and Samuel Lambert as his securities.

Peter G. Rives comes into open Court and with their consent was appointed guardean to Finley E. Barnett a minor orphan of William Barnett decd. who gave bond of three thousand dollars with Robert W. Barnett James Ruffin & Samuel Lambert as his securities.

Samuel Lambert comes into open Court & with the approbation of the Court was appointed guardean to Naoma M. Barnett a minor orphan of William Barnett decd. who Pggave bond of three thousand dollars with Cable Brook Green Pryor & Robert D. 67Barnett as his securities.

On motion and it appearing to the satisfaction of the Court that Henchey Hobbs died without making any will & testament & all things thereunto being properly understood ordered that John Rosson be allowed to administer on said estate who gave bond of five hundred dollars with Daniel Hughs as his security ordered that he have letters testimony & was qualified accordingly.

James Rogers came into open Court & with the consent of the Court was appointed guardean to Burlesson Warren and Margarett Ann Warren minor orphan of David Warren decd. who gave bond of sixteen hundred dollars with James Burlesson as his securities.

Pg
68
Willis Martin comes into open Court on motion & by consent of the court he was appointed guardean to William R. McKennie Elijah C. McKennie John L. T. McKennie Sarah Ann McKennie and Robert McKinnie minor children of John McKinnie who gave bond of ten thousand dollars with E. W. Boyt and Michael McKinnie as his securities.

Alexander Kirkpatrick comes into open court and records his stock mark then a cross and split in the right ear.

Ordered by the Court that Thomas Crosslin & William Hamblin be allowed to establish a Ferry across Hatchie River in this County who gave bond with Obediah Townsend & Warley Linvill as their securities.

A power of attorney from Edward Bass and Sarah Jacobs to Michael McKinnie was produced in open Court and the execution thereof was duly acknowledged by said Edward Bass & Sarah Jacobs to be their acts & deeds the same was ordered to be certified for registration.

Richard Lamb comes into open Court on motion & with the consent of the Court he is permitted to administer on the estate of Michael Pirtle decd. who gave bond of seven hundred dollars with Benjamin Gay & C. C. Collier as his security & was qualified . Ordered that he have letters testamentory.

Pg
69
On motion ordered by the Court that Francis Tedford widow of David Tedford Decd. be appointed guardean to John I. Tedford William C. Tedford, Millitha Tedford Sopprona O. Tedford and Amanda Tedford minor heirs of David Tedford Decd. by her comeing in open Court & giving bond of twenty five hundred dollars with good and sufficient securities.

Ordered that William Trewet have license to keep an ordinary at his now dwelling house who gave bond with Michael Read as his security and was qualified.

Ordered by the Court that Arthur Morrow have license to keep a public ordinary at his now dwelling home who gave bone with J. C. N. Robertson as his security & was qualified.

Samuel A. Neighbers was appointed constable who gave bond with Alexander McKenzie Garret Ford as his securities and was qualified.

John Thompson was appointed as Constable and gave bond with John M. Davis Garret Fitzgerald James Harder and Ephram Sparks as his securites and was qualified.

Jacob Pirtle Adm. produced in open court and account of sale of the chattel estate of Samuel Lewis decd. Ordered to be recorded.

Pg
69
An account of sales of the perishable property of William Barnett decd. was presented in open Court by the administratives ordered to be recorded.

Pg
70
Drucilla Saterwhite, a minor orphan came into open Court and was bound to Jeremiah Williams aged seven years until she arrive to the age of eighteen years.

An account of sales of the estate of Ashburn Gregory decd. returned in open Court by the administrator ordered to be recorded.

A settlement with Ezekial Owens administrator and Rachel Warren administratrix on the estate of David Warren Decd. was returned in open Court by the Commissioners ordered to be recorded.

A settlement with the administrator on the estate of Jefferson Key Dedd. was returned in open Court by the commissioners and ordered to be recorded.

An additional account of sales of the estate of Jefferson Key decd. returned in open Court and ordered to be recorded.

An inventory and account of sales of the chattel estate of Hampton Hopkins Decd. returned in open Court by the administrator. Ordered to be recorded.

A list of property and palls returned into open Court by the Sheriff as insolvents runaways etc. as also a list of land erroniously listed. Ordered by the Court that the same be received and recorded.

Pg
71
Ordered also that J. C. N. Robertson Shff. and Collector of the public taxes for the year 1827 have a credit with the State Treasurer & County Trustee etc. for the taxes of 4371 acres of land as the same appears to have been twice listed and on two slave polls and thirty nine free polls & one store house at $2 the season as thereon it appears cannot be found or insolvent.

An inventory & account sales of the estate of John K. Old decd. was returned into open Court by Jno. C. McKean adm. & Jacky Old adm. and ordered to be recorded.

An inventory & account sales of the property of Hamilton Cockburn decd. was returned into open Court by John C. McKean Adm. and ordered to be recorded.

It appearing to the satisfaction of the Court that I. C. Hensly was qualified last term of this Court as a magistrate of this County and which said circumstance was not put down on the record by the Clerk. Ordered by the Court that the same be entered of Record this term.

Ordered by the Court that the Commissioners appointed last term to settle with the late County Trustee have til next term to make a final settlement and report.

Pg
72
Ordered that Wm. W. Lennard oversee the cleaning out and keeping in repair the road leading from Bolivar toward Robt. Rivers house, commencing at the fork near John N. Arnolds and work south to Porters Creek Road and that the following hands W. Lennard W. Wright, E. P. Harris, Patton J. C. McKeans & all the hands East of said road except such as are allowed to Jno. H. Arnold work thereon under his directions.

Pg
72   Ordered that John Crowley be appointed overseer in the place of Moore Henley and that Eli Cox be also appointed overseer in the place of Obadiah Townsend.

Ordered by the Court that Watkins I. Hunt be permitted to change the road round his field, as marked out by the commissioners.

Ordered by the Court that the hands of Littleton Johnson hands Jesse Allsup Lemons Patterson James Burekley John Barkley & James Saunders work under John N. Arnold as overseer.

Ordered that George M. Pirtle oversee the clearing out keeping in repair that part of the road leading from Bolivar to Covington between Clear Creek
Pg and the west boundary of this County and all the hands that lives west of Clear
73 Creek and south of the sectional line between Section 425 west to the County line and south to include B. Needham East to Clear Creek thence down said Creek to said section line work thereon under his directions.

Ordered by the Court that V. D. Cossett be allowed to turn the Memphis road along the line between himself and Robert Rivers then a south west course to the old road.

Ordered by the Court that James Cody be appointed overseer in the room of James Bond on the road said Bond was overseer of.

Ordered that John Morgan be permitted to turn the road leading from Rivers to Middleburg about two hundred and fifty yards.

Ordered that George Hanks Saul A. Nabors Unah Stafford, Eli D. Hanks John Crawford Jesse Foster, William Rennick or any five of them appointed a jury of view to view and mark a road from the N. W. corner of Rennicks fence to Wm. Caldwells and make report to next term.

Pg   Ordered by the Court that Killiam Conner Vincent Willoughby Ross Herman
74 Cookseys hands, Green and Jacob Hartys hands work undr Solomon Willoughby overseer of the road leading from Hatchie toward Jackson in addition to the hands that he now has.

Ordered by the Court there being a majority of the justices present that James Ruffin, Robert Rosson and Newell Crain be appointed commissioners to enquire the expence or for what sum a bridge across Spring Creek near P. Colberts on the road leading from Simpsons ferry toward Memphis can be built then much thereof can be subscribed by individuals & that they be authorized to let said Bridge to the lowest bidder and that they appropriate all the monies paid by private subscriptions to the payment of said bridge.

Ordered by the Court that John Burns Daniel Cutbirth Thomas L. Duncan Wm. L. Duncan Robert Box, John Box Lewis Bolt, John May Hardin L. Adams and Wm. O. Mohundro or any five of them be a jury of view to view & mark a road leading from Michial Read by way of Lionel to the county line crossing Hatchie River at the best place toward Purdy etc.

Pg   Ordered by the Court that jurors summoned to the County Court for the
75 year 1828 be allowed one dollar per day for their service.

Ordered by the Court that John C. McKean Adm. & Jacky Old Adm. of the estate of John S. Old deceased do sell so many of the negroes belonging to said estate as will be necessary to satisfy the debts against sd. estate, after the other personal property of sd. estate is fully applied to that purpose.

Pg 75 Ordered by the Court that Edward Owens & Matthew Kirkendarfer be appointed commissioners to settle with Ezekiel Owens and Rachael Warner Adm.& Admx. of the estate of David Warren decd. and report to next Court.

Ordered that Wm. Robinson be appointed overseer of the road in the place of Alec Kirkpatrick.

Ordered that Abner Peeler be allowed to turn the Covington Road round his field provided it be on good ground as heretofore.

Ordered that John Wilkes be appointed overseer in the place of Thomas Wilkes.

Pg 76 Ordered by the Court that William H. Ragon be appointed overseer to cut out that part of the road leading from the mouth of Clover Creek to Summerville which was viewed and worked by a jury of view previous to last April term of this court crossing Clear Creek at or near Jesse Rufrells and intersecting the old road at the Buffalo licks and that he have all the hands living within two miles of said road to work under him for that purpose.

Ordered by the Court that V. D. Barry & N. Steele be appointed Commissioners to settle with the administrator of the estate of Hamilton Cockburn decd.

Ordered by the Court that Thomas Rivers oversee the clearing out and keeping in repair that part of the road leading from Robert Rivers to Bolivar, from said Rivers north to the junction of the Porters Creek road, and that the hands Kelly, Smith, Parkers, and all the hands within one and a half miles of said road and Bob Rivers & hands except tret. at one on other road work thereon under his directions.

Pg 77 Ordered by the Court that John H. Arnold overseer of the road leading from Bolivar to Simpson ferry road crossing Spring Creek be allowed to change the said road by a small deviation and that John H. Bills, William Ramsay & John H. Arnold be appointed commissioners to let to the lowest bidder the building of a bridge across Spring Creek and that said Commissioners be allowed to draw upon said Arnold for all the money that may be collected for fines and appropriate the same to the furthering of this object. And it is further ordered by the Court unanimously There being a majority of justices present that said Commissioners have leave to draw on the County Trustee for such balance as may be wanting to complete said bridge provided the same does not exceed fifty dollars, to be paid out of any moneys in his hand not otherwise appropriated and that they take bond for the building of said bridge.

Ordered that Isum Smith be appointed overseer to oversee the clearing out and keeping in repair the short part of the Brownsville road as marked out by a jury of view when leaves Wm. Dotsons house, leaving the old road at the view post, crossing Hickory Creek above Isum Smiths thence intersecting the road leading from Brownsville to the County line and that he have all the hands belonging to the old Brownsville Road from Wm. Dotsons to the County line.

Pg 78 Ordered that John Sheppard oversee the clearing out & keeping in repair the Covington road from Bolivar to Pleasant Run Creek & all the lands on T. D. Whites old place Rossers hands& John Shepherds work thereon under his direction.

Ordered by the Court that William Fulgham James Elkins & William B. Robin-

Pg son be appointed Commissioners to let to the lowest bidder the building of
78 a bridge across Porters Creek where the road crosses leading from Bolivar
to Simpsons Ferry and take bond and good security for the performance thereof.

Ordered that Commissioners who was heretofore appointed to lay off and
allot to the widow Barnett her proportion of her husbands estate be allowed
until next term to make their report.

Ordered that Edmund D. Tarver, Geo. M. Pirtle & R. S. Wilkerson be
appointed commissioners to settle with Chesley D. Key administrator of the
estate of Jefferson Key decd.

Ordered that John P. Boydston be appointed overseer in place of Robert
Hays on the road from Smiths ferry to the Eastern boundary of said Hays improvement and that he have all the hands that worked under said Hayes.

Pg Ordered that Gibson Merritt be appointed overseer in the room of Ran-
79 dolph Mott on the road from Water Street Bolivar on toward Jackson and have
all said Motts an that they open said road 30 feet.

Ordered that Benjamin Bowers oversee the clearing out and keep in repair the Memphis road from the west bank of Spring Creek to Allsups Prairie
and that all the hands James Ruffin, R. A. Dandridge, Lucy Robinson, L.
Rodd, Bery Riddle Dunaway and his own hand work thereon under his directing.

Ordered that Thomas Washburn oversee the Memphis road as far as Isaah
Davisons road, and that Woodson Vaden William Marvil, Wm. B. Roberson hands
Wm. Rogers, John S. Harris King Henderson & Michial Read work under said
Washburn.

Ordered that Isaah Davis be appointed overseer in the place of Michial
Reed. Cart from sd. Davis to Shirley Goodwin and that he be allowed all the
hands one mile north of the road and as far south as to take in Hills & David-
sons hands.

Ordered by the Court that Green Pryor oversee the clearing out and keep
in repair that part of the Covington Road from Pleasant Run to A. Peelers
and that all the hands of Rob Moore, Peeler, E. Crawford, Josu P. Durley
A. Foster, T. D. White Rowley & Jno. Gray & said Pryor hands work etc.

Pg
80 Ordered   that W. L. Duncan & John Rosson be appointed Commissioners
to settle with the administrator of the Estate of David Tedford decd. & make
report etc.

Ordered that Wm. Todd, Chesley D. Kay, George M. Pirtle, Isaac L. Moody,
Richard L. Wilkerson, James Steele & Wm. Ragon or any five of them be a jury
of view to view and mark a road round A. Conleters clearing commencing at
a pond west of George M. Pirtles and running in a direction to the county
line etc.

Ordered that David Harris oversee the clearing out and keep in repair
that part of the Jackson Road from Isaac Brewers house to Mill Creek, and that
he have all the hands of Jesse Pipkin, James Pipkin, James Piles, Hanson Day,
Milton Day, Rob D. Jackson, Armon P. Jackson, George L. Gibson, Aden Laveghan
& John Henson to work thereon under his direction.

Ordered that Nath K. Norment oversee the clearing out and keepin repair

Pg the road from Killpatricks mill to the west boundary of this county, and
80 that he have his own hands, the hands of Wm. Love, E. Peters Wm. Porter,
E. T. Tarver and I. Mitchie to work under his directions.

Pg   Ordered by the Court that Eli Cox be permitted to turn the Simpson ferry
81 road leading on to Memphis around his field.

Ordered by the Court that so soon as the Hatchie Bridge is completed
and recd. by the Commissioners that all ferries within three miles thereof
shall be disannulled.

Appropriations

Present E. D. Tarver, N. Steele, D. Champion, E. Gossett, M. Taylor, E.
Owens, James Ruffin, Alex McKenzie, John Slaughter & J. B. Hensley Esqs.
Justices.

Ordered unanimously there being ten ayes that the County Trustee pay
W. W. Shackelford four dollars for repairs done to the jail.

Ordered also unanimously as above that the County Trustee pay Thomas
J. Hardeman the sum of sixteen dollars for Blank Books furnished by him
for the use of the County.

Ordered also unanimously as above that the County Trustee pay Nathan
Avery seven dollars fifty cents erroniously collected as a County tax for
1826.

Pg
82   Ordered also unanimously as above that Duguid Mims be paid by the County
Trustee the sum of fifty dollars and fifty cents for jailers fees, provisions
to gourd etc. as appears by his a/c on file in the Clerk's office.

Ordered by the Court present same magistrates as above, unanimously that
the County Trustee pay Jeremiah Williams fifty three dollars twelve and half
cents for furnishing clothing and provision to the orphan children of the
widow Satterwhite.

A deed of trust from Duguid Mims to Roger Barton was exhibited in open
Court and the same acknowledged by said Mims & Barton to be their instruct
for the purpose, thence expressed and it was ordered to be certified for
registration.

A deed of conveyance from Needham Stevens to Littleton Johnson for one
town lot was exhibited in open court and the execution thereof duly proven
by the oaths of Wm. F. Jefferies & E. R. Belcher subscribing witnesses and
it was ordered to be certified for registration.

A deed of conveyance from V. D. & E. Gossett to Wm. N. Fleming for
Pg 24 acres of land was exhibited in open Court and the execution thereof duly
83 acknowledged by said Gossetts and it was ordered to be certified for registration.

A deed of conveyance from Wm. C. Sparks to Wm. N. Fleming for 80 acres
of land was exhibited in open Court and duly acknowledged by said Sparks
and ordered to be certified for registration.

A deed of conveyance from John Mollery to Nath Steele for 50 acres of
land was exhibited in open Court and acknowledged by said Mollery. Ordered
to be certified for registration.

A deed of conveyance from David Jefferies to Stephen Hinant for 390

Pg
83
acres of land was produced in open Court and the execution thereof was duly proven by the oath of Nincan Steele and hand writing of Samuel F. Steele the other witness and who is dedd. was proven by the oath of the said Ninican Steele ordered that it be certified for registration.

A deed of conveyance from the commissioners of the town of Bolivar to Needham Stevens for one town lot was exhibited in open Court and the execution thereof duly proven by the oaths of D. Fentress & E. R. Bibb subscribing witnesses thereto and it was adhered to be certified for registration.

Pg
84
A mortgage from Peter C. Reeves to Thomas Towles father was exhibited in open Court, and the same acknowledged by the said Reeves to be his act and deed for the purposes therein expressed & moved to be certified for registration.

A deed of conveyance from Nath Steele to John H. McKennie for 8 poles of land was exhibited in Court and acknowledged by said Steeld. Ordered to be certified for registration.

A deed of conveyance from Samuel Dickens to Edmund D. Tarver for 200 acres of land was exhibited in open Court and the execution thereof proven by the oath of Allen Dillard one of the subscribing witnesses and who also proved the hand writing of Sam Hannie the other subscribing witness thereto decd. and who he saw sign it. Ordered to be certified for registration.

A deed of conveyance from Samuel Neely to John Neely for 10 acres of land was produced in open Court and the same duly acknowledged by said Samuel Neely. Ordered to be certified for registration.

Pg
85
A power of attorney from Edward Boss & Sarah Jacobs to Michial Mckennie was produced in open court and acknowledged by said Edward & Sarah to be their act and deed for the purposes therein expressed. Ordered to be certified for registration.

A deed of conveyance from John McKinnie to John Mollory for 50 acres of land was produced in open Court and duly proven by the oath of James Steele and Cheeley D . May subscribing witnesses thereto. Ordered to be certified for registration.

A deed of conveyance from Andrew Taylor to Benj. Bowers for 190 acres of land was exhibited in open Court and the execution thereof acknowledged by said Taylor. Ordered to be certified for registration.

A power of attorney from Cyrus Bailey to Nincian Steele was produced in open Court and the execution thereof was duly proven by Mark Harvey one of the subscribing witnesses thereto and the hand writing of Sam F. Steele the other subscribing witness was duly proven by the oath of James Steele, Ordered to be certified for registration.

Pg
86
Two deeds of conveyance from Joseph Burlison to Blackstone Hardeman one for 60 acres and one for 5 acres was produced in open Court and acknowledged by the said Burleson. Ordered to be certified for registration.

A deed of conveyance from John Wallin to Isaac Ricks for 144 acres of land was exhibited in open Court and acknowledged by said Wallin. Ordered to be certified for registration.

A deed of trust from John McKinnie to Elisha W. Boyte & Will Morton was

Pg produced in open Court and duly acknowledged. Ordered to be certified for
86 registration.

An inventory and a/c sales of Drusilla Satterwhites Estate deceased
was returned into Court by the Administrator and ordered to be recorded.

Ordered that the following persons be summoned by the Sheriff to attend
as jurors at the next Circuit Court in the 4th Monday in May, John Y. Cockeran,
George M. Pirtle, Thomas Shaw, William Posten, E. W. Boyte, Benjamin Munell,
Thornton Jones, Jesse Crosby, Charles Cook, Francis Shoemake, Thomas Cox,
Pg James McDaniel Gabrial Bumpass, Howell Myrick, William Myrick, William L.
87 Duncan, Wm. M. Crisp, James Rutherford, George Martin, Robert A. Dandridge,
W. L. Hunt, Josiah Hatley, Ebenezer Killpatrick, William Todd & Caleb Brock
adm. Martin A Ramsay & Charles Jones Constable and that a Venni Facias issue
accordingly.

Ordered that the Sheriff summon the following persons to attend as jurors
at our next County Court to be held on the 1st Monday in July next viz Will-
iam Duncan John B. Justice David Lane, John H. McKennie, William Truett,
Jacob Read, William Crane, Garnett Fitzgerald, David Woods, Daniel E. Harper,
Allen Carroll, Jason Wilson, Joseph Hicks, John M. Neely, Woodson Vaden, Thomas
Washburn, Thomas Hutcherson, Chesley D. Key, Arthur Fulghum Wesley Linvill,
John Caldwell, John Ruffin, Josiah Short, Cumberland Robinson & Jesse Pipkin
constable and that a Venni Facias issue accordingly.

The magistrates appointed at last term to tax a list of taxable property
& polls for the present year returned their respective lists into Court.

Court then adjourned untill tomorrow morning nine O'clock.
                                        Edmund D. Tarver
                                        West Harris
                                        John Y. Cockeran J. P.

Pg _____ Tuesday April 8, 1828 _____
88   C
Court met according to adjournment. Present the worshipful Edmund D.
Tarver John Y. Cockeran, Francis Shoemake Esquires Justice Thomas J. Hardeman Clerk, J. C. N. Robertson Sheriff & V. D. Barry, Solicitor.

Proclamation being made as the form is the Sheriff returned into open
Court & Venirafacias in the following words & figures (towit) State of Tennessee Hardeman County January term 1828. Ordered by the Court that the
following persons be summoned to attend at the Court House in the town of Bol-
ivar on the first Tuesday after the first Monday in April next to serve as
jurors at said County Court (to wit) James McDaniel, Randolph Mott, Aquilla
Combs, Russell Cane, Alec Dean, Nincen Steel, Edmond Kirkland, William Love,
Edward Burlesson Champion Blythe, Richmond Carroll, Stephen Jones, Thomas
Crossland Andrew Blackwood Moore Bendley Johnathan Lindley Elisha W. Harris,
Thomas Gillum James Fippett, William Mayfield, James Lane Enoch Carter Henry
Reagon James Davis Josiah Chandler Snr and Nathaniel E. Normant also Andrew
Thomas and Henry W. Brown to serve as Constables at said term etc. To the
Sheriff of Hardeman County greeting. You are hereby commanded to summon all
of the above named persons to attend as directed above and have you then there
this writ witness, Thomas J. Hardeman Clerk of the Court of Pleas & Quarter
Session of said County at office the first Monday in January 1828. Thomas
J. Hardeman.

Pg   On the back of which was Venirafacias to April Court of Pleas and Quarter
89 sessions 1828. Issd. 19th Jany. 1828 came to hand January 21st 1828.

I hereby certify that I have summoned all of the within named jurors

Pg
89 and that they are all freeholders or house holders over the age of twenty one
years and inhabitants of Hardeman County given under my hand this 8th day
of April 1828. J. C. W. Robertson Shff. out of whom the following persons were
elected empannelled charged and sworn as grand jurors (to wit) James Mc-
Daniel, foreman, Josiah Chandler Serv. Moore Hendley Ninigan Steel, Richmond
Carroll Edmond Kirkland William Mayfield James Tippett Randolph Mott, Henry
Reagan, Edward Burlesson Aguilla Combs and Russell Cane who retired under
the care of Henry W. Brown a constable sworn for that purpose to inquire into
the body of the County etc.

Francis Tedford who was appointed on yesterday guardean to her children
gave bond of twenty five hundred dollars with William L. Duncan, E. L. Duncan and Noren Blackwood as her securities.

Elizabeth Murphey and William Caldwell who was allowed on yesterday to
administer on the estate of Joseph Murphey decd. came into open Court & gave
bond of one thousand dollars with Richmond Carroll and George Read as their
securiteis & was qualified accordingly & received letters testamentory.

On motion ordered that William R. Cockeran be allowed to have license to
keep an ordinary at his now dwelling place in the town of Bolivar who gave
Pg
90 bond with Thomas H. Giles & D. W. Love as his securities and was qualified accordingly.

A deed of conveyance from James Brown to Paul & John W. Williams for
343 acres of land was exhibited in open Court and the execution thereof was
duly proven by the oaths of John H. Arnold and David F. Brown the subscribing
witnesses thereto & the same was ordered to be certified for registration.

A transfer on an occupant claim from Isaac Cronyan to John Wright was
exhibited in open Court and the execution thereof was duly proven by the oath
of E. W. Boyt one of the subscribing witnesses thereto and the same was ordered to be so certified.

Whereas it appears by the certificate of the Ranger that Henry Reagan
posted under the stray law on the 25th July 1826 nine hogs appraised to ten
dollars and from failing to pay for the same as required by law has been com-
pelled to pay the full amount of appraisement. It is therefore ordered
by the Court that he be refunded by the Constable or County Trustee the sum
of five dollars.

An additional inventory & account of sales of the estate of Ezekial Polk
decd. presented in open Court & was ordered to be recorded.
Pg
91 Two bills of sale from John Y. Cockeran to Joel Langhorn was produced
in open Court and the execution thereof was duly acknowledged by said John
Y. Cockeran to be his act and deed and the same was ordered to be certified
for registration.

A transfer on a plot and certificate from David Webb and Absolem Henson
to Hiram Casey was produced in open Court and the execution thereof was
duly acknowledged by said David Webb and Abraham Henson to be their acts and
deeds for the use & purpose therein expressed the same was ordered to be so
certified.

A bond for a conveyance from Thomas A lsop to William Crane for one
hundred and eighty acres of land was produced in open Court and the execution thereof was duly proven by the oath of James McKenzie one of the subscribing witnesses thereto ordered to be so certified.

A deed of conveyance from John Murray to Vivian B. Holmes and William

Pg Arnold for 43 acres of land was produced in open Court and the execution
91 thereof was duly acknowledged by said Murray the same was ordered to be certified for registrations.

A deed of conveyance from William Johnson to Elijah Rudolph for 20 acres
of land was produced in open Court and the execution thereof was duly acknowledged by said William Johnson and the same was ordered to be certified for registration.

Pg
92   A deed of conveyance from Hugh Caruthers and Jane Caruthers his wife
to William Doyle for 300 hundred acres of land was produced in open Court
and the execution thereof was duly acknowledged by Hugh Caruthers to be
his act and deed and Jane Caruthers having been privily examined seperate
and apart from her husband touching her voluntary consent acknowledged that
it was done of her own free will without the coertion or persuasion of her
husband and the same was ordered to be certified for registration.

A deed of conveyance from the Commissioners of the town of Bolivar to
David Fentress for one town lot was exhibited in open Court and the execution thereof was duly acknowledged by John H. Bills Thomas J. Hardeman
and John Y. Cockeran three of the Commissioners who signed the same and it
was ordered to be certified for registration.

Edward Tisdale produced in open Court the scalp of one wolf adjudged to
be over four months old, ordered that he have his certificate.

Jonathan Lindley Elisha Harris Thomas Crosby James C. Davis Steven
Jones Thomas Gillum & Champion Blythe who was summoned as jurors to this
term be excused from further attendance.

Pg
93   Ordered by the Court that John Alsop be fined the sum of three dollars
for contempt of this court by comeing in the Courthouse drunk & misbehaving
while the court was sitting.

Andrew Kirk   )   Present E. D. Tarver, John Y. Cockerank &
    vs. 0   Motion No. 1   )   Thornton Jones Esquire Justices.
Duguid Mims   )
        On motion and it appearing to the satisfaction of the Court that an
execution had issued against the defendant by Francis Shoemake Esq. a Justice of the Peace for this County and which had come to the hands of Philip
I. Kearney a constable of said County, and by him in defect of personal property levied on one town lot No. 2 in Block No. 12 on the 1st day of March
1828. It is therefore ordered adjudged and dedreed by the Court that said
Town Lot be exposed for sale as required by law to satisfy the said execution & debt of seven dollars & fifty eight cents together with costs, as
also the costs of this motion etc. and that a vendituna exponas issue accordingly,

Ennis Ury   )   Present the same Justices as above.
    vs.   ) Motion No. 2)
Duguid Mims   )
        On motion and it appearing to the satisfaction of the Court that an ex-
ecution had issued against the defendant for thirty dollars debt, & costs
by Thomas James Esquire a justice of the peace for this county, and which
Pg said execution had come to the hands of Philip L. Kearney a constable of this
94 County and by him for want of personal property do by on, had levied on one
town lot, in the town of Bolivar known as lot No. 2 in Block 12. It is therefore ordered adjudged and decreed by the Court that the said Town Lot be ex
posed to sale as required by law to satisfy the said debt of thirty dollars

Pg
94 togather with costs and the costs of this motion and that a Venditum Exponsas issue accordingly.

John Carrin   ) Present same Justices as Before.
  vs) Motion No. 3)
Duguid Mims   )
  O On motion and it appearing to the satisfaction of the Court that an execution had issued against the defendant by Joseph W. McKean Esqs a
Cr. Justice of the Peace for this County for the sum of forty four dollars
$13.93 81¼ cents debt & costs and which said execution had come to the hands of Philip I. Kearney a Constable of said County, and by him for want of personal property to by or land levied on my Town Lot in the Town of Bolivar known as Lot no. 2 in Block No. 12. It is therefore ordered adjudged and decreed that the said Town Lot be exposed to sale as required by law to satisfy the said debt of forty four dollars 81¼ cents, together with the costs & also the costs of this motion and that Venoritan Exposas etc.

Pg
95 Allen Hamlin   )
  vs.) Motion No. 4) Present same justices as before.
Duguid Mims   )
  On motion and it appearing to the satisfaction of the Court that an execution had issued against the defendant by Thomas James Esquire a Justice of the Peace for said County for the sum of seven dollars and fifteen cents debt costs and which said execution had come to the hands of Martin A. Ramsay a constable of said County and by him for want of personal property levied on one town lot in the town of Bolivar known as lot No. 2 in Square No1 12. It is therefore ordered adjudged and decreed that the said town lot be exposed to sale as required by law to satisfy the said debt & costs together with the costs of this motion & that a Venditions exponas issue accordingly.

Thomas Sneed   )
  vs) Motion No. 5) Present same Justices as before.
Cr. D. Mims   )
$10.00 On motion and it appearing to the satisfaction of the court that an execution had issued against the defendant by Joseph W. McKean Esq. a Justice of the Peace for this County for the sum of fourteen dollars sixty two and a half cents debt& costs and which said execution had come to the hands of Martin A. Ramsay a constable of said County, and by him for want of personal property levied on one town Lot in the town of Bolivar known as Lot No. 2 in Square No. 12.

  It is therefore ordered adjudged and said that the said Town Lot be exposed to sale as to satisfy said execution & costs together with the costs of this motion and that a Venortima exponas issue accordingly.

Pg
96 Alexander Kirkpatrick   ) Present same Justices as before.
  vs.) Motion No. 6)
Duguid Mims   )
  On motion and it appearing to the satisfaction of the Court that an execution had issued against the defendant by Thomas James Esq. a Justice of the Peace for this County for four dollars sixty cents debt & costs and which said execution had come to the hand of Martin A. Ramsay a constable for said county and by him in defect of personal property levied on one town lot in the town of Bolivar known as Lot No.2 and Block No. 12. It is therefore ordered adjudged & decreed that the said Town Lot be exposed to sale required by law to satisfy the said debt & costs, as also the costs of this motion and that a venditina Exponas issue accordingly.

Pg Thomas N. Giles   )   Present same Justice as Before.
98   vs.) Motion No. 7   )
Duguid Mims   )

On motion it appearing to the satisfaction of the Court that an execution
had issued against the defendant by Thomas James Esq. a justice of the Peace
for this County for the sum of fifteen dollars, seventeen cents debt and costs
Pg and which said execution had come to the hand of Martin A. Ramsay a Constable
97 of said County and by him in defect of personal property levied on one town lot
in the town of Bolivar known as Lot No. 2 in Block No. 12. It is therefore
ordered adjudged and decreed that& the said town lot be exposed to sale as required by law to satisfy the said debt & costs as also the costs of this motion
and that a venditioni exponas issue accordingly.

Walter Robertson   )
      vs) Motion No. 8   )   Present the same Justices as Before.
Duguid Mims   )

On motion and it appearing to the satisfaction of the Court that an execution had issued against the defendant by West Harris Esq. a Justice of the
Peace for this County for the sum of eleven dollars and twenty seven cents debt
& costs and which said execution had come to the hands of Morton A. Ramsay
a constable of said County and by him in defect of personal property levied on
one town lot in the town of Bolivar known as Lot No. 2 in Block No. 12. It is
therefore ordered adjudged and decreed that the said Town Lot be exposed to sale
as required by law to satisfy the said debt & costs as also the costs of this
motion and that a venditiona exponas issue accordingly.

Pg Samuel Pettegrew   )
98n   vs.) Motion No. 9   )   Present the same Justices as Before.
Duguid Mims   )

On motion and it appearing to the satisfaction of the Court that an execution had issued from Thomas James Esquire a Justice of the Peace for this County
for sixteen dollars debt & costs against the defendant and which said execution had come to the hand of Martin A. Ramsay a constable of said County and a
defect of personal property levied on one town lot in the town of Bolivar, known
as lot No. 2 in Block No. 12. It is therefore ordered adjudged & decreed that
the said lot be exposed to sale as required by law to satisfy the said debt &
costs as also the costs of this motion & that a venditiona exponas issue accordingly.

The Shff. returned into Court the following report of land liable for
single taxes for the year 1827 as yet unpaid.

I Julius C. N. Robertson, Sheriff and Collector of publick taxes for the County
of Hardeman do hereby report to Court the following tracts of land as having
been given in for the taxes for the year 1829. That the same is liable for
single taxes, that the single taxes thereon remain due and unpaid and the respective owners or claimants thereof have no goods or chattels within my
County on which I can distrain for said single taxes (to wit)

	Owners Names	No. Entry.	No. Acres.	District	Range	Section
Pg 99	William Bradshaw	143	500	10	3	1
	Joseph H. Bryant	486	274	"	1	4
	Same pt. of	900	320	"	4.5	4
	Alexander Bodenburg	935	640	"	4	5
	William Bryant	874	190	"	4	2
	Wm. Bradshaw & G. Pillow	693	500	"	5	3
	Peter Brown Pt. of 5000	466	1000	"	3	5.6
	John Jenkins pt of	1011	490		2	4.5
	Thos. Claiborn & others	953	2000		1	2

Pg 99 Taxes	Shffs fee	Clerks fees	Printers fee	Total
5.93 3/4	1.00	1.40	1.50	9.83 3/4
3.26	1.00	1.40	1.50	7.16
3.80	1.00	1.40	1.50	7.70
7.60	1.00	1.40	1.50	11.50
2.26				6.16
5.93½				9.83½
11.87½				15.77½
5.813/4				9.71 3/4
23.75				27.65

(Cont. from page 37)

Owners Names	No. Entry	No. Acres	District	Range	Section
John C. Doughty pt. of 1140					
Name of Jacob John	749	243		4	3
Geo. Doherty	358	170		3	1.2
Thos. P. Devenger	884	500		3	4
" " "	881	500		3	4
Geo. Doherty Devisers of	1084	630		4.5	3.4
Vinot Fine p. of	933	150		4	1
Wm. H. Hughes	983	125		1	3
" " "	939	36		1	5
Robt. & Tho. Love	396	500		3	6
" " " " pt. of	487	1175		3	1
Beryn Malloy pt. of	1762	200		4	6
Michial Moore					
Robt. Searcy pt. of	253	800		3	3
Gideon Pillow	690	250		3.4	2
" "		12½		3	1
William Polk	769	204	9	2	1
Thomas Polk	885	327	10	4	4
Tyre Rhodes	403	345	"	5	2
John Shanklin pt. of	949	375	"	3	4.5
John Givens	1101	100	"	4	4
William Willoughby	1146	640	10	1	2
Lewis D. Wilson	518	640		5	1
Thomas N. William pt. of					
Susan William pt of 1140 is the name of J. Johnson	2382	100		2	4
John Burleson	740	290		4	3
Malcom Ama Johnson	1114	150		4	6
Pleasant Branden	1918	200		4	6
George Brandon	2021	200		2	4
Littlebery Mason	2022	175		3	4
"	1524	50			
Thomas Farmer on Just of Pease	2052	50		3	4
Name of W Lawrence	2089	50		2	4
Hosea Harris	2091	50		3	5
Patterson C. Landers	2097	25		2.3	2
Samuel F. Moore	2178	50		5	1
Samuel Givens	2265	50		4	4

Pg 100

(Cont. from page 38)

Pg	Taxes	Shffs fee	Clerks fees	Printers fee	Total
99	2.88½				6.78½
	2.1¼				5.91 3/4
	5.93 3/4				9.83 3/4
	5.93 3/4				8.83 3/4
	7.48				11.38
	1.78				5.68
	1.48¼				5.38¼
	45				4.33
	5.93 ¼				9.83¼
	13.95 3/4				17.85 3/4
	2.37 ½				6.27½
	9.50				13.40
	2.97				6.87
	14 3/4				4.4 3/4
	2.42 ¼				6.32 ¼
	3.88½				7.78½
	4.09 3/4				7.99½
	4.45				8.35
	1.18 3/4				5.08 3/4
	7.60	1.00			11.50
	7.60	1.00			11.50
	1.18 3/4				5.8 3/4
	3.44½				7.34½
	1.78				5.68
	2.37½				6.27½
	2.57½				6.27½
	2.07½				5.97½
	.54¼				4.47¼
	.59¼				4.47
	..59¼				4.47
	.59¼				4.47
	.29½				4.19
	.59¼				4.47
	3.88½				7.78½

Owners Name	No. of Entry	No. of acres	District	Range	Section
William G. Murtry	2198	50		4	5
Menymen Lines	2261	50		1	6
Thomas G. Williams	2332	25		3	5
Alfred M. Walker	2378	59		4	6
James King	1251	100		2	3
Gideon Spalding	1517	9		3	1
" " pd.)	1508	10		3	1
Lawrence Prosteman)	853	480		4	2
James P. Peters	878	314½		4	1
do	1419	75		4	1
Thomas Hunt ap. of F. Tafor	141	640		5	2
Coerge Dougherty	877	260		1	2
John McIver	892	49		23	5
Adam C. Goodlett & Wm. Campbell	665	1000			

Pg	Owners Name	No. of Entry	No. of Acres	District	Range	Section
101						
	Adam G. Goodlett & Wm. Campbeal	665	1000	10	2	5	11.89½
	Duncun Carpenter pt. of	1114	171		3	3	2.03
	Alfred Balch pt. of 500 name of S. Polk	466	1500		3	5.6	17.81
	Archibald Murphy prt of same	466	500		3	5.6	5.93¼
	Thomas Taylor ¾ of same	466	250		3	5.6	2.97
	William Dickson	491	500		4	6	5.93 3/4
	Isaac Swindle	941	72		4	4	.85½
	Randall Johnson	357	320		4	3	3.80
	Same pt. of 1140	740	224		4	2.3	2.66
	Jenkins Whitesides	642	253½		4	3	3.45½
	Gabrial Bensen	968	44		1	3	.52½
	Lebulon Tarkington	2103	25		3	3	.29½
	Thos. L. Polk p. of	442	35		4	3	.41
	Ephriam A. Davidson pt. of 500 name of Jneb Harriss	809	1200		1.2	1	14.25
	John O. Davidson prt. of same	809	1100		1.2	1	13.06
	Edward H. Chaffin pt. of same	809	1400		1.2	1	15.43 3/4
	Wm. Wood pt. of 968 name of Wm. Bell	1153	358		5	4	4.25

Julius C. N. Robertson
Sheriff

Pg
100
&
101
(cont.)

Taxes	Shffs fee	Clerks fee	Printers	Amt.
.59½				4.47
.59½				4.47
.29½				4.17½
.70				4.60
1.18 3/4				5.18¼
.10½				4.00
.11¼				4.02
5.70				9.60
3.73½				7.63½

Pg	Taxes	Shffs Fee	Clerks fee	Printers fee	Amt.
100	.99				4.77
&	7.60				11.50
101	3.08 3/4				4.98 3/4
cont.	.58				4.48
		1.00	1.40	1.50	15.77½
					5.93
					21.71
					9.83 3/4
					6.87
					9.83 3/4
					4.75
					7.70
					6.56
					7.37½
					4.42 ¼
					4.19½
					4.31
					18.15
					16.96
					19.33 3/4
					8.15

Julius C . N. Robertson Sheriff

Whereupon it is considered by the Court that judgment be and it is hereby entered the aforesaid treaty and owners of the lands in the name of the state for the sum annexed to each being the amount of taxes costs & charges due generally thereon for the year 1827 & it is ordered by the Court that the said several tracts lf land or so mutch thereof or shall be sufficient of each of them to satisfy the taxes costs & charges annexed to them severally as be sold the case directs.

Pg
102   Daniel Simpson)   C ovenant -Present Edmond Tarver, John Y. Cockeran
             vs.   )   and Nathaniel Steele Esq. Justices.
       Robert Rivers   )

This day came the defendant in proper person and says that he cannot gainsay the plaintiffs cause of action and confeses judgment for one hundred and three dollars damages besides costs. Therefore it is considered by the Court here that the plaintiff recover of said defendant the sum of one hundred and three dollars damages aforesaid in form aforesaid confessed also his costs about his suit in this behalf expended etc.

       Robert Rivers   )
             vs.   )   Motion samme Justices as above.
       John McKinnier)

This day came the said Robert Rivers by his attorney and moved the Court for judgment against the said John McKinnie for one hundred and three dollars the amt. of a judgment that Daniel Simpson obtain against the said Rivers on a covenant made by said McKennie and said Rivers to said Simpson also the costs by the said Simpson recovered of the said Rivers on said judgment.

And it appearing to the satisfaction of the Court that said Rivers was only the security of the said McKinnie in said Covenant made to said

102 Simpson as aforesaid and that the said Simpson had on this day recovered
judgment against said Rivers in this Court for the sum of one hundred and
three dollars besides costs on said covenant. Therefore it is considered
Pg by the Court that the said Rivers recover of the said McKinnie the said
103sum of one hundred and three dollars the amount of said judgment also the
costs recovered by the said Simpson of the said Rivers by reason of the
promises together with his the said Rivers costs about this motiont in
this behald exposed etc.

Samuel Dickins   )
     vs.   )   Garnishment.
Thomas Hunt   )

     This day comes into open Court Henry M. Johnson as he is summoned as
garnishee in this behalf and being examined as the law direct states that
he is indebted to the said defendant in the sum of one hundred and twenty
five dollars. It is therefore considered by the Court that the plaintiff
recover agst. the said Henry M. Johnson the said sum of one hundred and
twenty five dollars together with the costs of this garnishment.etc.

A. Taylor Ranger   )
     vs.   )
Michael McKennie   )

     This day came the parties by their attornies and thereupon came a Jury
of good and lawful men, towit, Andrew Blackwood, Aubrey Dean, William Love,
A. P. Lockman, Elijah C. Hull, William Overall, Benjamin Gey, James Mc-
Millen, George Read, M. B. Roberts, John Croly, W . A. Moore, who being
elected tried and sworn the truth to speak upon the matter in dispute on
their oath do say that the defendant is indebted to the said Ranger for
the use of said County in the sum of twenty dollars. It is therefore considered by the Court here that the plaintiff recover against the defendant
as aforesaid the said sum of twenty dollars together with the costs by him
about his suit in this behalf expended etc. Where upon the said defendant
Pg moves the Courthere for a new trial in this behalf which without argument
104 is ordered accordingly.

John Wright   )
     vs.   )   Covenant
A. A. King   )

     This day came the parties by their attornies and thereupon came a
Jury of good and lawful men, to wit, William I. Riddle, N. Stevens, J. G.
Wilkes, Isaac Jones, Michael Reed, John B. Justice, Samuel Henson, Aden
Longhorn, Benjamin Rook, William Fellow, Robert A. H. Harris and Thomas
C. Wilson who being elected tried and sworn the truth to speak upon the
issue joined on their oath do say that the defendant hatn not performed his
covenant in manner and form as the plaintiff in applying hath alledged they
find the issues in favour of plaintiff and they assess his damages by reason
thereof to one hundred dollars. It is therefore considered by the Court
that the plaintiff recover against the defendant the said sum of one hundred dollars together with the costs by him about his suit in this behalf
expended etc. and thereupon after motion and solem argument by counsel a
new trial is granted.

Con P. Jamerson   )
     vs.   )   Case
Smith Williams & Co.)

     This day came the parties by their attornies and thereupon came a Jury
of good and lawful men, to wit, Andrew Blackwood, Aubry Dean, Benjamin
Rook, Benjamin Gey, R obert A. Farris, Miles Filley, Joseph P. Stockton,
William Overall, Elijah C. Hull, W illie I. Riddle, Jesse Cockeran & James

Pg McMillan who being elected tried & sworn the truth to speak upon the issue
104 joined on this oath do say that they cannot agree and thereupon a mistrial
is had by the withdrawing a Juror. And thereupon came the parties by their
attornies and by assent of said parties and the consent of the Court it is
agreed that said case be transmitted to the Circuit Court Next term on an
agreed case by said parties.

Pg Louis M. Basye
105   vs.   ) Debt
Ebenezer Frazer
     This day came the parties by their attornies and thereupon came a jury
of good and lawful men to wit Willie I. Riddle, N. Stevens, J. G. Wilkes,
Isaac Jones, Michial Read, John B. Justices, Samuel Henson, Aden Longhorn,
Benjamin Rook, William Fellow, Robert A. Farris and Thomas C. Wilson who
being elected tried and sworn the truth to speak upon the issue joined on
their oath do say that they find the issues joined in favor of the plaintiff and that the defendant has not paid the sum of fifty dollars in the
plaintiffs declaration mentioned and they assess the plaintiff damages
by reason of the detention thereof to three dollars. Therefore it is considered by the Court that the said plaintiff recover of the said defendant
the debt aforesaid, together, with his damages aforesaid in form aforesaid
assessed & costs about his suit in this behalf expended & it is agreed to
stay execution etc.

David Jernigan   )
     vs.   )
Josiah Halby & William Bogard Admins.)
p. Lete of Thomas Alsup decd.
     This day came the parties by their attornies and thereupon came a
jury of good and lawful men to wit; Wilie J. Riddle, N. Stevens, J. G.
Wilkes, Isaac Jones, Michael Read, John B. Justices, Samuel Henson, Aden
Longhorn, Benjamin Rook, William Fellow, Robert Farris, & Thomas C. Wilson, who being elected tried and sworn the truth to speak upon the issue
joined on their oaths do say that they find the issue in favor of the
plaintiff and that the defendant has not paid to the plaintiff the debt
Pg in the declaration mentioned and assess the plaintiffs damages in the sum
106 of nineteen dollars & twelve and one half cents for the detention of the
same . It is therefore considered by the Court that the plaintiffs recover of the defendants administrators as aforesaid to be levied of the
property of the said Alsup decd. in their hands to be administered the said
sum of two hundred and eighty eight dollars and seventy five cents his debt
aforesaid and the sum of nineteen dollars and twelve & one half cents his
damages in form aforesaid assessedtogether with costs about his suit in
this behalf expended and that execution issued accordingly. The Court
adjourned untill tomorrow morning nine O'clock.
                                        John C. Cockeran
                                        Edmund D. Tarver
                                        F. Shoemake

Wednesday 9th April 1828
Pg
107   Court met according to adjournemtn present the worwhipful Edmund D.
Tarver John Y. Cockeran Francis Shoemake Esquires Justices Thos. J. Hardeman Clerk, J. C. N. Robertson, Sheriff, V. D Barry, Solicitor.

     A deed of conveyance from Hezekiah Ward to John H. Bills for 25/160
acres of land was produced in open Court and the execution thereof was
duly proved by the oaths of Austin Miller and David F. Brown two of the
subscribing witnesses thereto and the same was ordered to be certified for
registration.

Pg
107
A deed of conveyance from William W. Bomer to John H. Bills and Charles Stewart for 147½/160 acres of land was produced in open Court and the execution thereof was duly acknowledged by said William W. Bomer to be his act & deed the same was ordered to be certified for registration.

A power of attorney from Francis Richardson to John H. Bills was produced in open Court and the execution thereof was duly proven by the oaths of Joseph H. Talbot and C. C. Collin two of the subscribing witnesses thereto the same was ordered to be certified for registration.

A title bond from Andrew Davidson to Daniel Davis was produced in open Court and the exedution thereof was duly proven by the oath of Sm. M. Carnery the subscribing witness thereto and the same was ordered to be certified for registration.

Pg
108
Two deeds of conveyance from the Commissioners of the town of Bolivar to John C. McKean for one town lot each was produced in open Court and the execution thereof duly acknowledged. John H. Bills Thomas J. Hardeman John Y. Cockeran & Nathaniel Steel who resigned the same to be their acts & deeds, the same was ordered to be certified for registration.

A deed of conveyance from the Commissioners of the town of Bolivar to Joseph W. McKean for one town lot was exhibited in open Court and the execution thereof was duly acknowledged by John H. Bills Thomas J. Hardeman, John A. Cockeran & Nathaniel S teel those who signed the same and the same was ordered to be certified for registration.

A deed of conveyance from the Commissioners of the Town of Bolivar to William A. Clun for one town lot was produced in open Court and the execution thereof was duly acknowledged by John H. Bills, Thomas J. Hardeman, John Y. Cockeran, & Nathaniel Steel those who signed the same & it was ordered to be certified for registration.

A Quit Claim deed or relinquishment from John H. Bills to Adam R. Alexander was produced in open Court and duly acknowledged by said John
Pg
109
H. Bills to be his act and deed the same was ordered to be certified for registration .

A Quit Claim deed from Adam R. Alexander to John H. Bills was produced in open Court and the execution thereof was duly acknowledged by said Adam R. Alexander to be his act and deed and the same was ordered to be certified for registration.

A deed of conveyance from Charles Stewart to Thornton W. Pinckard for 3-73 3/4 /160 acres of land was produced in open Court and the execution thereof was duly acknowledged by said Charles Stewart to be his act the same was ordered to be certified for registration.

A deed of conveyance from the Commissioners of the Town of Bolivar to Thornton Pinckard for one town lot was exhibited in open Court and the execution thereof was duly proven by the oaths of E. B. Belcher and Daniel M. Guinn the subscribing witnesses thereto and the same was ordered to be certified for registration.

Pg
110
A deed of conveyance from Rayford Crawford to Anthony Foster for one hundred acres of land was produced in open Court and the execution thereof was duly proven by the oaths of David W. Wood and M. D. Ramsay the subscribing witnesses thereto and the same was ordered to be certified for registration.

Pg   Robert A. Farris Joseph P. Stockton James McMillan Miler Filly,
110 William Overall Benjamin Gay, Willie I. Riddle, Benjamin Rook, Elijah
C. Hull and Jesse Cockeran proved two days attendance as jurors.

John Moore
    vs.) Motion No. 10) Present Edmund T. Tarver, John Y. Cockeran &
Josiah Dunn   F. Shoemake Esq.
        On motion and it appearing to the satisfaction of the Court that an
execution had issued from West Harris Esq. a Justice of the Peace for
this County against the defendant for fifteen dollars & costs and which
said execution had come to the hand of H. W. Brown a Constable of said
County and by him in defect of personal property levied on 25 acres of
land in said County in Range 3 Section 4. Therefore it is ordered adjudged & decreed that said tract of land be exposed for sale as required
by law to satisfy said debt and costs as also the costs of this motion &
that a vinditona exponas issue accordingly.

Pg John Moore
111   vs.) Motion 11) Present the same Justices as before.
Josiah Dunn
        On motion and it appearing to the satisfaction of the Court that an
execution had issued from West Harris Esq. a Justice of the Peace for this
County against the defendant for the sum of thirteen dollars fourteen cents
and which said execution had come to the hands of Harry W. Brown a Constable of said County, and for defect of personal property levied by
him on 25 acres of land in said County in the Range 3 Section 4. Therefore it is ordered adjudged and decreed that the said tract of land be
exposed to sale as required by law to satisfy said debt & costs, together with the costs of this motion and that a venditiona exponas issue
accordingly etc.

Raiford Crawford
    vs.) Motion No. 12) Present same Justices as Before.
Enoch P. Hannis
        On motion and it appearing to the satisfaction of the Court that an
execution had been issued from Frances Shoemake Esq. A Justice of the
Peace for this County against the defendant, for ninety two dollars &
costs, and which said execution had come to the hands of Martin A. Ramsay a Constable of said County and by him in defect of personal property levied on 200 acres of land entry 1995 in the name of E. P. Hannis
in the 10th District Range 3 & Section 3 on Spring Creek 9th of April
1828. It is therefore considered by the Court that the said tract of
land be exposed for sale as required by law to satisfy said debt & costs
& the costs of this motion & that he ven ex etc.

Pg Raiford Crawford
112   vs.   ) Motion No. 13) Present the same Justices as before.
Enoch P. Hannis
        On motion and it appearing to the satisfaction of the Court that an
execution had issued from Francis Shoemake Esq. a Justice of the Peace
for this County against the defendant for fifty dollars & costs and
which said execution had come to the hands of Martin A. Ramsay a Constable
of said County and in defect of personal property levied on 200 acres
of land entered by No. 1975 in the name of E. P. Hannis in the 10th District Range3 & Section 3 on Spring Creek the 9th of April 1828. Therefore it is considered ordered adjudged and decreed that the said tract
of land be exposed for sale to satisfy said debt & costs as required by
law together with the costs of this motion and that a vinditiona exponas issue accordingly.

Pg Benjamin Arnold   )
112   vs.   ) Case No. 7) Present same Justices as Before.
     Benjamin Gay   )

     This day came the parties by their attornies and thereupon came a
Jury of good and lawful men To Wit, Richard Lambert, Isaac Brewer, Tensil
Jasper, James Burleson, A. S. Lockman, Charles Stewart, Robert Box, Gesson
Moss, David F. Owens, Daniel Davis, James Slaughter & Arthur Fulghum who being electioned and sworn the truth to speak upon the issue joined upon their
oath do say the defendants are not guilty in manner and form as charged in
the plaintiff declaration.

Pg   Therefore it is considered by the Court that the defendants depart hence
113 without day and recover of the plaintiff their costs in this behalf unjust-
ly expended. From which said judgment of the Court the plaintiff prayed
and obtained an appeal to the next Circuit Court for this County and gave
bond with John M. Davis as his security.

John Foster   )
     vs.   ) Appeal No. 9)   Present same Justices as before.
Thomas L. Oliver   )

     This day came the parties by their attorney and thereupon came a Jury
of good and lawful men to wit Richard Lamb, Isaac Brewer, Terrel Jasper
James Burlesson Archebald S. Lockman Charles Stewart Robert Box Gesson Moss,
David F. Owens Daniel Davis James Slaughter and Arthur Fulgham who being
elected tried and sworn the truth to speak upon the matter in dispute upon
their oaths do say they find for the defendant and that the said plaintiff
is justly indebted to said defendant the sum of thirteen dollars twelve &
one half cents and costs of suit. Therefore it is considered by the Court
that the defendant go hence without day & recover of the plaintiff the
said debt aforesaid & costs aforesaid assessed & that he have his execution from which judgment the plaintiff prayed and obtained an appeal to
the next Circuit Court for the County and gave bond with John H. McKinnie
as his security.

Pg
114 John H. McKennie   )
        vs.   ) Case No. 16) Present same Justices as Before.
     Gesson Moss   )

     This day came the parties by their attornies and thereupon came a jury
of good and lawful men To wit Andrew Blackwood, Alsey Deen, Benjamin Rook,
Benjamin Gay, Robert A. Farris, Miles Filley, Joseph P. Stockton, William Overall, Elijah C. Hull, Wilie I. Riddle, Jesse O ockeran & James Mc-
Millan who being elected empannelled tried and sworn the truth to speak upon
the issue joined upon their oath do say they find the issue joined in favor
of the defendant and that he is not guilty in manner and form as charged
in the plaintiff declaration. Therefore it is considered by the Court
that the said defendant depart hence without day and recover of the plaintiff his costs in behalf of said suit expended etc.

Daniel Hughes   )
adm.)   Covenant
   vs.) No. 15 Writ of Inquiry) Present sa me Justices as Before.
John H. Arnold   )

     This day came the parties by their attornies and thereupon came a
jury of good and lawful men To Wit Andrew Blackwood, Alsey Deen, Benjamin
Rook, Benjamin Gay, Robert A. Farris, Miles Filley, Joseph I1 Stockton,
William Overall, Elijah C. Hull, Wilie I. Riddle, Jesse Cockeran & James
McMillan who being elected empannelled and sworn the truth to speak upon the
issues joined upon their oath do say they find the issue joined in favor
of the defendant and that he is not guilty in manner and form as charged in
the plaintiff dedlaration. Therefore it is considered by the Court that
the said defendant depart hence without day and recover of the plaintiff

Pg day and recover of the plaintiff his costs in behalf of said suit expended etc.
114

Daniel Hughes
Adm.) Novenant
    vs.) No. 15 Writ of Inquiry)   Present same Justices as before.
John H. Arnold
    This day came the parties by their attornies and thereupon came a Jury of good and lawful men To Wit Andrew Blackwood, Alsey Deen, Benjamin Rook, Benjamin Gay, Robert A. Farris, Miles Filley, Joseph I. Stockton William Overall, Elijah C. Hull, Wilie I. Riddle, Jesse Cockeran, & James McMillan who being elected empannelled and sworn well and truly to enquire of the damages the said plaintiff has sustained by reason of the non performance of the Covenant in the plaintiffs declaration mentioned upon their oath do
Pg say that the said plaintiff has sustained damages by reason of the non-
115 performances aforesaid to the amount of one hundred and thirty three dollars in which this is credit of thirteen dollars).
    Therefore it is considered by the Court that the plaintiff recover of said defendant the said sum of one hundred and thirty three dollars damages aforesaid by the Jury aforesaid in form aforesaid assessed also his costs about his suit in this behalf expended.

Michial Pirtle   )
    vs.   ) Case No. 18)   Present same Justices as Before.
James Pirtle   )
    This day came the parties by their attornies and thereupon came a Jury of good and lawful men To Wit, Richard Lambert, Isaac Brewer, Tenill Lasper, James Burleson, Archibald S. Lockman, Charles Stewart, Robert Box, Gesson Moss, David F. Owens, Daniel Davis, James Slaughter & Arthur Fulghum, who being elected emapnnelled and sworn the truth to speak upon the issue joined upon their oath do say they find in favor of the plaintiff and that the defendant did assume in manner and form as charged in the said plaintiff dedlaration and they assess the plaintiff damages by reason of the defendants non performance of his said <u>assumpsit</u> to sixty dollars.
    Therefore it is considered by the Court that the plaintiff recover of the defendant the said sum of sixty dollars damages aforesaid by the Jury aforesaid in form aforesaid assessed also his costs by him about his suit in this behalf expended etc.

Pg
116 Hiram Casey for the use of Newell W. Cram)
        vs.) Debt No. 19   ) Present the same Justices as
James Wright   ) Before.

    This day came the parties by their attornies and thereupon came a Jury of good and lawful men To Wit Andrew Blackwood, Alsey Deen, Benjamin Rook, Benjamin Gay, Robert A. Farris, Miles Filley, Joseph S. Stockton, William Overall, Elijah C. Hull, Wilie J. Riddle, Jesse C ockeran & James McMillan who being elected empannelled and sworn the truth to speak upon the issues joined upon their oath do say they find the issues in favour of the plaintiff and that the defendant hath not paid the debt of two hundred and forty three dollars and seventy five cents in the plaintiff declaration mentioned and they do assess his damages by reason of the detention thereof to fifteen dollars and seventy five cents. Therefore it is considered by the Court here that the plaintiff recover of the defendant for the use of the said Newell W. Cram the said sum of two hundred & forty three dollars and seventy five cents his debt aforesaid, together with his damages aforesaid in form aforesaid assessed also his costs about his suit in this behalf expended etc.

Pg   V. D. Barry)
116   vs.   )   Motion
      C. D. Key   )

This day comes the plaintiff by his attorney and C. D. Key thereupon
it appearing to the satisfaction of the Court that an execution has issued from a Justice of the Peace against said defendant in behalf of said
plaintiff for the sum of ten dollars and interest from the 6th day of
Pg   October   1827 with lawful costs which said execution for want of per-
117 sonal estate is levied upon 112½ acres of land in range 4 section 4, tenth
District, it is ordered by the Court that a Scirifacias issue requiring
the heirs of Jefferson Key decd. to appear at the next term of this Court
to show cause if any they have or can why said land should not be ordered for sale to satisfy the said plaintiff his debt and costs aforesaid.

The Grand Jury return into open Court under the care of their officer and present a bill of indictment against Henson A. Day and George W.
Graves for an affray and a bill of indictment against John Jones for an
assault and battery severally endorsed " a true bill James McDowell foreman of the Grand Jury."

Davis W. Wood for the use of Wm. Todd)
      Vs.   ) Present same Justices as Before.
Ch. D. Key Adm.   )
This day comes the plaintiff by his attorney and thereupon it appearing to the satisfaction of the Court that an execution had issued from
a Justice of the Peace against said defendant in behalf of said plaintiff
for the use of etc. for the sum of eighty four dollars sixty seven cents
with interest & costs which said execution for want of personal estate
is levied upon 112½ acres of land in Range 4 Section 4 tenth District, it
is ordered by the Court that a Sciri Facias issue requiring the heirs of
Jefferson Key decd. to appear at the next term of this Courtto show
cause if any they have or can why said land should not be ordered for sale
to satisfy the said plaintiff his debt & costs aforesaid etc.

Pg   David W. Wood for the use of Wm. Todd)
118   vs.   ) Motion   ) Present the same Justices
      C. D. Key adm.   ) as Before.
This day came the plaintiff by his attorney and thereupon it appearing to the satisfaction of the Court that an execution had issued from
a Justice of the Peace against said defendant in behalf of said plaintiff
for the sum of eighty four dollars & sixty seven cents debt with interest
& costs which said execution for want of personal estate is levied upon
112½ acres of land in Range 4 Section 4 in the Tenth District. It is
ordered by the Court that a Sciri Facias issue requireing the heirs of
Jefferson Key deceased to appear at thenext term of this Court to show
cause if any they have or can why said land should not be ordered for sale
to satisfy the said plaintiff his debt & costs aforesaid.

John Lea & James Lea   )
Firm of John Lea   )   Present same Justices as before.
      vs.   ) Case No. 8   )
Chesley D. Key Adm.   )
Jefferson Key deceased   )
This day came the parties by their attorneys and thereupon came their
Jury of good and lawful men To wit Andrew Blackwood, Alsey Deen, Benjamin
Rook, Benjamin Gay, Robert A. Farris, Miles Philley, Joseph P. Stockton,
William Overall, Elijah C. Hull, Wilie J. R iddle, Jesse Cockeran &
James McMillan who being elected empannelled and sworn the truth to speak
upon the issue joined upon their oath do say, that the defendant has fully

Pg

119 administered all and singular the good & chattels of the said Jefferson
Key deceased which at the time of his death came into the defendants
hand to be administered. And the jury aforesaid upon their oath aforesaid do further say that they find that said Jefferson Key deceased in
his life time did assume to the said plaintiff in manner and form as
alleged in the said plaintiffs declaration and they assess their damages
try reason of the non performance of his said undertaking to eighty three
dollars and thirty two cents.

Therefore it is considered by the Court that the said plaintiff recover of the said defendant the said sum of eighty three dollars and
thirty two cents aforesaid to be levied of the goods & chattel etc. of
Jefferson Key which have or may come to his hand to be administered together with costs etc. And thereupon on motion to the Court and because
it appears that the said Chesley D. Key administrator aforesaid has fully
administered the personal estate of said Jefferson Key deceased as
found by the Jury aforesaid. It is ordered that Sciri Facias issue
against the heirs of the said Jefferson Key deceased to appear at the
next term of this Court & show cause if any they have why execution
against the land and tenements of the said J efferson Key deceased at
the time of his death should not be awarded etc.

George Stull   )
            vs.) Debt No. 24)   )   Present same Justices
Thos. James Adm. James L. Nelson decd.)   as before.

This day came the parties by their attornies and thereupon came

Pg   a Jury of good and lawful men To Wit Andrew Blackwood, Alsey Deen, Ben-
120 jamin Rook, Benjamin Gay, Robert A. Farris, Miles Philley, Joseph Pl
Stockton, William Overall, Elijah C. Hull, W illie I. Riddle, Jesse
Cockeran & James McMillan who being elected empannelled and sworn the
truth to speak upon the issues joined upon their oath do say that they
find the same in favor of the plaintiff and that the defendant hasx not
paid the debt of one hundred and seventy two dollars in the plaintiffs
declaration mentioned and they assess the plaintiffs damages by reason
of the detention thereof to thirty four dollars forty cents. Therefore
it is considered by the Court that the plaintiff recover of the defendant his debt aforesaid together with the damages aforesaid in form aforesaid by the Jury assessed and his costs about his suit in this behalf
expended etc. to be levied of the goods & chattels which were of the
said James L. Nelson deceased in the hands of the said defendant to be
administered.

Herbert Newsum   )
        vs.) Debt No. 31)   Present as before the same Justices.
John C. McKean adm.   )

This day came the parties by their attornies and thereupon came a
Jury of good and lawful men to wit Anderson Blackwood, Alsey Deen, Ben-
jamin Rook, Benjamin Gay, Robert A. Farris, Miles Philley, Joseph P.
Stockton, William Overall, Elijah C. Hull, Wilie I. Riddle, Jesse

Pg   Cockeran, & James McMillan who being elected empannelled and sworn the
121 truth to speak upon the issues joined upon their oath do say they find
the issues joined in favor of the plaintiff and that the defendant has
not paid the debt of four hundred & eighty dollars in the plaintiffs declaration mentioned and they assess his damages by reason of the detention thereof to sixty seven dollars. Therefore it is considered by the
Court that the Plaintiff recover of the defendant his debt aforesaid
together with the damages aforesaid in form aforesaid by the Jury in
form assessed and his costs about his suit in this behalf expended etc.
to be levied of the goods & chattels which were of the said John C.
Old deceased in the hand of the said defendant to be administered etc.

Pg Elizabeth Smith   )
      vs.   )   Present the same Justices as above.
121 Alvan F. Reese   )

    The judgment of a Justice of the Peace this day came the plaintiffs
attorney and moved the Court to dismiss the defendants appeal for want
of security and it appearing to the Court that the defendant had failed
to give security for his said appeal. It is ordered that the same be
dismissed and that the plaintiff recover of the said defendant his costs
of this Court & that a prosedendo issue to the magistrate to issue execution etc. in this case etc.

Pg
122 David Jernigan   )
      vs.   )   Covenant Present same Justices
Wm. B. Robison Adm. of   )
Thomas B. Hughes Decd.   )

    This day came the parties by their attornies and thereupon came a
Jury of good and lawful men to wit, Andrew Blackwood, Alsey Deen, Benjamin Rook, Benjamin Gay, Robert A. Farris, Miles Phelley, Joseph P.
Stockton, William Overall, Elijah C. Hull, Willie J. Riddle, Jesse Cockeran, and James McMillan, who being elected empenneled and sworn well
and truly to enquire of the damages which the plaintiff hath sustained by
the breach of the defendants covenant upon their oath do say they find
the issue joined in favor of the defendant on his plea of fully administered
whereupon they find that the said plaintiff hath sustained damages in the
sum of five hundred and four dollars & twenty cents for the said breach
in the plaintiffs declaration mentioned. It is therefore considered by
the Court that the plaintiff recover of the said defendant the sum of five
hundred and four dollars & twenty cents his damages for manner and form
aforesaid assessed for the breach aforesaid to be levied of the goods and
chattels of the said Thomas B. Hughes when they may come to the hands of
the said administrator. Whereupon on motion and it appearing to the
Court that sufficient assets have not yet come inot the hands of the
defendant as aforesaid to satisfy said damages aforesaid. It is ordered
by the Court that Scira facias issue to the hands of the said Thomas
requiring them to show causes if any they can why execution shall not
be issued against the lands and tennants of the said Thomas at the time
his death or to which legal title may hand vested in said lands by
virtue of the equity in the said Thomas at the time of his death and also
the costs about this, sent in this behalf expended.

Pg
123 David W. Wood   )
      vs.   ) Debt)   Present same Justices
John Molloy   )

    This day came the plaintiff by his attorney and says he will no
further prosecute his said suit, and thereupon comes the defendant in
proper person and assums the costs. It is therefore considered by the
Court that the said plaintiff recover of the said defendants his costs
aforesaid etc.   And the Court adjourned to tomorrow morning 9 O'clock.
                                Edmund D. Tarver
                                F. Shoemake
                                Wm. L. Duncan

_____Thursday 10, April 1828_____

Pg   Court met according to adjournment present the worshipful Edmund D.
124 Tarver, John Y. Cockeran and Francis Shoemake Esquires Justices Thomas
J. Hardeman Clerk, J. C. N. Robertson, S hff., V. D. Barry Solicitor.

    A deed of conveyance from Duguid Mims to Francis Shoemake for 90½

Pg   acres of land was produced in open Court and the execution thereof was
124 duly acknowledged by said Mims to be his act & deed the same was orderer-
     ed to be certified for registration.

     The grand jury returned into open Court under the care of their
sworn officer the following bills of indictment and presentments:a
bill of indictment against John O. Brian for an assault and battery a
bill of indictment against Walden Fuller for extortion a bill of indict-
mant against Robert Hays Junior & Silas Hart for an assault & battery
severally indorsed a true bill James M. Daniel foreman of the Grand
Jury also a bill of presentment against Walden Fuller for extortion a
bill of presentment against Walden Fuller as overseer of road a bill of presentment against Walden Fuller for extortion a bill of presentment against
John C rane overseer severally endorsed a true bill James M. Daniel
foreman of the Grand Jury & signed by all the other Jury.

Pg   Ordered that Francis Shoemake Thomas James & William Ramsay be app-
125 ointed Commissioners to divide the personal property between the heirs
     of Henry G. Kearney & make report to next Court.

     State   )
       vs.   )   A & B)
     John E. Mayfield)
          This day came the Solicitor general on the part of the state and
     the defendant being solemly called to come into Court and answer the
     state of Tennessee on a bill of indictment as you are bound to do or you
     will forfeit your reconisence who came not but made default therefore it
     was considered by the Court that the state recover of the defendant the
     sum of two hundred dollars the amount of his recognisence & costs of
     this prosecution etc.

     State   )
       vs.   )
     John Foster   )
          This day came into open Court John Foster and Andrew Blackwood who
     acknowledged themselves severally to be indebted to the State of Tenn-
     essee in the sum of three hundred dollars John Foster in the sum of two
     hundred dollars & Andrew Blackwood in the sum of one hundred dollars to
     be levied of their goods & cattels lands & tenements but to be void on
     condition that John Foster do make his personal appearance at our next
     County Court and answer the state of Tennessee on a bill of indictment
     against him & not depart without leave first had etc.

Pg   State   )
126   vs.   ) A & B Justices Present E. D. Tarver, Francis Shoemake, John
     Levy Todd   ) Y. Cockeran.
          This day came the Solicitor General on the part of the state and the
     defendant in proper person who being arraigned & charged upon the bill
     of indictment plead not guilty and for his trial puts himself on the
     County and the Solicitor General likewise and thereupon came a Jury of
     good & lawful men (to wit) John Foster Daniel Culbirth Richard Lamb
     William Cockeran, John Henson Thomas Newland Willie I. Riddle Mark R.
     Roberts, William L. Haynes Andrew Blackwood Alsey Dean, & Thomas I.
     Oliver who being elected empannelled charge d & sworn the truth to speak
     upon the issue of traverse upon their oaths do say they find the defend-
     ant is guilty in manner and form as charged in the bill of indictment
     therefore it is considered by the Court that the defendant be fined the
     sum of twenty dollars and pay the costs of this prosecution & he be taken
     etc. from which judgment the defendant prays & obtains an appeal to the

Pg next Circuit Court to be held for this County and gave bond J. W. Mc-
126 Keen as his security.

State   )
   vs.   )Presentment Effray) Justices as above.
Francis Pusby)

     This day came the Solicitor General on the part of the State and
the defendant in proper person who being arraigned & charged upon the
Pg   Bill of Presentment pleads not guilty and for his trial puts himself
127 on the County and the Solicitor likewise and thereupon came a Jury of good
and lawful men to wit John Foster Daniel Culbirth Richard Lamb William
Cockeran, Thomas Newland, Willie I. R iddle, Mark R. Roberts, William
S. Haynes Andrew Blackwood, Alsey Dean Thomas J. Oliver & Walden Fuller
who being elected empannelled charged & sworn the truth to speak upon the
issue of traverse upon their oaths do say they find the defendant is
guilty in manner & form as charged in the Bill of Presentment therefore
it is considered by the Court that the defendant be fined the sum of
twenty five cents and pay the costs of this prosecution & that he be taken
& remain in custody of the Sheriff until fine & costs are paid or secured.

State   )
   vs.   ) Affray) Same Court as heretofore.
Shaderick Owens)

     This day came the Solicitor General on the part of the State and the
defendant in proper person who being arraigned & charged on the bill of
presentment pleads guilty and puts himself upon the mercy of the Court
whereupon it is considered by the Court that the defendant be fined the
sum of five dollars and pay the costs of this prosecution & that he be
taken etc.

State   )
   vs.   ) Scirifacias.
William B. Duncan   )

     This day came the Solicitor on the part of the State and the defend-
ant in proper person and move the Court to set aside a judgment entered
against him having filed his affadavit setting out grounds on which he
Pg   applied whereupon it is considered by the Court that the forfeture be set
128 aside on this Scifa & that the County pay the costs etc.

State   )
   vs.   ) Sciri facias) Court as before.
John Garrison   )

     This day came the Solicitor General on the part of the State and
the defendant in proper person and move the Court to set aside a judgment entered against him the cause having been shown it is considered by
the Court that the forfeiture be set aside on this sciri facias & that
the County pay the costs etc.

State   )
   vs.   ) Sciri Facias) Court as before.
John Garrison   )

     This day came the solicitor Gen. on the part of the state & the
defendant in proper person and move the Court to set aside a judgment
entered against him the cause having been shown it is considered by the
Court that the forferture be set aside on this Sciri facias & that the
County pay the costs.

State   )
Pg vs.   ) Sciri Facias
Jason Cloud)

128 This day came the Solicitor General on the part of the state and the defendant in proper person and thereupon on motion the judgment of default against said defendant was set aside for cause shown. And it is considered by the Court that the County pay the costs.

State   )
 vs.) Sci Fa)
James A. Barker)

Pg This day came the Solicitor General on the part of the state and on motion and it appearing that two Sci Facias had been returned against
129 the defendant "Not Found". It is thereupon considered by the Court that final judgment be had against said James A. Barker for the sum of one hundred and twenty five dollars & costs of this prosecution and that execution issue accordingly.

State   )
 vs.) Sci Fa)
Benjamin Rook)

  This day came the Solicitor General on the part of the state and the defendant in proper person and on motion the Sciri Facias is set aside in this case for cause shown on the defendants paying costs.

  Therefore it is considered by the Court that the state recover of the defendant the costs aforesaid etc.

State   )
 vs.   ) Forfeiture.
James W. Townsend)

  This day comes the Solicitor General on the part of the State and thereupon the defendant being solemnly called to come into Court and bring with him the body of John E. Mayfield according to his recognizance came not but made default according to the tenor thereof. It is therefore considered by the Court here that the State recover against the defendant the sum of one hundred dollars unless he appears at the next term of this Court and show cause if any he has or can why judgment final and execution thereof should not be had against him and that Sciri facias issue accordingly etc.

State   )
 vs.   ) Forfeiture
Thirley Goodwin)
Barney Skipper)

  This day came the Solicitor General on the part of the state and thereupon the said defendant being solemnly called to come into Court and bring with him the body of John E. Mayfield according to their recognizance came not but made default according to the tenor thereof. It is therefore considered by the Court that the state recover against the said defendants the sum of one Hundred dollars unless they appear at the next term of this Court serve cause if any they have or can why judgt. final and execution thereof should not be had against them & that Servi facias issue accordingly.

John Briscoe)
Pg vs.   )No. 23 Covenant) F
130 Joseph Coe) Present Edmund D. Tarver John Y. Cockeran & Frances Shoemake Esq. Justices.

  This day came the parties by their attornies and thereupon on motion

Pg of the plaintiff counsel and after solemn argument had thereon the 1st
130 and 2d plan of the defendant to the sd. plaintiff declaration is adjudged by the Court to be struck out.

And thereupon came a jury of good and lawful men To Wit, John Foster,
Daniel Cutbirth, William Cockeran, Thomas Newland, Willie O. Riddle, Mark
R. Roberts, Wm. L. Haynes, Andrew Blackwood, Alsey Deen, Thomas J. Oliver,
Gossett Fitzgerald, & William Thornton, who being elected empannelled
& sworn the truth to speak upon the issues joined upon their oath do say
they find the issues joined in favor of the plaintiff and that he has not
kept his covenant as alleged on the plaintiffs declaration and they assess his
damages by reason of the non performance thereof to three hundred and
thirteen dollars and four cents. Therefore it is considered by the Court
here that the plaintiff recover of the defendant the said sum of three
hundred thirteen dollars & four cents damages together with his costs in
his suit in this behalf expended etc.

From which judgment the defendant prayed and obtained an appeal
in nature of a writ of error to the next Circuit Court he having give
bond & security as the law directs

Pg   John B. Fulkes   )
131   vs.   ) Debt No. 25) Present same Justices as before.
     Robert Rivers   )

This day came the parties by their attornies and thereupon came
this cause to be tried by the Court here and upon inspection and examination of the record it doth appear to the said Court that then is such
a record as the plaintiff in pleading hath alleged . Therefore it is
considered by the Court that the plaintiff recover of the said defendant his debt of one hundred & ninety four dollars fifty seven cents debt
in his declaration mentioned together with the further sum of thirty
five dollars and twenty five cents damages by reason of the detention
thereof also his costs about his suit in this behalf expended etc. and
it is agreed by plaintiff to stay execution 3 months.

     Rivers & Brown   )
         vs.   ) Debt No. 26
     Robert Rivers   )

This day came the plaintiffs by their attorney and moves the Court
that he be permitted to amend his declaration and it is thereupon considered by the Court that on the paying of the costs of said motion the
said plaintiff be allowed so to amend his sd. declaration.

     Hardey Derhago   )
         vs.   ) Debt No. 29) Present same Justices.
     Green Parrish   )

This day came the parties by their attorneys and thereupon came a
jury of good and lawful men to wit John Foster Daniel Cutbirth, William
Pg   Cockeran, Thomas Newland Willie I. Riddle, Mark Ro. Roberts, Wm. L. Hay-
132 nes, Andrew Blackwood, Alsey Deen, Thomas J. Oliver Garrett Fitzgerald
& William Thornton who being elected empanneled & sworn the truth to
speak upon the oath do say they find the issue joined in favor of the
plaintiff and they assess his damages by reason of the detention of the
debt of one hundred & twenty dollars debt in the sd. plaintiffs declaration
mentioned to ten dollars & twenty cents. Therefore it is considered by
the Court that the plaintiff recover of said defendant the said sum of
one hundred and twenty dollars debt aforesaid together with his damages
aforesaid on form aforesaid assessed by the Jury and his costs by him
about his suit in this behalf expended etc.

     N. W. Floyd   )
         vs   ) Debt No. 32) Present the same Justices as Before.
     Wm. L. London   )

Pg   This day came the parties by their attornies and thereupon came a
132 Jury of good and lawful men To Wit John Foster, Daniel Cutbirth, William
Cockeran, Thomas Newland, Wilie I. Riddle, Mark R. Roberts, Wm. L.
Haynes, Andrew Blackwood, Alsey Deen, ThomasJ. Oliver & Garrett Fitzgerald & Wm. Thornton who being elected empannelled and sworn the truth
to speak upon the issue joined upon their oath do say they find in
favor of the plaintiff and they assess his damages by reason of the
detention of the debt of seventy two dollars and thirty two cents debt
in the plaintiffs declaration mentioned, to four dollars and thirty
Pg three cents. Therefore it is considered by the Court that the plain-
133 tiff recover of the said defendant the said sum of seventy two dollars
and thirty two cents debt aforesaid, together with his damages aforesaid
in form aforesaid assessed and his costs by him about his suit in this
behalf expended etc. and it is agreed by the said plaintiffs attorney
to stay execution untill the 1st day of June next . Do not issue this
execution until I hear from plff.

Oney L. Harvey   )
       vs.   )   Covenant No. 33) Present same Justices as before.
John W. Philpot   )
       This day came the parties by their attornies and thereupon came a
Jury of good and lawful men To Wit John Foster, Daniel Cutbirth, William
Cockeran, Thomas Newland, Wilie I. Riddle, Mark R. Roberts, Wm. L. Haynes
Andrew Blackwood, Alsey Deen, Thomas L. Oliver & Garrett Fitzgerland &
Wm. Thornton who being elected empannelled and sworn well and truly to
enquire of the damages which the plaintiff hath sustained by reason of
the non performance of the said plaintiffs covenant upon their oath do
say they find the plaintiff hath sustain damages to the amount of three
hundred and fifteen dollars. Therefore it is considered by the Court that
the plaintiff recover of said defendant the said sum of three hundred
and fifteen dollars damages aforesaid by the jury aforesaid in form aforesaid assessed, also his costs about his suit in this behalf expended etc.

John Shute   )
       vs.   )   Covenant No. 34) Present as above.
Nathaniel Steele   )
PgP   This day came the parties by their attornies and thereupon came a
134 Jury of good and lawful men To Wit John Foster, Daniel Cutbirth, Wm.
Cockeran, Andrew Blackwood, Alsey Deen, Mark Rw. Roberts, Thomas J.
Oliver, Garrett Fitzgerald, Wm. L. Haynes, Wilie L. Riddle, Thomas Newland, & Wm. Thornton who being elected empannelled and sworn the truth
to speak upon the issue joinedu upon the oath do say they find the issue
joined in favor of the plaintiff and that the said defendant hath not
kept his covenant as charged in the plaintiffs declaration and they assess
the damages of the said plaintiff by reason of the non performance thereof
by the said defendant to one hundred and four dollars.
       Therefore it is considered by the Court here that the said Plainfiff
recover of the sd. defendant the said sum of one hundred four dollars
damages aforesaid by the jury aforesaid in form aforesaid assessed also
his costs by him about his suit in this behalf expended etc.

David White
       vs.   ) Covenant No. 35) Present the same Justices as Before.
Daniel Minner
Peter Minner
       This day came the parties by their attornies and thereupon came a
jury of good and lawful men To Wit John Foster, Daniel Cutbirth, Wm.
Cockeran, Andrew Blackwood, Alsey Deen, Mark R. Roberts, Thomas J.
Oliver, Garret Fitzgerald, Wm. L. Haynes, Wilie G. Riddle, Thomas New-
land & Wm. Thornton who being elected empannelled and sworn the truth

Pg
136
to speak upon the issue joined upon their oath do say they find the
issues joined in favor of the plaintiff and that the said defendants
hath not kept his covenant as charged in the plaintiffs declaration
and they assess his damages by reason of the said defendants not performing their said covenant to four hundred and nineteen dollars fifty
two cents. Therefore it is considered by the Court that the said plaintiff recover of the said defendants the said sum of four hundred and
nineteen dollars damages aforesaid by the jury aforesaid in form aforesaid assessed also his costs by him about his suit in this behalf expended,
etc.

Pg
135

John Terrill   )
     vs.   ) Case No. 36)   Justices Present Same as Before.
John Murray   )

This day came the parties by their attornies and thereupon came a
Jury of good and lawful men To Wit John Foster, Daniel Cutbirth, Wm.
Cockeran, Andrew Blackwood, Alsey Deen, Mark R. Roberts, Thomas J. Oliver
Garrett Fitzgerald, Wm. L. Haynes, Wilie I. Riddle, Thomas Newland, &
Wm. Thornton who being elected empanelled and sworn the truth to speak
upon the issues joined upon their oath do say they find that the defendant did assume upon himself in manner and form as the plaintiff against
him hath complained and they do assess his damages by reason thereof to
one hundred and twelve dollars and fifty cents. Therefore it is considered
by the Court that the plaintiff recover against the said defendant his
damages aforesaid in favor aforesaid assessed likewise his costs in this
suit in his behalf expended & the defendant in mercy etc.

Pg
136

Richard Lamb   )
    vs.   ) Debt No. 37) Present same Justices as Before.
John McKinnie   )

This day came the parties by their attornies and thereupon came a
jury of good and lawful men To Wit John Foster, Andrew Blackwood, Alsey
Deen, Mark R. Roberts, Thomas Newland, Wm. Thornton, Wm. Cockeran, Thomas
J. Oliver, Wilie I. R iddle, Daniel Cutbirth, Wm. L. Haybest, Garrett Fitzgerald who being elected empannelled and sworn the truth to speak upon
the issue joined their oath do say they find the issue joined in favor of
the plaintiff and that the defendant has not paid the debt of one hundred
and two dollars in the plaintiffs declaration mentioned and they assess his
damages by reason thereof to four dollars, and fifty cents. Therefore it is
considered by the Court that the plaintiff recover of the defendant the
said debt aforesaid together with his damages aforesaid in form aforesaid
assessed and his costs by him about his suit in this behalf expended and
that he be etc.

Thomas W. Norman   )
    vs.   )) Debt No. 39) Present the same Justices as Before.
John N. Pulliam   )

Pg
137
This day came the parties by their attornies and thereupon came a
jury of good and lawful men To Wit John Foster, Mark R. Roberts, Thomas
J. Oliver, Andrew Blackwood, Thomas Newland, Wm. Cockeran, Wm. Thornton,
Alsey Deen, Daniel Cutbirth, Wm. L. Haynes, Gerrett Fitzgeraldn & Wilie
I. Riddle, who being elected empannelled and sworn the truth to speak
upon the issues joined upon their oath do say they find the issue joined in
favor of the plaintiff and that the defendant has not paid the debt of two
hundred & twenty seven dollars in the plaintiffs declaration mentioned
and they assess the plaintiffs damages by reason of the detention thereof
to five dollars and fifty three cents. Therefore it is considered by the
Court that the plaintiff recover of the defendant his debt aforesaid to-

Pg
137 gether with his damages aforesaid together with his damages aforesaid in
form aforesaid, assessed also his costs by him about his suit in this behalf
expended etc. and the plaintiff agrees to stay execution untilthe 1st day
of July next.

George Conly   )
    vs.) Debt No. 40) Present the same Justices as before.
Walden Fuller   )
        This day came the parties by their attorneys & thereupon came a jury
of good and lawful menk to wit John Foster Mark R. Roberts, Thomas J.
Oliver, Andrew Blackwood, Thomas Newland, Wm. Cockeran, Wm. Thornton, Alsy
Deen, Daniel Cutbirth, Wm. Haynes, Garrett Fitzgerald and Willie J. Riddle,
who being elected tried & sworn to try the issues joined upon their oath
Pg do say they find in favour of the plaintiff and that the defendant hath
138 not paid the debt of seventy eight dollars and twenty five cents in the
plaintiffs declaration mentioned and they assess his damages by reason of
the detention thereof to seven dollars whereupon the Court proceeded to the
trial of the plea of nil till record and on inspection of the said record
it doth appear that there is such a record as the plaintiff in his declaration hath alledged. Therefore it considered by the Court here that the
plaintiff recover of the defendant the said sum of seventy eight dollars
and twenty five cents debt aforesaid also his costs about his suit in this
behalf expended etc.

Abner Pillow   )
    vs.   ) Present the same Justices as Before.
Stephen W. Russell   )
Ann P. Russell   )
        This day came the parties by their attornies and thereupon came a
jury of good and lawful men To Wit John Foster, Willie I. Riddle, Wm.
Cockeran, Andrew Blackwood, Alsey Deen, Mark Rm. Roberts, Thomas Newland,
Wm. Thornton, Thomas J. Oliver Garrett Fitzgerled, Daniel Cutbirth, & Wm.
L. Haynes, who being elected empannelled and sworn the truth to speak
upon the issues joined upon their oath do say they find the issues joined
in favor of the plaintiffs and that the said defendant hath not kept their
Pg covenant as complained of in the plaintiffs declaration and they assess his
139 damages by reason thereof of the said defendants non compliance with his
said covenant to the sum of six hundred and ten dollars and fifty cents.
Therefore it is considered by the Court that the said plaintiff recover of the
defendants the said sum of six hundred & ten dollars and fifty cents damages
aforesaid by the Jury aforesaid in form aforesaid assessed. Also his costs
by him about his suit in this behalf expended, etc.

John Fitzgerald   )
    vs.   )   Assumpsit . Same Justices as before.
Garet Ford   )
        By the consent of parties it is ordered that each party on application
have a commission to take dipositions of witnesses on giving the opposite
party on their attorney fifteen days notice of the time & place.

A. R. Alexander   )   Debt- Same Court as above.
Jnos. H. Pills   )
    vs.   )
George Seaton   )
        This day came the parties by their attorneys and thereupon came a jury
of good and lawful men to wit John Foster, Willie I. Riddle, William Cockeran,
Andrew Blackwood, Alsey Deen, Mark R. Roberts, Thomas Newland, Wm. Thornton,
Thomas J. Oliver Garrett Fitzgerald, Daniel Cutbirth & W. L. Haynes who being

Pg
139

Pg
140

elected impannelled & sworn the truth to speak upon the issues joined
upon their oath do say that they find in favour of the plaintiffs and
and the defendant has not paid the whole of the debt in the declaration
mentioned but that there remains a balance of two hundred and ninety
dollars thereof unpaid and they assess their damage by reason of the detention of that balance to twenty three dollars 75 cents. Therefore it
is considered by the Court that the plaintiffs recover against the defendant the balance of debt aforesaid and the damages in favour aforesaid
assessed together with his costs by him about his suit in this behalf expended & that etc. From which said judgment the defendant prayed and
obtained an appeal to the next Circuit Court for this County and gave bond
with Wm. Todd as his security.

Thomas W. Norman)
adm. of John N. Pulliam) Present same Justices as Before.
  vs.) Debt No. 45)
John H. McKinnie)

 This day came the parties by their attornies and thereupon came a
Jury of good & lawful men To Wit John Foster Mark R. Roberts, Thomas J.
Oliver Wm. Cockeran, Wilie I. Riddle, Garrett Fitzgerald Daniel Cutbirth,
Wm. Thornton, Thomas Newland, Andrew Blackwood, Wm. L. Haynes & Alsey
Been who being elected empannelled and sworn the truth to speak upon the
issues joined upon their oath do say they find the issues joined in favor
of the plaintiff and that the defendant has not paid the sum of one hun-
dred and seven dollars in the plaintiffs declaration mentioned, and they

Pg
141

assess his damages by reason of the detention thereof to one dollars &
eighty two cents. Therefore it is considered by the Court that the plaintiff recover of the defendant his debt aforesaid and the damages in form
aforesaid assessed together with his costs by him about his suit in this
behalf expended etc.

Cox & Jameson)
  vs.) Debt No. 46) Present same Justices as Before.
Edmund R. Anderson)

 This day came the parties by their attornies and thereupon came a
jury of good & lawful men To Wit John Foster, Mark R. Roberts, Thomas
J. Oliver, Wm. Cockeran, Wilie I. Riddle, Garrett Fitzgerald, Daniel
Cutbirth, Wm. Thornton, Thomas Newland, Andrew Blackwood, Wm. L.
Haynes & Alsey Deen who being elected empannelled and sworn the truth
to speak upon the issues joined upon their oath do say they find the issues
joined in favor of the plaintiffs and that the defendant has not paid
the sum of one hundred and forty six dollars in the plaintiffs declaration mentioned and they assess his damages by reason of the detention
thereof to nine dollars & nine cents. Therefore it is considered by the
Court that the plaintiff recover of the defendant his debt aforesaid,
and his damages aforesaid in form aforesaid assessed together with all
his costs about his suit in this behalf expended and that he have his execution etc.

Pg
142

Nathaniel Steele)
  vs.) Debt No. 51) Present the same Justices as Before.
John B. Justice)

 This day came the parties by their attornies and thereupon came a jury
of good and lawful men To Wit John Foster, Mark R. Roberts, Wm. Cockeran,
Wm. Thornton, Thomas J. Oliver, Wilie I. Riddle, Alsey Deen, Daniel Cutbirth, Andrew Blackwood, Garrett Fitzgerald, Thomas Newland, & Wm. L.
Haynes, who being elected empannelled and sworn the truth to speak upon
the issues joined on their oaths do say the defendant has not paid the
whole of the debt in the declaration mentioned but that there remains a
balance of three hundred and seventy five dollars thereof unpaid and they
assess his damage by reason of the detention thereof of that balance to

Pg six dollars 50 ¼. Therefore it is considered by the Court that the plain-
142 tiff recover of the defendant the balance of debt aforesaid and the damages in favor aforesaid assessed together with his costs about his suit in
this behalf expended etc.

Francis Shoemake & Brice Wilson)
firm of F. Shoemake) Present as Before) Debt No. 52
   vs.)
William A. Allen

  This day came the parties by their attornies and thereupon came a Jury
of good & lawful men To Wit John Foster, Mark R. Roberts, Wm. Ccokeran,
William Thornton, Thomas J. Oliver, Willie I. Riddle, Alsey Deen, Daniel Cut-
Pg birth, Garrett Fitzgerald, Andrew Blackwood Thomas Newland & Wm. L. Haynes,
143 who being elected empannelled and sworn the truth to speak upon the issues
joined upon their oath do say they find the issues joined in favor of the
plaintiffs and that the defendant has not paid the debt of eighty nine
dollars and twelve and a half cents the debt in the plaintiffs declaration
mentioned and they assess his damages by reason of the detention thereof
to one dollar and sefenty eight cents.

  Therefore it is considered by the Court that the plaintiff recover
against the defendant the debt aforesaid and the damages in form aforesaid
assessed together with his costs about his suit in this behalf expended etc.

Joseph P. Stockton)
  vs.)
Elijah C. Hull)

  Ordered by the Court that the plaintiff in this case have leave to take
the deposition of William M. Beal in New Orleans by giving forty days
notice to be read in evidence in this case.

xPg Arthur Jones)
   vs.)
 William Renecks)

  Ordered by the Court that the plaintiff in this case have leave to
take the deposition of Isaac Winstead Thomas Wooldridge & Thomas I. Winstead citazens of the State of Alabama to be read in evidence in favour of
the plaintiff by giving fifteen days notice.

Pg
144 Ordered by the Court that David Fentress be fined the sum of fifteen dollars for contempt of this Court by rising in the bar immediately after the
Court had delivered an opinion and saying to the jury in his argument and
refered to them when the case was submitted that he did not care what the
Court said, that the jury were men of sense and were judges of law &
fact the Court then stopped him and he said that he did not wish to in-
sult the Court from which judgement the said D. Fentress prays an appeal
in the nature of a writs of Error which is granted.

William Porton)
  vs.) Debt
M. Read)
This day
  This day came the parties by their attornies and thereupon came a
jury of good and lawful men to wit, James McDowell, James Lippett Ninican
Steele, Edmund Kirkland, Henry Ragan, Josiah Chandler, Moore Hurly, Randolph Mote, Russell Cain William Mayfield Aquila Combs & Richmond Carroll
who being elected tried and sworn the truth to speak on the issue joined
on their oath do say that they find in favour of the defendant.

  It is therefore considered by the Court that the defendant depart hence

Pg
144 without day and recover against the plaintiff his costs about his defence
in that behalf expended etc.

And the Court adjourned to meet tomorrow morning 9 O'clock.

Edmund D. Tarver
John Y. Cockeram
Martain Taylor

Pg
145 _____ Friday 11th April 1828

Court met according to adjournment present Edmund D. Tarver, John Y.
Cockeram and Francis Shoemake Esq. Justices Thomas J. Hardeman Clerk,
J. C. N. Robertson Sheriff V. D. Barry Solicitor.

A deed of conveyance from the Commissioners of the town of Bolivar to
William Ramsey for one town lot was exhibited in open Court and the execution thereof was duly acknowledged by John H. Bills Nathaniel Steel John
Y. Cockeram & Thomas J. Hardeman those commissioners who signed the same
and it was ordered to be certified for registration.

A deed of conveyance from the Commissioners of the town of Bolivar to
Lenin H. Coe for two town lots was exhibited in open Court and the execution
thereof was duly acknowled by John H. Bill, Nathaniel Steel, John Y. Cockeram
& Thomas J. Hardeman those commissioners who signed the same and it was
ordered to be certified for registration.

A deed of conveyance from James McDaniel to W illiam Todd for fifty
acres of land was produced in open Court and the execution thereof was duly
acknowledged by said James McDaniel to be his act and deed the same was of-
dered to be certified for registration.

Pg
146 A deed of conveyance from the Commissioners of the town of Bolivar
to Thomas James for one town lot exhibited in open Court and the execution
thereof was duly acknowledged by John H. Bills John Y. C ockeran, Nathaniel
Steel & Thomas Hardemen those commissioners who signed the same and it was
ordered to be certified for registration.

A bond for a deed of conveyance from Thomas Alsop to William Crane was
produced in open Court and the execution thereof was duly proven by the oath
of William Boguard one of the subscribing witnesses thereto and the same
was ordered to be certified for registration.

A deed of conveyance from Peter G. Rives to James Wood for 200 acres
of land was produced in open Court and the execution thereof was duly proven
by the oaths of John C. McKean and Duguid Mims the subscribing witnesses
thereto and the same was ordered to be certified for registration.

It appearing to the Court from personal knowledge that Edward Burlesson Joseph Burlesson and Akins with others unknown have been guilty
of a riot & that no one will prosecute for the same it is ordered that the
solicitor ex officio a Bill of indictment against said persons for said
offence.

Pg
147 The grand jury came into open Court under the care of their sworn officer and
presented a bill of Inditement against Edward Burlesson Joseph Burlesson and
Akins for a riot endorsed a true bill James M. Daniell foreman of the Grand
Jury.

V. D. Barry   )
     vs.)   ) Present Edmund D . Tarver, John Y. Cockeran
Chesley D. Key administrator   ) & Joseph W. McKean Esq.

Pg
147   This day came the plaintiff by his attorney and thereupon it appearing to the satisfaction of the Court that an execution had issued from a Justice of the peace against said defendant in behalf of said plaintiff for the sum of twenty dollars sixty five cents debt with interest from the seventeenth day of October 1827 and lawful costs which said execution for want of personal estate is levied upon one hundred and twelve & one half acres of land in range four section four in the tenth district it is ordered by the Court that a Sira facias issue requireing the heirs of Jefferson Key deceased to appear at the next term of the Court to shew cause if any they have why said land should not be ordered for sale to satisfy the said plaintiffs debt & costs aforesaid.

A. O. Harris   )
    vs.   )   Justices as above.
Duguid Mims   )
William Stulman   )

    On motion and it appearing to the satisfaction of the Court that an execution had issued against the defendant by Joseph W. McKean Esq.

Pg
148 a Justice for this County for the sum of twenty five dollars with interest from the 2nd day of January 1828 & 50 cents costs and which said execution had come to the hands of P. M. McKinnie a Constable of said county and by him in defect of personal property levied on one town lot in the town of Bolivar known as Lot No. 3 in Square No. 9. It is therefore ordered adjudged & decreed that the said town lot was exposed to sail as required by law to satisfy said debt & costs as also the costs of this motion and that a venditioni exponas issue accordingly.

A. O. Harris   )
    vs.   )   Justices as before.
Duguid Mims   )

    On motion and it appearing to the satisfaction of the Court that an execution had issued against the defendant by Josft. W. McKean Esquire a Justice of the Peace for this County for the sum of twenty five dollars with interest from the 2 day of January 1828 & 50 cents costs and which said execution had come to the hands of P. M. McKennie a constable of said County & by him in defect of personal property levied on one town lot in the town of Bolivar known on the plan as Lot No. 3 in Square No. 9. It is therefore ordered adjudged & decreed that the said town lot be exposed to sail as required by law to satisfy said debt & costs as also the costs of this motion and that a venditionas exponas issue accordingly.

Pg
149 n David Harris   )
    vs.   )   Same Justices as before.
Duguid Mims   )
S. P. Smith   )

    On Motion and it appearing to the satisfaction of the Court that an execution had issued against the defendants by Nathaniel Steel Esquire a Justice for said County for the sum of thirty one dollars and 90 cents with interest from the   day 18 2   and one dollar costs and which said execution had come to the hands of P. M. McKinnie a constable of said County & by him in defect of personal property levied on one town lot in the town of Bolivar known as lot No. 3 and Square No. 9. It is therefore ordered adjudged and decreed that the said Town Lot be exposed to sail as required by law to satisfy said debt & costs as also the costs of this motion and that a venditioni exponas issue accordingly.

William Poston   )
    vs.   ) Debt) Justices E. D. Tarver, John Y. Cockeram
Michael Read   )   William L. Duncan.

Pg
149
This day came the parties by their attorneys and thereupon came a jury of good and lawful men to wit James McDaniel James Tippet Ninian Steel Edmund Kirkland Henry Reagan Josiah Chandler Moore Hendley Randolph Mott Russell Cane William Mayfield Richmond Carroll & Andrew Blackwood who being elected tried and sworn the truth to speak on the issue joined on their oath

Pg
150
do say that they find in favour of the defendant. It is therefore considered by the Court that the defendant depart hence without day and recover off the plaintiff his costs about his defence in this behalf expended etc.

William Poston)
    vs.) Debt) Same Court
Michael Read)

This day came the parties by their attorneys and thereupon came a jury of good and lawful men to wit James McDaniel James Tippett Ninican Steel, Edmond Kirkland Henry Reagon Josiah Chandler Moore Hendley Randolph Mott Russell Cane William Mayfield Richmond Carroll & Andrew Blackwood who being elected tried and sworn the truth to speak upon the issue joined upon their oaths do say they find the issues joined in favor of the plaintiff and they assess his damage by reason of the detention of the debt of ninety seven dollars sixty two and one half cents in the declaration mentioned. Therefore it is considered by the Court that the plaintiff recover against the defendant the damages aforesaid in form aforesaid assessed and his costs by him about his suit in this behalf expended & that he have his execution.

William Poston)
    vs.) Debt) Court as above.
Michael Read)

This day came the parties by their attorney and thereupon came a jury

Pg
151
of good and lawful men (to wit) James McDaniel James Tippett Ninion Steel Edmund Kirkland Henry Reagan Josiah Chandler Moore Hendley Randolph Mott Russell Cane William Mayfield Richmond Carroll & Andrew Blackwood who being elected tried & sworn the trooth to speak upon the issue joined upon their oaths do say that they find in favour of the defendant. It is therefore considered by the Court that the defendant depart hence without day & recover against the plaintiff his costs about his defence in this behalf expended etc.

Anderson Sheppard)
    vs.) Appeal No. 56)
Robert Hays Jr.)

This day came the parties by their attornies and thereupon came a Jury of good and lawful ment To Wit Lewis Bolt, Garrett Fitzgerald James N. Allen, Alsey Deen, Thomas M. Pattrick, Wm. B. Duncan, Wm. Ramsay, Sampson Edwards John Jones, John Archy, Josiah Hadley & Michial Reed who being elected empannelled and sworn the truth to speak upon the matter in dispute upon their oaths do say they find in favor of the plaintiffs and they assess their damages by reason thereof to twenty six dollars and fifty cents. Therefore it is considered by the Court that the plaintiffs recover of the defendant the damages aforesaid in form aforesaid assessed by the Jury together with their costs by them in their suit in this behalf expended.

A   Andrew Blackwood & Alsey Deen served 4 days attendance as jurors.

Pg
152
David Webb
    vs.)Appeal 57
W. L. Duncan

Pg
152   This day came the parties Wm. L. Duncan by their attornies and
thereupon came a jury of good and lawful men To Wit Garret Fitzgerald
James N. Allen, Alsey Deen, Thom. M. Patrick, Wm. B. Duncan, William
Ramsay, John Hichy, Josiah Hatley, Michial Read, Stephen Russell &
Andrew Cavett & Andrew Blackwood who being elected tried and sworn
the truth to speak upon the matter in dispute upon their oath do say
they find in favor of the plaintiff and assess his damages to five
dollars fifty nine per cents. Therefore its considered by the Court
that the plaintiff recover of the defendant the damages aforesaid
in form aforesaid assessed to be levied of the goods & chattels of
John Duncan deceased which have or may come to his hands as administrator if so much there be together with his costs etc. and if not
so much of those goods & chattels there to be levied of the proper
goods and chattels of said W. L. Duncan.

State   )
   vs.) A & B   )
John O. Brien   )
     This day came the Solicitor General on the part of the State &
the defendant in proper person who being arraigned upon the Bill of
Indictment pleads guilty and puts himself on the mercy of the court.
Whereupon it is considered by the Court that the said defendant be
fined five dollars and pay the costs of this prosecution and that he
remain in custody of the Sheriff until the fine & costs aforesaid are
paid or secured.

Pg
153 Stephen Russell   )
          vs.   ) No. 53 Debt)
     John Moore   )
     This day came the parties by their attornies and thereupon came a
jury of good and lawful men To Wit Garrett Fitzgerald, James N. Allen,
Alsey Deen, Thos. M. Pattrick, Wm. B. Duncan, Wm. Ramsay, John Archy,
Josiah Hatley, Michial Read, Stephen R ussell, Andrew Cavett & Andrew Blackwood, who being elected empannelled & sworn the truth to
speak upon the issues joined upon their oath do say they find the issues joined
in favor of the plaintiff, and that the said defendant has not paid
the debt of three hundred dollars in the plaintiffs declaration mentioned and they assess his damages by reason of the detention thereof to
five dollars and twenty five cents. Therefore it is considered by the
Court that the plaintiff recover of the defendant his debt aforesaid
and his damages aforesaid in favor aforesaid assessed as also his costs
by him about his suit in this behalf expended etc. From which said
judgment the defendant prayed and obtained an appeal to the next Circuit Court and gave bond with Hugh A. Reynolds Walven Fuller & Thomas
Pattrick as his securities.

George Briscoe   )
     vs.) No. 58 Appeal)
James Hubbard   )
     This day came the parties by their attornies and thereupon came a jury
of good and lawful men To W it Garrett Fitzgerald Lewis Bolt James N.
Allen Alsey Deen, Thomas M. Pattrick Wm. B. Duncan, Wm. Ramsay, Sampson
Edward John Jones John Archy. Josiah Hatley and Michial Read who being
elected empannelled and sworn the truth to speak upon the matter in den pro-
versy upon their oath do say that they confirm the judgment of the Justice
of the Peace and that the defendants have not paid the debt of seventy
one dollars & seventy five cents and they assess his damages by reason of

Pg the detention thereof to one dollars and eight cents. Therefore it is con-
154 sidered by the Court that the plaintiff recover of the defendants and on
motion against the security John Faggart the debt aforesaid & damages aforesaid in form aforesaid assessed his costs by him expended etc.

Abner Pillow)
    vs.) 41 Covenant
Stephen Russell &)
Ann P. Russell)
    This day came the plaintiff by their attorney and the defendant by
their attorney and the defendant moved the Court for an appeal in this case
to the next Circuit Court which was granted and thereupon gave bond & security
with Andrew Cavett and Garrett Fitzgerald as their securities.

    The Grand Jury discharged the 4th day except Edward Burleson the 3d day
N. W. Brown 5 days as Constable.

Pg
155 Oney S. Harvey)
    vs.) No. 33
John W. Philpot)
    This day came the defendant by his attorney and prayed and obtained
and appeal to the next Circuit Court for this County and gave bond with
James Haslett as his security.

Raiford Crawford)
    vs.) Debt)
Anthony Foster)
Richard Lamb)
    This day came the plaintiff by his attorney and says he will no further
prosecute his suit and pays costs. Therefore it is considered by the Court
that the defendants recover of the plaintiff his costs etc.

James Alsup)
    vs.)
Benjamin Merrill)
    This day came the parties by their attornies and by consent of parties
the said suit is dismissed. And thereupon came the said parties and each
one assumes his equal proportion of costs. Therefore it is considered by the
Court that the Clerk have execution etc.

Joseph Cutton)
    vs.)
Samuel A Hamner)
    This day came the plaintiff by his attorney and says he will not fur-
ther prosecute his suit against the defendant. Therefore it is considered
by the Court that the defendant recover against the said plaintiff his costs
by him expended etc. and that he have execution etc.

Pg Hugh A. Reynolds)
156   vs.)
Mattin Taylor)
    This day came the plaintiff by his attorney and says he will no further
prosecute his suit against the defendant. Therefore it is considered by
the Court that the defent. recover of the plaintiff his costs by him expended
etc.

Josiah Hatley Adm.)
    vs.) Debt
Garrett Fitzgerald)

Pg
156
     This day came the parties by their attornies and thereupon the defendant his demurrer being withdrawn says that he cannot gainsay the plaintiffs action in this behalf but that he justly owes the said plaintiff the sum of one hundred and thirty five dollars and fifty cents together with eight dollars and eight & one half cents his damages accassioned by the detention thereof. It is therefore considered by the Court that the plaintiff recover against the defendant his debt and damages aforesaid together with his costs about his suit in this behalf expended etc. and the plaintiff stays exedution three months.

Duguid Mims   )
    vs.   ) Motion
C. Davenport   )

    This day came the plaintiff by his attorney and thereupon it appearing to the satisfaction of the Court that an execution has been levied on one town lot No. 6 and block 1 Nol 14 the property of said defendant for want of personal estate. It is therefore considered by the Court that said Lot be exposed to sale to satisfy the judgment of said plaintiff together with the costs on this behalf expended and that a venditioni exponas issue accordingly.

Pg
157
Haley Buckner   )
    vs.   )
Philip M. McKinnie   )   Motion
Securities   )

    This day came the parties by their attorneys and it appearing to the satisfaction of the Court here that anexecution which issued heretofore to wit on the 21st day of January 1828 and since the last term of this Court from Joseph W. McKean Esquire a Justice of the Peace in & for said County of Hardeman commanding the said Philip M. McKinnie as constable to make the sum of forty seven dollars & cents the sum of money on said execution specified together with costs etc. of the goods & chattels, lands & tenements of William S. London to satisfy a judgment for said sum of forty seven dollars & county besides costs that said Haly Buckner obtained against the said London before the said Joseph W. McKean Justice as aforesaid on the 2 day of January 1828 and the said execution having come into the hands of the said P. M. McKinnie constable as aforesaid and he having failed to make the money therin specified agreeable to the direction of said execution within twenty days from the time of its coming into his hands ahd having failed to pay over the moneys therein specified to said Buckner. It is therefore considered by the Court here that the plaintiff recover of the said P. M. McKennie constable as aforesaid and Joseph W. McKean & John H. McKinnie his securities the sum of forty seven dollars and 87 cents it being the amount of the principal & interest due on said execution also his costs about this motion in this behalf expended etc.

Pg
158
John Catron   )
    vs.   )   Present E. D. Tarver, John Y. Cockeran, and Nathaniel Steel Esquires Justices.
William Whittaker   )
& William Crain   )

    This day came the defendants in open Court and confess judgment for four hundred and twenty four dollars & 25 cents debt and seven dollars & 25 cents damages. Therefore it is considered by the Court here that the plaintiff recover of the said defendants the said debt of four hundred & twenty four dollars 25 cents debt aforesaid also the sum of seven dollars & 25 cents damages aforesaid in form aforesaid also his costs about this suit in this behalf expended etc. And plaintiff stays execution until next Court.

Pg James L. Nelson)
158 vs.) Writ of Enquiry
Duguid Mims)

T   This day came the parties by their attornies and said interlocutory indictment being revived in the name of Thomas James Adm. of said decd. plaintif the defendant confesses judgment for the sum of ten dollars and eighty cents. It is therefore considered by the Court that the plaintiff recover agst. the defendant the damages aforesaid in form aforesaid confessed together with the costs about his suit in this behalf expended etc.

    And the Court adjourned to meet in the morning at 11 O'clock.

                       N. Steele
                       B. D. Tarver
                       John G. Cockeram

Pg
159   **Saturday 12th April 1828**

    Court met according to adjournment present Edmund D. Tarver John Y. Cockeram & Francis Shoemake Esquires Justices.

                     Thomas J. Hardeman Clerk
                     J. C. N. Robertson, Sheriff
                     V. D. Barry, Solicitor

    A deed of conveyance from R. P. T. Stone to John H. Arnold for 125 acres of land was produced in open Court & the execution thereof was duly acknowledged by said Stone to be his act & deed for the use and purposes therein expressed & the same was ordered by the Court to be certified for registration.

George Conly)
    vs.) Debt)
Walden Fuller)

    This day comes the defendant into Court & prays an appeal to the next Circuit Court which is granted on his giving bond with Hugh A. Reynold and William P. Haden his securities.

John Ferrill)
    vs.) Case)
John Murray)

    This day comes the defendant in proper person who prays & obtains an appeal to the next Circuit Court which is granted on his giving bond with William M. Crisp and Edward Burleson his securities.

William Poston)
    vs.)
Michael Read)

    This day comes the plaintiff in proper person who prays & obtains an appeal to the next Circuit Court which is granted on his giving bond with D. Fentress & V. D. Barry his securities.

Pg
160 John Shute)
    vs.)
Nathaniel Steel)

    This day came the defendant in this case in open Court & pray an appeal to the next Circuit Court which is granted who gave bond with William G. Steel and V. D. Barry as his securities.

Littleton Johnson)
    vs.) Debt)
Edmund R. Anderson)

Pg
160   This day came the plaintiff by his attorney and says he will no further prosecute his said suit at this term. Therefore it is considered by the Court that the defendant recover of the plaintiff his costs etc.

Rhea & McCrabb   )
    vs.   ) Debt)
John Jack   )

This day came the parties by their attornies and thereupon came the plaintiffs attorney and dismisses his said suit at their costs etc.

William Poston   )
    vs.   )
Michael Read   )

This day came the plaintiff in open Court who prayed & obtained an appeal to the next Circuit Court who gave bond with David Fentress & V. D. Barry as his securities.

William Poston   )
    vs.   )
Michael Read   )

This day came the plaintiff in open Court who prayed and obtained an appeal to the next Circuit Court who gave bond with David Fentress & V. D. Barry as his securities.

Pg   State   )
161   vs.   )
Jno. O Brien   )

This day comes into Court the Solicitor General on the part of the state and the defendant in proper person whereupon it is considered by the Court that the fine of five dollars assessed against the defendant be remitted. Thereupon comes into Court Walden Fuller who donfesses judgment for the costs in this behalf jointly with said defendant. It is therefore considered by the Court here that the state recover against the said Walden Fuller & John O'Brien his costs in this behalf expended and that execution issue accordingly.

N. Steele   )
    vs.   )Certiovari- Motion)to dismiss. Present Francis Shoemake
Pitser Miller   )John Y1 Cockeram and Edward D. Tarver.

This day came the parties by their attorneys and the said Miller by his attorney moved the Court to dismiss said Certiovari and upon solemn aggusment being had thereon it is ordered that the said motion be sustained & that the said Miller recover of the said state and Philip I. Kearney his security the sum of thirty seven dollars and 60 cents the principal and also one dollar costs it being the amount of the judgment rendered by the Justice of the Peace together with the sum of one 81/100 dollars interest thereon at the rate of 12½ percent per annum from the 14th of November 1827 the term of the rendition of said judgment by said Justice up til this time also his costs about this suit in this behalf expended etc.

Pg   Andy Kirk   )
162   vs.   ) Motion) Present Edm. D. Tarver F. Shoemake & N. Steele
B. W. Boyte   ) Esq. Justices, etc.
O. L. Harvey   )
John Y. Cockeram
Isaac Jones securities of David S. Hanniss)

This day came the parties by their attornies and it appearing to the satisfaction of the Court that two executions which issued heretofore to wit on the 21 day of March 1827 from Joseph W. McK een esquire a justice pf the for Hardeman County for twnety six dollars 2½ cents each besides

Pg
162 costs which came into the hands of said David P. Hannis as a Constable
as aforesaid to satisfy two judgments that said Kirk obtained against
Henry G. Wells for the said amt. on the day of Dec. 1826 and stayed by
said Chancy Davenport before said Kean Justice as aforesaid of Hardeman
County. And the said Hannis constable as aforesaid having fail to make
& pay over the money & therein specified agreeable to the command of said
executions and the said D. P. Hannis Constable as aforesaid having not
proceeded according to law by not returning said execution within thirty
days and it appearing to the Court that the said defendants had been duly
notified that this motion would be made at this term. It is therefore considered by the Court that the plaintiff recover of the said E. W. Boyt
O. S. Harvey John Y. Cockeram & Isaac Jones securities of the said Hannis
the sum of thirty four dollars and twenty five cents the balance due on
said executions also his costs about this motion expended etc.

Pg
163

Peter a free man of	)	
colour	)	Demurer same Court as before.
vs.	)	
John Saunders	)	

This day came the parties by their attorneys and solemn argument
being heard on the demurer of the plaintiff to the said defendants plea
as it is considered by consent of parties that the plea be withdrawn
and the defendant have leave to plead over in bear to the plaintiffs action
and that the defendant pay the costs of this amendment.

Babench	)	Babench & Gardiner	)	
G. Gardiner	)	vs.	)	Attachment.
vs.	)	Samuel A. Hamner	)	
Gardiner	)		)	

This day came the parties by their attornies and thereupon all matters arising upon the motion of the defendant to quash the attachment of
of the plaintiffs being heard and by the Court here fully understood.
It is considered by the Court that the said attachment be quashed and
that the defendant recover against the plaintiffs his costs about his
defence in this behalf expended. From which judgement the plaintiffs
pray an appeal to the next Circuit Court which is granted theron bond
and security being given as the law requires.

Alex McClanhan		
vs.	)	Petition for Certiovari)
Lazarus Stewart		

The Court having heard and understood the petition of the plaintiff
it is on motion ordered that the petitioner have writs of certiovari &
supersedcas on his giving bond and security as required by law.

Pg
164

Thos. W. Norman	)	
vs) No. Debt	)	
John H. McKennie	)	

This day came the defendant into Court and prays the Court to
grant him an appeal to the next Circuit Courtian this case which is
done and thereupon the said defendant comes and gives bond with Knuckles
& Nathaniel Steele as his securities etc.

W. L. Duncan	)	
vs.) Attachment	)	
M. Hays	)	

This day came the plaintiff by his attorney and the defendant being
solemnly called to come in and reply his property attached came not
but made default. Therefore it is considered by the Court that judgment
final be given in this case for the sum of one hundred & eighteen dollars

the sum in the plaintiffs declaration mentioned and that he have his execution etc. together with his costs in this behalf expended.

Andrew Kirk   )
    vs.   )   Motion
Wills & Davenport)

  This day came the plaintiff by his attorney & thereupon it appearing to the satisfaction of the Court that an execution had been issued by Joseph W. McKean a Justice of the Peace for said County against the defendant which came to the hands of P. I. Kearney a constable for said County for the sum of twenty seven dollars & 68 cents & costs & by him in defect of personal property be levied on one town lot in the town of Bolivar known on the plan of said town by lot No. 6 and Square No. 14 the property of said Davenport.

It is therefore considered by the Court that the said lot be exposed to sail to satisfy the said plaintiff debt & costs together with the costs of this motion in this behalf expended & that a venditionas exponas issue accordingly.

Andrew Kirk   )
    vs.   )
Wills & Davenport)

  This day came the plaintiff by his attorney and moved the Court for an order of sale to sell a town lot in the town of Bolivar and it appearing to the satisfaction of the Court here that an execution had lately issued from Joseph W. McKean Esq. an accounting Justice of the Peace for said County of Hardeman for twenty seven dollars and sixty eight cents besides coststo satisfy a judgment that said Kirk obtained against said Wills & stayed by said Davenport before the said McKean Justice as aforesaid which came into the hand of P. I.Kearney a constable of said County and because there was no personal property to buy the same on the said executor was bond on Lot No. 6 in the town of Bolivar the property of said Davenport. Therefore it is considered by the Court that an order of sale issue to the Sheriff to sell said lot to satisfy said execution & costs also the costs of this motion etc.

Alexander McClanahan   )
& Hamilton McClanahan   )
        vs.   )
Lazaras Stewart   )

  On motion supported by petition & affidavit it is ordered that costs of certiovari & supercedus issue agreeable to the prayer of said petition to bring up this cause on the petitioners giving bond & security as the law directs etc.

William Lyttle   )
    vs.   )   Debts
Thomas Sammons   )

  Ordered by the Court that the defendant have leave to take deposition generally by giving ten days notice in the state and twenty days notice out of the state as agreed by the parties by their command and that notice given to the counsel shall be sufficient.

James F. Smith   )
    vs.) Certiovari   )
Wm. Todd   )

  On motion it is ordered by the Court that an petitioner give additional

Pg 166 secutity for the prosecution of this suit, and it appearing to the Court that this order is not complied with. It is considered by the Court that the Certiovari be dismissed and that an execution issue against the said Smith for the debt & costs etc. by the 2'd day of next term unless the said Smith comes in and gives good additional sedurity.

```
Gabriel a free man )
of Colour          )    Debt
        vs.        )
John Lucky         )
```

This day came the plaintiff by his attorney and says he will no further prosecute his suit against the defendant. Therefore it is considered by the Court that the defendant go hence and recover his costs against said plaintiff and on motion against his security Alfred Shelby and that he have execution etc.

Andrew Thomas served five days as Constable

Pg 167

```
John H. McKennie   )
      vs.  ) Case  )
Gesson Moss        )
```

This day came the plaintiff by his attorney and moves the Court to grant him an appeal in this cause to the next Circuit Court for this County which is thereupon granted by the Court. And the plaintiff comes and gives bond with Valentine D. Barry as his security in said appeal.

Ordered by the Court that Joseph W . McKean and David W. Wood be released from further responsibility as securities for the well performance of Medicas R. T. Outlaw as constable and that said Outlaw be suspended from his said office as constable until he give new security.

And the Court adjourned to
Court in caurse
Edmund T. Tarver
N. Steele
John Y. Cockeram

Pg 168

Monday July 7, 1828

At a Court of pleas and Quarter sessions began and held for the County of Hardeman at the Court House in the town of Bolivar on the 7th day of July A. D. 1828 it being the first Monday present the worshipful James Boguard Walter Scott John Y. Cockeram Martin Taylor Edward Owens Thornton Jones Edmund D. Tarver, Elijah Gossett James Ruffin Nathaniel Steel Esquires Justices.
Thomas J. Hardeman Clerk
J. C. N. Robertson Sheriff
V.D. Barry, Solicitor

Ordered that the County Trustee pay to William W. Shackleford the sum of thirteen dollars for furnishing bedding & vessels for the use of the jail also the sum of twenty dollars for building a meat house for the use of the jail.

Ordered that the County Trustee pay Thomas J. Hardeman Clerk for making out the tax list for the year 1828, $16.62½.

Isaac Sanders produced in open Court the scalps of four wolves adjudged to be under four months old ordered that he have his certificate.

Pg
168 Henry Webster petitioned to the Court to allow him license to keep an ordinary in this County after examination ordered that he have license who gave bond & qualified.

Pg
169 Also ordered that Robert C. Friar have license to keep an ordinary who gave bond & qualified.

Thomas Musgrove produced in open Court the scalp of one wolf adjudged to be over four months old. Ordered that he have his certificate.

The Court proceeded to elect the following persons as Constables (viz) Elihu C. Duncan in Capt. Rosses Company William Boyt in Boyts Company & Miles Birdsong in Bonds Company who severally gave their bonds & was qualified according to law.

A plat & certificate with a transfer thereon from John T. Rogers to George M. Pirtle was produced in open Court & proven by the oaths of John A. Pirtle & Peter Rogers the subscribing witnesses thereto ordered that it be so certified.

A plat and certificate with the transfer thereon from John A. Pirtle to George M. Pirtle was exhibited & acknowledged in open Court & ordered to be so certified.

Ordered by the Court that John Miller be bound to Alexer Kirkpatrick to learn the halling business untill he arrive to the age of twenty one years and the said Kirkpatrick enters in bond with the chairman with the the conditions etc.

Ordered that A. Colter have leave to turn the road round his field as marked out by the jury of view by putting it in good order.

Pg
170 Ordered by the Court that Elijah Cossett & Lazarus Stewart be appointed commissioners to take the privy examination Mrs. Elenor Thompson touching her voluntary act in signing a deed of conveyance to a tract of land in N. Carolina Rockingham County & make report, etc.

Ordered that John Crowley oversee the clearing out and keeping in repair that part of the Brownsville road from the Jackson Road to Clover Creek & that all the hands on the west of said road between Hatchie & Clover Creek Vincent Willoughby John Read More Henleys hands Timothy Shaw & the hands living with them East of said road work under his directions.

Drew Champion resigns his Commission as magistrate in this County.

Ordered by the Court that Caleb Brock executor to the last will & testament of Willie Jones deceased have leave to sell so mutch of the negro property as will pay the debts against said estate.

Ordered that Jesse Story oversee the clearing out and keep in repair the road from the mouth of Clover Creek through the bottom to the foot of the Hill near John Pirtles & he have the hands of John Pirtle Jas. Pirtle Martin Pirtle J. C. Hail Charles Jones K. Shultz Jacob Finley Cannibil Parker Joel Parker Daniel Davis & hands Higgins John Wilson Richard C. Ponel Daniel Cadwell John C. Cadwell Joshua Cadwell Sidney P. Smith Calvin Stevens Edwin Stevens Ashley Stevens Tigerts hands Joseph Chandler John Huddleston & Zacheriah Chandler work thereon under his directions.

Pg
171   Ordered that George Taylor oversee the clearing out and keep in repair that part of the road leading from Bolivar in a direction for Trenton & Brownsville from one mile North of Pirtles Creek to where it intersects the road from Jackson to the mouth of Clover Creek and that all the hands north of Pirtles Creek to the north boundary of said County east of said road so as to include Ruffin Jacob Davis Zacheriah Thomas Squire Pirtle William Dean Isaac Williams John Daniel Maurice George Taylor Moses Cadwell Casy Isaac Pirtle Robert Pirtle Walter Scott Henry Davis Timothy Davis & James Ferrester work thereon under his directions and class.

    Ordered that Mark Lea oversee the clearing out and keep in repair the road leading from Cindeville to the McNairy County line crossing Hatchie River at Crosslands Ferry as lately viewed by a jury & that all the hands south of said road for three miles & south of Hatchie & all on the north of Hatchie & south of said road as far as to include Allen Kirk & East to the County line work thereon under his directions 2nd class.

    Ordered that Thomas Crossland have leave to establish a ferry across Hatchie River by giving bond agreeable to law.

Pg
172   Ordered that John Crane oversee the west half of the Memphis Road that he is now overser of & that he have all the hands that worked under him heretofore west of the halfway ground that he formerly worked.

    Ordered that John B. Lacy oversee the clearing out and keep in repair the road from Bolivar in a direction to Memphis half the distance that Crain formerly worked on & that he have all the hands East of the dividing line between said Crane & Lacy Mat formerly worked on said road.

    Ordered that E. D. Tarver William Todd Jesse Russell, James Pirtle John Pirtle and Elijah Rudolph or any five of them be appointed a Jury of view to view & mark out a road leading from the mouth of Clover Creek in a direction for Somerville with the least in-jury to individuals & make report to next term.

    J. C. Henley comes into open Court and resigns his Commission as Justice of the Peace for this County but returned no papers.

    Ordered that Stephen Jarman be allowed the hands Robert Barnett Zekial Owens & James Duffhand in addition to the lands already assigned him.

    Ordered that Henry W. Brown Henry Stevens John Moore James Hubbard Rowden Gray John Caldwell Ezekial Key or any five of them be appointed a jury of view to view & mark out a road from the three mile post on the Brownsville Road to pass the six mile post the nearer & best way so as to
Pg intersect the Brownsville road near Major S haws the nearest & best way
173 & make report etc.

    Ordered that Matthew Farrow oversee the clearing out and keep in repair the cotton gin road from the bank of the branch near Mark R. Roberts house south as far as Taylor worked& that all the hands of John H. McKinnie A. Taylor the hands that live where Brodk & Steel formerly lived Hester Davis Brown Whitlock & all the hands living within one mile of said road not already mentioned North of Little Spring Creek between Big Spring Creek & said road work thereon under his directions.

173 Ordered that David Harris overseer have the hands of HughsPipkins
& from thence by a line direct so as to include Asa Robinson thence so as
to include all the hands subject to said road south of Mill Creek work
thereon under him.

Ordered that John Doxey oversee the clearing out and keep in repair
the road from John Hodges west to the County line & all the hands within
one mile of said road work thereon under his directions.

Ordered that John Hardeman oversee the clearing out and keep in repair that part of the Cotton G in Road lately overseen by Mark R. Roberts
and that he have the hands of Barney Clifft, Gaunt, Blount, Jas. Allsup,
Mark R. Roberts, Kimbrough Livingston & Wilkerson & Blackstone Hardeman

Pg
174
Nichols A. Hazlewood & Allens work under his directions.

Ordered that Eli Cox overseer have Kinckin Kaisdale & hand Embers &
two Baunsons to work under him in addition to other hand allotted him.

Ordered by the Court that the report of West Harris relative to the
disposal of the children of John Mitcham be confirmed and it further ordered that said children be continued under the direction of said Harris and
that he make such arrangements as may seem to him necessary for the further
maintenance of said children.

Ordered that A. Cavett, John C. McKean, Geo. Thompson, Benjamin Alexander, L. M. Hardeman, W. W. Lennard & John Kelly be appointed a Jury
of view to view and mark a road south from Bolivar to intersect the Porters
Creek Road at some suitable place East of Spring Creek.

Ordered by the Court that James Ruffin and Edmund Tarver be appointed
Commissioners in conjunction with Edward R. Belcher to settle with the
County Trustee for the year 1824, 1825, 1826 and 1827 and report to next
Court they being appointed in the room of D. W. Wood removed and James O.
Leitch deceased.

Ordered that William B. Duncan, Isaac Ricks, Martain Taylor, Joseph
Rogers, Henry Jones, William Porter, Thomas Wilkes and Elijah Rudolph
or any five of them be a jury of view to lay out and mark a road upon Dun-

Pg
175
cans landing on Hatchie near the mouth of Hickory Creek to intersect the
road leading from Bolivar to Brownsville near Martain Taylors.

Ordered that L. W. McKean F. Shoemake, N. Steele, Wm. Ramsay, Needham
Stevens, W. W. Lennard, Thomas James, Allen Hill and R. C. Friar or any
five of them be appointed a jury to view out and mark a road from the town
of Bolivar to the new bridge on Hatchie on to the place when it is intended
to build it and make report to this Court.

Ordered that Cumberland Robinson oversee the clearing out and keeping in repair that part of the Mount Pinson Road from where it strikes the
County line near Martin Houston to the Jackson Road near Robt. H. Vaughans
and all the land east of the dry fork of Clover Creek, and north of the
Main Creek and West of Carn Creek work thereon under his directions.

Ordered that Wm. Gage oversee the clearing out and keeping in repair
the road from Fowlers ferry on Hatchie River the distance of eight miles
toward the Madison County line as marked out by the jury of view and that
he have all the hands immediately east and west of said road living within
three miles thereof to work under his direction.

Pg
176

Ordered by the Court that Bernet Highfield be appointed to oversee the cutting out that part of the way as marked out by the jury of view from the eight mile point running from Fowlers Ferry to Main Piney Creek in a direction toward the Madison County line, and that he have all the hands immediately then miles East and West of said way to work under his direction 2'class.

Ordered by the Court that Alsey Deen be appointed overseer to oversee and keep in repair a road from Main Piny Creek to the Madison County line as marked out by a Jury of View and that he have all the hands immediately East & West of said way within three miles thereof to work under his directions 2'd class.

Ordered that John Y. Cockeram Wm. Ramsay, John C. McKean, Thomas Hazlewood, Needham Stevens, Thomas James, Hugh A. Reynolds, W. B. Peck, Alex Kirkpatrick, & T. D. White or any five of them be appointed a jury of view to view and alter the road leading from Bolivar to Brownsville near the north East corner of Thompson D. White's field, so not to intersect the present road a short distance beyond said White's field.

Pg
177

Ordered that Isaac Ricks oversee the clearing out and keep in repair that part of the Brownsville road from the north Bank of Clear Creek to the north Bank of Hickory Creek and that he have all the hands that worked under Wm. G. Dotson commencing at Clear Creek running with the line dividing the 5 & 6th Range then with Hatchie Creek thence with said Creek to Saul Duncans then on a direct line to Elijah Ruloph thence on a straight course to the beginning.

Ordered that Miles Davis, Wm. Rennick Daniel Harper A. G. Harper & Rob McMillan be appointed a jury of view to view and mark out a road from Cun Goodals on the state line in a southwest direction to the southwest corner and make report to next term of this court.

Ordered by the Court that following persons be summoned by the Sheriff to attend at the next term of this Court as jurors To Wit, Coleman Draper, Isaac Saunders, Eli Ammons, Robert Jones, Joel Grantham, Thomas Grantham, James Elkins, Joel Rainer, Humphrey O. Warren Henry Rueller, Andrew Blackwood William Duncan George Floid Allison Cox, Isaac L. Moody, Wm. Ow en
Wm. H. Moers, James Marsh, Jesse Kerby, Daniel Muntz, William Pirtle, Isaac Rick James Wood, William Whitaker, Alexander Kirkpatrick, Randolph Mott, John

Pg
178

Polk, and that a Venni Facias issue accordingly, Jesse Pipkin, Con.

A deed of conveyance from Jacob Read to John Brantley for five acres of land was exhibited in open Court and the execution thereof acknowledged by said Read to be his act and deed and ordered to be certified for registration.

A plat & certificate from Hardy McCoy to Walter Robinson with the transfer thereon was produced in open Court and the execution thereof duly proven by the oaths of Walter Scott & Thomas Chisam and ordered to be certified.

A bill of sale from William B. Ervin to Robert D. Frost was exhibited in open Court and proven by the oaths of I. C. Henslyand Asa Robinson. Ordered to be certified for registration.

A bill of sale from Johathan Joyner & Elizabeth Joyner his wife to Robert D. Hart was exhibited in open Court and proven by the oaths of Asa Robertson to I. C. Hensly ordered to be certified for registration.

Pg
178

A bill of sale from John W. Pattrick to William S impson was exhibited in open Court and proven by the oath of Houston McKaughn. Ordered
to be certified for registration.

A deed of conveyance from John Murray to John Burris for 339 acres
of land was exhibited in open Court and acknowledged by said Murray to
be his act and deed. Ordered to be certified for registration.

Pg
179

A deed of conveyance from Charles Goldston to Humphrey Warren for
40 acres of land was exhibited in open Court and the execution thereof
duly proven by the oaths of R. P. McNeal and John H. Bills. Ordered
to be certified for registration.

A plat & certificate with the transfer thereafrom Wm. A. Allen to
David Dickinson was exhibited in open Court & the execution was duly
proven by the oath of C. C. Crisp one of the subsdribing witnesses thereto
ordered that it be so certified.

Three deeds of conveyance from Geo. W. Earle & Jesse Birdsong (one
of ten acres, one of twenty five acres & one of 109 acres) to Benjamin
Arnold & William Overall was produced in open Court and proven by the
oaths of Ichabod Watkins and Miles Birdsong. Ordered to be certified for
registration.

A deed of conveyance from William Polk to Richard Rainey for 80
acres of land was exhibited in open Court and acknowledged by said Polk
to be his act and deed/ Ordered to be certified for registration.

Pg
180

A deed of conveyance from William Polk to George D. Cain for 274
acres was exhibited in open Court and acknowledged by said Polk to be
his act and deed. Ordered to be certified for registration.

A deed of conveyance from James B. Clary to John S. Clary for 100
acres of land was exhibited in open Court and duly acknowledged by said
James B. Ordered to be certified for registration.

A deed of conveyance from John I. Clary to Jacob Reed for 100 acres
of land was exhibited in open Court and acknowledged by said Clary.
Ordered to be certified for registration.

A plat & certificate with the transfer thereon from Hardy McCoy
to Walter Scott was produced in Court and proven by the oaths of
Walter Robinson & James Robinson. Ordered to be certified.

The last will and testament of Levi Moore was produced in open
Court and the execution thereof proven by the oath of Andrew Stockwood one
of the subscribing witnesses and ordered to be recorded. And thereupon
came into open Court James Moore & William Moore who were appointed executors to said will and gave bond in the sum of five hundred dollars with
Daniel Hughs & Andrew Blackwood as their securities and were qualified
according to law. Ordered that hey have letters testamentary.

Pg
181

A deed of conveyance from Daniel Minner to Littlebery Mason for 60
acres of land was exhibited in open Court and acknowledged by said Minner
to be his act & deed. Ordered to be certified for registration.

A marriage contract between John D. Carroll & Rachael Rennich was
produced in open Court and the execution thereof duly proven b y the oaths

Pg of Miles Davis & Nathaniel Atkinson two of the subscribing wintesses
181 thereto and ordered to be recorded.

A plat & certificate with the transfer thereon from John N. McKennie
to Cessom Moss was produced in open Court and proven by the oaths of W. R.
Belcher & Amos Warner and ordered to be certified.

A deed of conveyance from Raiford Crawford to Thompson D. White for
110 acres of land was exhibited in open Court and proven by the oaths of
E. R. Belcher & A. Stevens. Ordered to be certified for registration.

An inventory of the Estate of Hanchia Hobbs decd. was returned into
Court and ordered to be recorded.

An account of the Estate of Michial Pirtle decd. was returned into
open Court and ordered to be recorded.

Pg
182

This day comes into open Court Frances Tedford and on motion and
by consent of the Court she was appointed Guardian to Polly Ann Tedford
one of the minor children of David Tedford decd. and who thereupon game
bond as the law directs in the sum of four hundred dollars with Curtis
Moon & Dutton Sweeten as her securities.

This day came into open Court Walter Robinson and on motion and by
consent of the Court the said Walter Robinson and on motion and by consent of the Court the said Walter is appointed guardian to Richard Hill
minor orphan son of James Hill decd. and who thereupon came into Court
and gave bond in the sum of one thousand dollars with James Chisam &
J. C. N. Robertson as his securities.

This day came into open Court Caleb Bright and on motion and by
consent of the Court he is appointed guardian to Judy Bright and Susan
Bright minor children of said Caleb, and thereupon he came into Court
and gave bond in the sum of five hundred dollars with John Nuckolls as his
security.

Pg
183

This day came into open Court Green Dupriest and prayed the Court
to be admitted as administrator on the estate of Joseph C. Dupriest which
in consideration by the Court is granted and thereupon the said Green gave
bond in the sum of six thousand dollars with Robert Robson & Wm. M. Crisp
as his securities and was qualified according to law. Ordered that he have
letters of administration.

A power of attorney from Caleb Bright to Samuel Bright was produced
in open Court and acknowledged by said Caleb to be his act & deed. Ordered that it be so certified.

An additional settlement of Edward Owens & Matthew Penkerd Com-
missioners appointed to settle with the administrator of the estate of
Davis Warren decd. was returned into open Court and ordered to be recorded.
And the Court adjourned to meet at 10 O'clock tomorrow morning.

James Ruffin, Chairman
John Y. Cockeram
Jas. Bogever

Pg
184

Tuesday 8th July 1828

Court met according to adjournement, present the worhipful James

Pg
184 Ruffin Edmund D. Taryer & John Y. Cockeram Esquires Justices,
Thomas J. Hardeman Clerk
J. C. N. Robertson, Sheriff
V. D. Barry, Solicitor.

      Proclamation being made as the form is the Sheriff returned into
Court a Venira facias in the words & figures (to wit), The State of Tenn-
essee to the Sheriff of Hardeman County Greeting you are hereby commanded
to summons the following persons to attend as jurors at our next County
Court to be held on the first Monday in July next viz William Duncan, John
B. Justice David Lane, John H. McKinnie William Trevett Jacob Read William Crane Garrett Fitzgerald David Woods Daniel E. Harper Allan Carroll
Jason William Joseph Hicks John M. Neelfy Woodson Doden Thomas Washburn
Thomas Hutchinson Chesley D. Key Arthur Fulgham Worley Lindvill John
Caldwell John Ruffin Josiah Short and Cumberland Robertson also Jessee Pip-
kin to act as Constabla here in fail not and have you then and there this
writ witness Thomas J. Hardeman Clerk of one said Court of Pleasant Quarter Sessions at office the 1st Monday in April A. D. 1828.
                        Thos. J. Hardeman Clerk
On the back of which was State of Tennessee Venira facias to County Court,
the Sheriff of Hardeman County J. P. April 19th 1828.

Pg
185   Came to hand same day issued I do hereby certify that I have summoned
all of the within named jurors except Thomas Hutchinson not found and that
they are all householders or free holders over the age of twenty one years
& inhabitants of Hardeman County given under my hand this 7th day of July
1828 J. C. N. R obertson, Shff. Out of whom the following were duly se-
lected as a Grand Jury viz Chesley D. Key foreman John Ruffin David Woods
David Lane William B. Duncan Jason Wilson Arthur Fulgham John B. Justice
Cumberland Robertson Josiah Short Woodson Vaden Garrett Fitzgerald John
Caldwell & who being elected empannelled charged and sworn retired under
the care of Henry W. Brown a Constable sworn for that purpose to inquire
for the body of the Court.

     A power of attorney from Samuel McIver to Robert McIver was exhibited
in open Court and the execution thereof was duly acknowledged by said Samuel & ordered to be certified for registration.

     A deed of conveyance from William Benbow & Alfred M. Briton to
Nathaniel Steels for 150 acres of land was produced in open Court and the
execution thereof was duly proven by the oaths of Wm. G. Steel & Joseph
W. Graves two of the subscribing witnesses thereto & the same was ordered
to be certified for registration.

     A deed of conveyance from Nathaniel Steel to Wm. G. Steel for 150
acres was exhibited in open Court and acknowledged by said Nathaniel or-
Pg dered to be certified for registration.
186

     A deed of conveyance from William B. Duncan to Isham Smith for 50
acres of land was produced in open Court & duly acknowledged by said Duncan ordered to be certified for registration.

     A deed of conveyance from David Laird to Daniel McGuinn & E. R.
Belcher for a town lot was exhibited in open Court and the execution thereof
was duly proven by the oaths of Jno. H. Bills & D. Fentress the subscribing
witnesses thereto ordered to be certified for registration.

Pg
186   A deed of conveyance from John I. Hibbett to Milton Moore for 4
acres of land was exhibited in open Court & duly acknowledged by said
Hibbell ordered to be certified for registration.

A bill of sale from Milton Moore to John I. Hibbett was exhibited
in open Court & acknowledged by said Moore ordered to be certified for
registration.

A deed of conveyance from R. P. T. Stone to Joseph P. Atwood was
exhibited in open Court & the execution thereof was duly proven by the
oaths of Austin Miller & Pitser Miller the subscribing witnesses thereto
ordered to be certified for registration.

The Grand Jury returned into open Court under the care of their
officers a Bill of Indictment against James Gunter for an assault &
battery endorsed a true bill Chesley D. Key foreman of the Grand Jury.

Pg
187   William McKinnie   )
          vs) Motion   )   Present James Ruffin E. D. Tarver & John Y.
James Lane   )   Cockeram Esq.
Elisha W. Boyte   )

On motion and it appearing to the satisfaction of the Court that
an execution had issued from John Slaughter Esquire an acting Justice
of the Peace for this County against the defendants and in favor of the
plaintiff for the sum of sixty one dollars & seventy cents debt & costs
and which had come to the hands of H. Williams a Constable of said
County, said execution bearing date the 29th day of March 1828, and in
defect of personal property levied on fifty acres of land Entry No.
1971 in range two and section 3. Therefore it is considered ordered
and adjudged that the said Tract of Land be exposed for sale to satisfy
said debt & costs as required by law together with the costs of this
motion and that a venditiona exponas issue accordingly.

Hugh A. Reynolds   )
      vs.) Petition for Certiovi)
James Hill   )
This day came into Court Hugh A. Reynolds and prays the Court for
writs of Certioavi and Supercedias directed to Thomas James Esquire a
Justice of the Peace for this County to send up a transcript of this
case. On the hearing of his said petition it is ordered that writs etc.
do issue accordingly on the said Reynold giving bond & security as required by law.

Pg   State |
188   vs.) Recognizance   )
    James Gunter   ))
This day came into open Court James Brown and acknowledged himself
to be indebted to the State of Tennessee in the sum of one hundred and
twenty five dollars to be levied of his goods and chattels lands and
tenements. But to be void on condition that he do make his personal
appearance at our next Court of pleas & quarter sessions and give evidence on behalf of the state against James Gunter and not depart without
leave first had/

Ordered that Josiah Hatley & William Bougard administrator on the
estate of Thomas Allsup deceased, do sell a negro girl by name Mary to
satisfy debts against said estate.

Pg Joshua Wright)
188   vs.) Cawe No. 1   )
James Burleson)

     This day came the parties by their attornies and thereupon came a Jury of good and lawful men To Wit William Truett William Cram Daniel E. Harper Allen Carroll, Joseph Hicks, John Mills, Robert C. Moore, David C. Powell Richard Saunders, Hardin S. Adams, Wm. P. Haden & Charles A. Hutcherson who being elected empannelled and sworn the truth to speak upon the issue joined upon their oath do say they find in favor of the plaintiff and assess his damages by reason of the non-

Pg
189
performance of the promise and undertaking of the defendant in the plaintiff declaration complain of to fifty five dollars and eighty eight cents. Therefore it is considered by the Court that the plaintiff recover of the defendant the said sum of fifty five dollars and eighty eight cents the damages in form aforesaid assessed by the Jury together with his costs about his suit in this behalf expended etc.

Andrew Taylor Ranger)
    vs.) No. 2 Appeal)
Michial McKennie)

     This day came the parties by their attornies and thereupon came a Jury of good and lawful men to wit David F. Owen Joel Ferguson, Michial Read, Samuel B. Jackson, Pleasant Colvert, Abram Smith, Robert Forbush , John Wilson Jr. Thomas Duncan, Benjamin Pirtle, James Musgrove, & Robert Berc who being elected empannelled and sworn the truth to speak upon the matters in controversary upon their oath do say they find in favor of the appelle Andrew Taylor Ranger and that the said Michial McKinnie is indebted to him in the sum of twenty dollars.

     Therefore it is considered by the Court that the judgment of the magistrate below be confirmed and that the Range recover of the said Michial McKennie the said sum of twenty dollars as found by the Jury aforesaid together with his costs about his suit in this behalf expended from which judgment the said McKennie pray and obtains an appeal to the next Circuit Court and gave N. Stevens as his security.

Pg   John Wright)
190   vs.) Nol 3 Covenant)
Austin A. King)

     This day came the parties by their attornies and thereupon came a Jury of good and lawful men To Wit Wesley C. Brown, Joseph Morman, Williams Truett William Crane, Daniel E. Harper, Allen Carroll, Joseph Hicks, John Mills, Robert C. Moore, Hardin S . Adams, William P. Haden, & Charles A . Huthcerson who being elected empannelled and sworn the truth to speak upon the issues joined upon their oath do say they find the issues joined in favor of the plaintiff and that the defendant hath not performed his covenant in manner and form as the plaintiff in replying hath alleged and they assess his damages by reason thereof to one hundred & twenty four dollars & fifty cents. It is therefore considered by the Court that the plaintiff recover against the defendant the said sum of one hundred and twenty four dollars & 50 cents, together with the costs by him about his suit in this behalf expended etc. and the plaintiff releases fourteen dollars of the above damages.

George C. Barfield)
    vs.) No. 4 Case)
John Lea)

     This day came the parties by their attornies and thereupon came a Jury of good and lawful men To Wit Wesly C. Brown Joseph Morman, William Truett William Crane Daniel E. Harper, Allen Carroll, Joseph Hicks, John

Pg 191   Mills, Robert C. Moore, Hardin I. Adams, William P. Haden & Charles A. Hutcherson who being elected empannelled and sworn the truth to speak upon the issues joined upon their oath do say they find in favor of the plaintiff and they assess his damage by reason of the non performance of the defendants promise and undertaking to eighty three dollars twenty five cents. Therefore it is considered by the Court that the plaintiff recover of the defendant the said sum of eighty three dollars & eighty five cents by the Jury in form aforesaid assessed together with his costs about his suit in this behalf expended from which said judgment the defendnat prays and obtains an appeal gave bond with Edward R. Belcher as his security to the next Circuit Court.

Peter A Man of Color)
     vs.) No. 5 Trespass)
John Saunders)

     This day comes the parties by their attornies and thereupon came a Jury of good and lawful men to wit Champion Blythe, Richard Lamb, John P. Darley, John Foster, John Moore, Israel Jones, Mark R. Roberts, Jesse Grive, Daniel Dodd, James Bond, John Alsop & Thomas Read who being elected empannelled and sworn the truth to speak upon the issues joined upon their oath do say they find the defendant Guilty in manner and form as charged in the plaintiffs decleration and they assess the plaintiffs damages to

Pg 192   seven hundred and sixteen dollars and seventy five cents. Therefore it is considered by the Court that the plaintiff recover of the defendant the said sum of seven hundred and sixteen dollars and seventy five cents the damages in form aforesaid assessed by the Jury together with his costs by him about his suit in this behalf expended etc.

William Harvey)
     vs.) Covenant)
Caleb Brock)

     This day came the plaintiff by his attorney and sayd he will no further prosecute his suit but takes a non suit and thereupon came the defendant in open Court and assumes all costs.

     Therefore it is considered by the Court that the plaintiff recover of the defendant his costs by him about his suit in this behalf expended etc.

John McKinnie)
     vs.) Certiovari)
William Cane)

     In this case came the said William Cane by his attorney and moved the Court to set aside the non pros. entered against him at the October term 1827 he being the plaintiff in the Court below and the parties to the case having been transposed in this Court. Whereupon come both parties by their attornies and said William Canes, motion came on to be heard once which being fully understood hereby the Court and after solemn argument had thereon by counsel both for the plaintiff and the defendant and it appearing to the satisfaction of the Court that the said William Cane had not notice that this cause was summoned from before the justice of the peace into this Court. It is therefore the opinion of the Court and

Pg 193   it is so ordered and adjudged that the non pros. in this cause be set aside and that this cause be placed upon the docket for trial.

     Richmond Carroll, this day came into Court and records his stock mark, a swallow fork in each ear.

     Court adjourned until tomorrow morning nine O'clock.

                         James Ruffin, Chm.
                         Edmund D. Tarver
                         John G. Cockeram

Pg
194
Court met according to adjournment present the worshipful James
Ruffin Edmund D. Tarver & John Y. Cockeram Esquires Justices.

Thomas J. Hardeman Clerk
V. D. Barry Solicitor General
J. C. N. Robertson Sheriff

William Davis and Henry W. Mosely came into open Court presented the license as attorneys who were qualified as such.

Thomas J. Oliver)
vs.)
John Foster)

This day came the parties in proper person and dismisses their suit and the defendant assumes all cost in this case. Therefore it is considered by the Court that the plaintiff recover against the defendant the costs about his suit in this behalf expended & that he have his execution.

Amos Warner)
vs.) Petition for Certiovari)
John Lea & Co.)

This day came into Court Amos Warner and prays the Court for writs of certiovari and supercedias directedto Joseph W. McKean Esquire Justice of the Peace fob the County of Hardeman to send up a transcript of this case on the hearing of his said petition it is ordered that writs etc. issue accordingly on said Warner giving bond and security as required by law.

The last will and testament of Levi Moore was exhibited in open Court and the executor thereof proved by the oath of William Kerr one of the subscribing witnesses thereto it having been proven on Monday the first day of the term of Andrew Blackwood the other subscribing witness thereto and ordered to be recorded.

Pg
195

State of Tennessee)
vs.)
John R. Rhea and Thomas N. Giles)

The Grand Jury returned into open Court under the care of their officer and presented an title of indictment against John Rhea and Thomas N. Giles for an afray endorsed a true bill Chesly D. Key foreman of the Grand Jury.

Samuel B. Harper)
& Walter Shinault) Present James Ruffin, Edmund D. Tarver John
vs.) Y. Cockeram, Esquires Justices.
Robert Rivers)

This day came the parties by their attorneys whereupon came a jury of good and lawful men to wit

William Truett	Richard Lamb
William Crane	George Campbell
Allen Carroll	Wm. L. Steele
Joseph Hicks	Mark R. Roberts
Charles A. Hutchen	William Todd
Thomas J. Oliver	Archa Chaffin

who being elected empannelled and sworn well and truly to enquire the damages the said plaintiffs have sustained by reason of the defendants not performing the covenants in the declaration mentioned upon their oath do say they find the plaintiffs damages to the sum of four hundred and twenty four dollars and fifty cents.

Pg
195   Therefore it is considered by the Court that the plaintiffs recover of the said defendant the damages aforesaid by the jury aforesaid in form aforesaid assessed also his cost about his suit in this
behalf expended etc. From which the defendant prayed and obtained an
Pg   appeal in the nature of a writ of error to the next Circuit Court and
196   give Willie B. Peck and W. D. Barry security.

John Fitzgerald)
    vs.   )
Garrt Ford   )
    By consent it is ordered that the parties have leave to take de-
positions on giving the adverse party reasonable notice on twenty days.

    A deed of conveyance from Charles Stewart to Littleton Johnson
for one town lot was exhibited in open Court & the execution thereof
duly acknowledged by said Stewart ordered to be certified for registration.

Duguid Mims   )
    vs.   )   Trespass) James Ruffin, Edmund D. Tarver, John
Mark R. Roberts)   Y. Cockeram
    This day came the parties by their attorneys and thereupon came a
Jury of good and lawful men to wit Daniel H. Harper, W. B. Hill, Roderick
Oliver, Solomon Tuttle, Robert Box, Hardin S. Adams, Sampson Edwards,
John Robertson, Enoch P. Hannis Edward Burlesson, Jesse G. Grice &
Michial Read who being elected tried empanneled & sworn the truth to
speak upon the issues joined upon their oaths do say they find defendant
guilty in manner and form as charged in the plaintiffs declaration and
they assess the plaintiffs damages to seven dollars and seventy five
Pg   cents.
197   Therefore it is considered by the Court that the plaintiff recover
off the defendant the said sum of seven dollars and seventy five cents
the damages in form aforesaid assessed by the jury together with the
costs by him about his suit expended etc.

Thomas McNeal   )
    vs.   ) Case) James Ruffin, Edmund D. Tarver, John Y. Cockeram
Fortan B. Gray   )
    This day came the parties by their attorneys and thereupon came a
Jury of good and lawful men to wit, John Foster, John Crane, Williams
Trewett, William Crane, Allen Carroll, Joseph Hicks, Charles A. Hucherson
John Nuckols, Richard Lamb, George Campbell, William G. Steel & William
Todd who being elected empaneled and sworn the truth to speak upon the
issues joined upon their oaths do say find the defendant guilty in manner
& form as charged in the plaintiffs declaration and they assess the plaintiff damages to forty dollars. Therefore it is considered by the Court
that the plaintiff recover of the defendant the said sum of forty dollars
the damages in form aforesaid assessed together with his costs by him
about his suit in this behalf expended.

Philip I. Kearney)
    vs.   ) Case) Justices Present James Ruffin Edmund D. Tarver
Henry W. Brown   )   John Y. Cockeram
    This day came the parties by their attorneys and thereupon came a
jury of good and lawful men (to wit) Daniel E. Harper W. B. Hill Robert
Box H. S. Adams, Sampson Edwards, E. P. Hannis, Edward Burlesson, Jesse
Pg   G. Grice, Charles Stewart James L. McDonald George Read and Jesse Blount
198   who being elected empaneled and sworn the truth to speak upon the issue
joined upon their oath do say they find the defendant guilty in manner

Pg
198 and form as charged in the plaintiffs declaration and they assess the plaintiffs damages to eighteen dollars & thirty seven & one half cents. Therefore it is considered by the Court that the plaintiff recover of the defendant the sum of eighteen dollars thirty seven and one half cents the damages in form aforesaid assessed together with his costs by him about his suit in this behalf expended etc. and thereupon came the plaintiff in open Court and acknowledged his satisfaction for the aforesaid damages.

Robert Rives & Alexander   Brown)
Surviving partners   )   Justices as before
Rives Murphy & Brown   )   Debt No. 10
    vs.   )
Robert River   )

    This day came the parties by their attorneys and thereupon came a Jury of good and lawful (to wit) Williams Trewet, Wm. Crane, Allen Carroll, Joseph Hicks, Charles A. Hucherson, John Nuckols, Richard Lamb, George Campbell, Wm. G. Steel, Mark R. Roberts, William Todd, & Archebald Chaffin who being elected tried & sworn the truth to speak upon the issue joined on their oaths do say they find the issues joined in favor of the plaintiffs and they assess their damage by reason of the detention of the debt of fifty three dollars and twenty eight cents in the declaration mentioned to eighteen dollars fifty five cents. Therefore it is considered by the

Pg
199 Court that the plaintiff recover against the defendant the debt aforesaid and the damages in form aforesaid assessed and his costs by him about his suit in this behalf expended and that he have his execution.

    Ordered by the Court on the application of Ephriam Sparks one of the securities for John Thompson a Constable of this County, to be released as such security, that the said Thompson be suspended from office until further and sufficient security be given.

John Wilson   )
    vs.   )   No. 15 Debt } Present Same Justices.
Chaucey Davenport   )
Henry G. Wells   )

    This day came the parties by their attornies and thereupon came a Jury of good and lawful men To Wit

John Foster   Charles A. Hutcherson
John Crane   John Nuckolls
William Crane   Richard Lamb
Allen Carroll   George Campbell
Joseph Hicks   Wm. G. Steel &
William Truett   William Todd

who being elected empannelled and sworn the truth to speak upon the issue joined upon their oath do say they find the issues joined in favor of the plaintiff and that the defendants have not paid the debt in the plaintiffs declaration mentioned of one hundred fifty dollars and they assess his damages by reason of the detention of the said debt to sixteen dollars and fifty cents. It is therefore considered by the Court that the plaintiff recover of the defendants his debt aforesaid and his damages in form aforesaid assessed by the Jury & also his costs by him about his suit in this behalf expended etc.

Pg
200 Robert L. Caruthers
  z Bechariah G. Goodall
    Administrator of all etc.
    of William Goodall decd.
        vs.   )   Debt No. 18)
John Crawford, John McKinnie, Henry Stevens& Rarford Crawford

Pg
200 Present James Ruffin, Edm. D. Tarver, John Y. Cockeram, Justices etc.

This day came the parties by their attornies and thereupon came a
Jury of good and lawful men To Wit Daniel E. Harper Edward B. Hill Robert Box, Hardin S. Adams, Sampson Edward Enoch P. Hannis Edward Burleson, Jesse G. Grice, Charles Stewart, James L. McDaniel, George Read,
& Jesse Blount who being elected empannelled and sworn the truth to speak
upon the issues joined upon their oath do say they find the issues joined
in favor of the plaintiffs and that the defendants have not paid the
debt of one hundred forty dollars in the plaintiffs declaration mentioned
and they assess them damages by reason of the detention thereof to four
dollars and twenty two cents. It is therefore considered by the Court
that the plaintiffs recover of the defendants the debt aforesaid and the
damages aforesaid in form aforesaid assessed by the jury together with
their costs by them about their suit in this behalf expended and that
they be in mercy etc.

Pg
201

Zechariah G. Goodall   ) Present James Ruffin Edm. D.
       vs.   ) Debt No. 19   ) Tarver, John Y. Cockeram, Esq.
John Crawford   ) Justices.
Henry Stevens & Raiford Crawford   )

This day came the parties by their attornies and thereupon came a
Jury of good and lawful men To Wit Daniel E. Harper, Edward B. Hill,
Robert Box, Hardin S. Adams, Sampson Edward, Enoch P. Hannis, Edward
Burleson, Jesse G. Grice, Charles Stewart, James L. McDaniel, George
Read, & Jesse Blount who being elected empannelled and sworn the truth
to speak upon the issues joined upon their oath do say they find the issues
joined in favor of plaintiff and that the defendants have not paid the debt
of one hundred & ninety eight dollars in the plaintiffs declaration mentioned and they assess their damages by reason of the detention thereof
to five dollars and ninety four cents.

It is therefore considered by the Court that the plaintiff recover
of the defendants the debt aforesaid and the damages aforesaid in form
aforesaid assessed by the Jury together with his costs by him about his
suit in this behalf expended and that they be in mercy etc.

John C. McKean for   ) Present same Justices as Before.
the use of etc.   )
       vs.   ) Debt No. 25   )
James T. Scott & Joseph Savage   )

Pg
202

This day came the parties by their attornies and thereupon came a
Jury of good and lawful men To Wit Daniel E. Harper, Edward B. Hill, Robert Box, Hardin S. Adams, Sampson Edward, Enoch P. Hannis, Edward Burleson,
Jesse G. Grice, Charles Stewart, James L. McDaniel, George Read & Jesse
Blount who being elected empannelled and sworn the truth to speak upon the
issues joined upon their oath do say that they find the defendants have not
paid the whole of the debt in the declaration mentioned but that there
remains a balance of fifty eight dollars and seventy five cents thereof unpaid and they assess the plaintiff damages by reason of the detention of
said balance to five dollars fifty two cents. It is therefore considered
by the Court that the plaintiff recover against the defendants the balance
of the the debt aforesaid and the damages in form aforesaid assessed together with his costs by him about his suit in this behalf expended & that
he have his execution., etc.

Edmund D. Tarver   )
       vs.   ) No. 30 Debt)
James Bond   )
Benjamin Arnold   )

Pg
202

Present James Ruffin John T. Cockeram Nath Steele Esq.

This day came the parties by their attornies and thereupon came a
Jury of good and lawful men To Wit Daniel E. Harper Edward B. Hill
Robert Box Hardin S. Adams, Sampson Edward, Enoch P. Hannis, Edward Burleson, Jesse G. Grice, Charles Stewart, James L. McDaniel, George Read,
and Jesse Blount who being empannelled and sworn the truth to speak upon

Pg
203

the issues joined upon their oath do say they find the issues joined in
favor of the plaintiff and that the defendants have not paid the debt of one
hundred dollars in the plaintiffs declaration mentioned and they assess his
xdamages by reason of the detention thereof to three dollars.

Therefore it is considered by the Court that the plaintiff recover of
the defendants the debt aforesaid and the damage aforesaid in form aforesaid assessed together with his costs about his suit in this behalf expended & that they be etc.

Thomas Grantham   )
    vs.   ) Debt No.   )   Present same Justices as before.
John H. McKinnie   )

This day came the parties by their attornies and thereupon came a jury
of good and lawful men to wit Daniel C. Harper Edward B. Hill, Robert Box,
Hardin S. Adams, Sampson Edward, Enoch P. Hannis, Edward Burlison, Jesse
G. Grice, Charlie Stewart, James L. McDaniel, George Read & Jesse Blount,
who being elected empannelled and sworn the truth to speak upon the issues
joined upon their oath do say they find the issues joined in favor of the
plaintiff and that the defendant has not paid the whole of the debt in the
declaration mentioned but that there remains a balance of six hundred &
thirty eight dollars & seventeen cents thereof unpaid and they assess his
damages by reason of the detention of that balance to three hundred forty

Pg
204

eight dollars and seventy cents. Therefore it is considered by the Court
that the plaintiff recover against the defendant the balance of the debt
aforesaid and the damages in form aforesaid assessed together with his
costs by him about his suit in this behalf expended etc.

Court then adjourned until tomorrow morning half past eight O'clock.
                      James Ruffin Chm.
                      Edmund D. Tarver
                      Jas. W. McKean

Pg
205

Thursday July 10, 1828

Court met according to adjournment present the worshipful James Ruffin
Edmund D. Tarver & Joseph W. McKean, Esquires Justices of the Peace for
Hardeman County, Valentine D. Barry Solicitor General, Thomas J. Hardeman
Clerk and Julius C. N. Robertson, Sheriff.

Rhea L. Jameson   )
    vs.   )
William R. Robinson   ))

On motion & by consent of parties it is ordered by the Court that the
parties have leave to take depositions generally on giving the adverse party
thiry days notice of time and place if end of the state and twenty days notice of time and place if and in the state.

A platt & certificate of survey for two hundred acres of land with a
transfer of the same to Joseph W. McKean was produced in open Court and
the executions of said transfer was duly acknowledged by Carter C. Collin
to be his act and deed for the use and purposes expresse d therein, ordered
that the same be certified accordingly.

Pg
205 Peter, a free man of colour)
    vs.) Motion for new trial.
John Sanders)
  This day came the parties by their attorneys and thereupon all the
matters and things arising on said motion being heard and by the Court here
fully understood whereupon after solemn argument had thereon. It is
Pg considered by the Court that a new trial should be granted in this behalf
206 on the costs accruing upon this motion for a new trial being paid by the
defendant.

  A deed of conveyance from John H. Bills to Josiah Chandler for
eighty acres of lands in Hardeman County was produced in open Court and
the execution thereof duly acknowledged by John H. Bills to be his act
and deed for the purposes therein expressed and the same ordered to be
certified for registration.

State)
  vs.) Indictment overseer of the road.
Mark R. Roberts)
  This day came the Soliciter General on the part of the state and
thereupon says he will no longer prosecute this suit and with leave
of the Court enters a Noli Proroqui in this behalf.
  It is therefore considered by the Court that the defendant go
hence without day and that the County pay the costs of this prosecution
etc.

Thomas Hardeman use of)
Atlas Jones)
  vs.)
Hiriam Casey)
  In this case by consent of parties., it is ordered by the Court that
the defendant have leave to amend his pleas so as not to prevent a trial at
this term.

Pg State of Tennessee)
207   vs.) Indictment
John R. Rhea) Affray Nol-pros-
  This day came the Solicitor General on the part of the state and on
motion and by consent of the Court a Nolli Prosequi is entered in this case
as to Rhea. And thereupon came into Court the said Joseph A/ Rhea and confesses judgment for the costs. Therefore it is considered that the state
recover of the defendant her costs etc. expended.

William M. Crisp)
for the use of Wm. Lemmond) Debt
  vs.)
Peter G. Rieves)
  This day came the plaintiff by his attorney whereupon came the defendant
Peter G. Rives and Caleb Brock and Samuel Lambert and confessed judgment
for one hundred ten dollars debt in the plaintiffs declaration mentioned also
the sum of two dollars and twenty five cents the interest thereon. Therefore
it is considered by the Court that the plaintiff recover of the said Rieves,
Brock, and Lambert, the said sum of one hundred and ten dollars debt and two
dollars and 25 cts. damages aforesaid in form aforesaid confessed also the
costs about his suit in this behalf expended etc. And the plaintiff agrees
to stay execution for nine months.

Pg
207 State   )
  vs.) Affray)
Thomas N. Giles)

  This day came the Solicitor General on the part of the state and on motion and by consent of the Court in Nolli Prorequi is entered as to Giles in this case and thereupon came the said Thomas N. Giles and confesses judgment for costs. Therefore it is considered by the Court that the state recover of the defendant his costs expended etc.

Pg John Foster   ) Present James Ruffin, Edmund D. Tarver, John Y.
208   vs.   ) Cockeram, Justices.
John M. Davis &)
William S. London)

  This day came the parties by their attorneys and thereupon came a jury of godd and lawful men to wit Williams Truett, William Crain, Jos. Hicks, Charles A. Hutcheson Dahiel W. Harper, John Crain, Cresson Moss, Wm. H. Tisdale, Moore Henley, Sampson Edward Yancy Rainey & James Elkins who being elected empannelled and swron the truth to speak upon the issue joined upon their oath do say that the defendants have not paid the said plaintiff the debt of fifty one dollars in the plaintiffs declaration mentioned and they do assess the damages by reason of the non performance of the condition to the writing obligatory in the declaration mentioned to forty one dollars and fifty cents. Therefore it is considered by the Court that the plaintiff recover of said defendant the said debt of fifty one dollars in the declaration mentioned which may be discharged by the payment of forty one dollars & fifty cents the damages aforesaid also the costs about his suit in this behalf expended etc.

State   )
  vs.)A & B)
Thomas Deen)

  This day came the Solicitor General on the part of the state and on motion and by consent of the Court a Nolli Proreqeri is entered in this case and thereupon came into open Court James T. Scott and confesses judgment for all

Pg costs. Therefore it is considered by the Court that the state recover of
209 the defendant his costs about this prosecution expended and the defendant in mercy.

State   )
  vs) Overseer)
John Crane   )q

  This day came the Solicitor General on the part of the state, and on motion and by consent of the Court a Nolli Proseqin is entered in this case, and the state pays the costs.

State   )
  vs.) Recognizance)
John Foster)

  This day came into open Court John Foster and acknowledged himself to be indebted to the State of Tennessee in the sum of two hundred dollars to be levied of his goods and chattels lands and tenements but to be void on condition that he domake his personal appearance on the first Thursday after the first Monday in October next before our Court of Pleas & Quarter Sessions to answer the state of Tennessee on a Bill of Indictment for Malicious Mischief and not to depart without leave first had and obtain etc.

  The Grand Jury returned into open Court under the charge of the proper officer a Bill of Indictment the State vs. James Burbran for A. & Battery

Pg
210

indorsed a true Bill Chesley D. Key foreman of the Grand Jury.

State   )
   vs.) Affray)
Walden Fuller)

This day came the Solicitor General on the part of the State and the defendant in proper person who being arraigned and charged on the Bill of Indictment plead not guilty and for his trial puts himself on the County and the Solicitor General likewise and thereupon came a Jury of good and lawful men To Wit William Truett, Wm. Crain Joseph Hicks, Daniel T. Harper, John Crain, Cessom Moss, Moore Henley, Sampson Edward, Yanyecy Rainey, Thomas Read. Allan Carroll, who being elected empannelled and sworn the truth to speak upon the issue of Travari joined upon their oath do say they find the defendant Not Guilty in manner and form as charged in the Bill of Indictment. Therefore it is considered by the Court that the defendant go hence without day and recover of the state his costs etc.

The Grand Jury returned into open Court under the charge of their lawful officer a Bill of Presentment against Wm. N. Fleming for abstracting a full road endorsed by all the Grand Jury.

State   )
   vs.) A & B   )
John Jones   )

This day came the Solicitor General on the part of the State and on motion and by consent of the Court a Nolli Prosequi is entered in this cause and thereupon came the said John Jones & Thornton Jones and confess judgment of all costs. Therefore it is considered that the State recover of the defendant his costs etc. expended etc.

Pg
211

Willie I. Riddle   ) Present James Ruffin, Esq. Edmund D. Tarver
        vs.   ) Debt No. 34) Esq. John Y. Cockeran Esq. etc.
Daniel Davis   )

This day came the parties by their attornies and thereupon came a Jury of good and lawful men To Wit Joseph Roger Williams Truett, William Crane Allen Carroll, Joseph Hicks, Daniel E. Harper, John Crane, Gesson Moss, William H. Tisdale, Moore Henley, William Ramsay, Yancey Rainey who being elected elected empanelled and sworn the truth to speak upon the issues joined upon their oath do say they find the issue joined in favor of the plaintiff and that the said plaintiff has not paid the debt of one hundred and nineteen dollars in the plaintiffs declaration mentioned and they assess his damages by reason of the detention thereof to three dollars and ninety seven cents. It is therefore considered by the Court that the Plaintiff recover of the defendant the said debt in the declaration mentioned and his damages in form aforesaid assessed by the Jury and also his costs by him about his suit in this behalf expended etc.

William Justice   )
        vs.) Covenant No. 35) Present same Justices as before.
Josiah Hatley Adm.   )
of Lewis Dillahunty decd.   )

This day came the parties by their attornies and thereupon came a Jury of good and lawful men To Wit Williams Truett William Crane, Joseph Hicks, Daniel E. Harper, John Crane, Gessom Moss, Moore Henley

Pg
212

Sampson Edward, Yancy Rainey, James B. Reves, Thomas Read & Allan Carroll, who being elected empannelled and sworn the truth to speak upon the issues joined upon their oath do say they find the issues joined in favor of the plaintiff said that the defendant hath not performed his covenant in manner and form as the Plaintiff in his declaration hath alleged and they assess his damages by reason thereof to one hundred and

Pg
212 two dollars. It is therefore considered by the Court that the plaintiff
recover against the defendant the damages aforesaid in form aforesaid
assessed and his costs by him about his part in this behalf expended to
be levied of the goods and chattels rights and credits which were of the
said Lewis Dillahunty do at the time of his death in the hand of the
defendant to be administered of so much then he, and if so much then
he not then the said Huny owe upward and two dollars damages aforesaid &
costs of the proper good & chattels lands & tenements of the defendants
etc.

Robert Gordon   )
    vs.   ) Covenant No. 36) Present same Justices as before.
John Foster   )
John H. McKennie   )
    This day came the parties by their attornies and thereupon came a
jury of good and lawful men To Wit William Truett, William Crain, Joseph
Hicks, Daniel E. Harper, John Crain, Gesson Moss, Moore Henley, Sampson
Edwards, Yancey Rainey, James Elkins, Thomas Read & Allan Carroll, who
being elected empannelled and sworn the truth to speak upon the issue joined
on their oath do say they find the issues joined in favor of the plaintiff
and that the said defendants have not kept their covenant as the Plaintiff
in his declaration hath alleged and they assess his damages by reason
thereof to one hundred and eighty nine dollars & twenty five cents. It is
therefore considered by the Court that the plaintiff recover of the defendants the damages aforesaid in form aforesaid assessed and his costs by
him about his suit in this behalf expended from which judgment the defendants prayed and obtained an appeal to the next Circuit Court & gave bond
& security according to law.

Littleton Johnson   )
        vs.   ) Debt- Same Justices as above.
Raeford Crawford   )
& Needham Stevens   )
    This day came the parties by their attorneys and their upon came a
jury of good and lawful men to wit Williams Truett, William Crain, Gresson
Moss, Moore Henly, Sampson Edwards, Yancy Rainy James Elkins and Allen
Carroll who being elected empannelled and sworn the truth to speak upon
the issues joined upon their oath do say they find in favour of the plaintiff and that they has not paid the debt of three hundred and two dollars
and 87 cents in the declaration mentioned assess the plaintiff damages
by reason of the detention thereof to six dollars & six cents. Therefore
it is considered by the Court that the plaintiff recover of the said defendant the said sum of three hundred and two dollars & 87 cts. debt together with the damages aforesaid by the jury aforesaid and in form
aforesaid assessed also the costs about his suit expended etc. Whereupon
Pg the said Needham Stevens came into Court and moved as a security on the
214 said writing obligatory in the plaintiff declaration named for judgment
against the said Raiford Crawford and William H. Maxwell principals in
said writing obligatory and it being proved to the Court here that the
said Needham Stevens is only the security for the said Crawford & Maxwell in manner aforesaid. Therefore it is considered by the Court here
that the said Needham Stevens recover against the said Crawford and Maxwell the said sum of three hundred and eight dollars and 93 cents the
amount of the judgment of the said Johnson against the said Crawford
& Stevens aforesaid, also his costs about this motion expended etc.

Pg
214 William Crawford ⟩
    Henry Hitchcock ⟩ Debt- Same Court as above
        vs. ⟩
    John McKinnie ⟩

This day came the parties by their attorneys whereupon came a jury of good and lawful men to wit William Truett William Crain, Joseph Hicks, Daniel E. Harper, John Crain, Gressom Moss, Moore Henly, Sampson Edward, Yancy Rainy, Thomas Read, James Elkins, and Allen Carroll who being elected impannelled and sworn tthe truth to speak upon the issues joined upon their oath do say they find in favor of the plaintiff and that the defendant hath not paid the debt of eighty five dollars in the declaration mentioned and assess their damages by reason of the detention

Pg thereof to twenty eight dollars and 52 cents damages by reason of the
215 detention thereof. Therefore it is considered by the Court here that the plaintiff recover of the defendant the debt and damages aforesaid in form aforesaid by the jury aforesaid assessed also the costs about this suit in this behalf expended etc.

Gideon Pillow ⟩
      vs.   ⟩ Debt No. 35 ⟩ Present James Ruffin, Edmund B. Tarver &
Robert A. Dandridge   ⟩ Martin Taylor Esq.

This day came the plaintiff by his attorney and the defendant also by his attorney and thereupon came a Jury of good and lawful men To Wit William Truett, William Crain, Joseph Hicks, Daniel E. Harper, John Crain, Gesson Moss, Moore Henley, Sampson Edward, Yancey Reiney, Thomas Read, James Elkins and Allen Carroll who being elected empannelled and sworn the truth to speak upon the issues joined upon their oath do say they find in favor of the plaintiff and that the defendant hath not paid the debt of six hundred & sixty seven dollars in the Plaintiffs declaration mentioned and they assess his damages by reason of the detention thereof to thirteen dollars & thirty four cents. Therefore it is considered by the Court here that the plaintiff recover of the defendant the debt and damages aforesaid in form aforesaid by the Jury aforesaid assessed also his costs by him about his suit in this behalf expended from which said judgment the defendant prays and obtains an appeal to the next Circuit

Pg Court and gave bond with James Ruffin as his security.
216

Francis Shoemake Brice Wilson   ⟩
Robert Gordon firm of Francis Shoemake ⟩ Present same Justices,
        vs, ⟩ Debt No. 39 ⟩ as before.
Reuben R. Stone   ⟩

This day came the parties by their attornies and thereupon came a Jury of good and lawful men to wit William Truett, Wm. Crain, Joseph Hicks, Daniel E. Harper, John Crain, Gessom Moss, Moore Henley, Sampson Edward Yancey Rainey James Elkins, Thomas Read & Allen Carroll, who being elected empannelled and sworn the truth to speak upon the issues joined upon their oath do say they find the issues joined in favor of the plaintiff and that the defendant has not paid the whole of the debt in the declaration mentioned but that there remains a balance of one hundred and seventy five dollars & twenty five cents thereof unpaid and they assess their damage by reason of the detention of that balance to five dollars & twenty five cents. Therefore it is considered by the Court that the plaintiff recover against the defendant the balance of debt aforesaid and the damages in form aforesaid assessed by the Jury together with their costs by them about their suit in this behalf expended & the defendant in mercy etc.

Pg
216 William Justice ⟩
⟩
vs. ⟩
Josiah Hatley Adm. ⟩Covenant No. 40) Present same Justices as
of Lewis Dillahunty decd. ⟩ Before.

Pg
217 This day came the parties by their attornies and thereupon came a
Jury of good and lawful men To Wit Williams Truett, William Crain, Joseph Hicks, Daniel R. Harper, John Crain, Gessom Moss, Moore Henley, Sampson Edward, Yancey Rainey, James Elkins, Thomas Read, Allen Carroll,
who being elected empannelled and sworn the truth to speak upon the
issues joined upon their oath do say they find the issues joined in favor
of the plaintiffs and that the defendant hath not performed his covenant in manner, and form as the plaintiff hath alleged in his declaration
and they assess his damages by reason thereof to four hundred and thirty
two dollars. It is therefore considered by the Court that the Plaintiff
recover against the defendant the damages aforesaid in form aforesaid
assessed and his costs by him about his suit in this behalf expended to
be levied of the goods and chattels rights and credits which were of the
said Lewis Dillahunty due at the time of his death in the hands of the defendant to be administered if so much there be and if so much there be not
then the paid sum of four hundred & thirty two dollars damages aforesaid
of the proper goods & chattels land & tenements of the defendants etc. to
be levied.

State ⟩
⟩
vs.) Debt No. 41)
⟩
Amos Warner ⟩
 This day came the Solicitor General on the part of the State, and
says he will no further prosecute this suit in behalf of the state and
on motion and by consent of the Court the same is dismissed. Therefore
it is considered by the Court that the defendant recover of the state
his costs about his suit in this behalf expended etc.

Pg
218 William F. Long ⟩
vs.) Debt No. 46) Present same Justices as Before.
Champion Blythe ⟩
 This day came the parties by their attornies and thereupon came a
Jury of good and lawful men To Wit William Truett, William Crane, Joseph
Hicks, Daniel E. Harper, John Crain, Gessom Moss, Moore Henley, Sampson
Edward, Yancey Rainey, James Elkins, Thomas Read, Allen Carroll, who
being elected empannelled and sworn the truth to speak upon the issue joined in favor of the plaintiff and that the defendant hath not paid the
debt of one hundred and two dollars for the declaration mentioned and
they assess his damages by reason of the detention thereof to nine dollars
eighteen cents.
 It is therefore considered by the Court that the plaintiff recover
of the defendant the debt aforesaid and the damages in form aforesaid
assessed by the Jury together with his cost by him about his suit in
this behalf expended from which said Judgment the defendant prays and
obtains an appeal to the next Circuit Court and gave bond with David Lane
as his security.

James Hodge ⟩
vs.) Debt No. 47) Present same Justices as before.
Duguid Mims)
 This day came the parties by their attornies and thereupon came a
Jury of good and lawful men to wit William Truett, William Crane, Joseph
Hicks, Daniel E. Harper, John Crain, Gesson Moss, Moore Henley, Sampson
Edward, Yancey Rainey , James Elkins, Thomas Rend & Allen Carroll who

Pg who being elected empannelled and sworn the truth to speak upon the
218 issues joine d upon their oath do say they find the issues joined in
favor of the plaintiff and that the defendant hath not páid the debt
of six hundred dollars in the plaintiffs decletion mentioned and they
Pg assess his damages by reason of the detention thereof to eighteen doll-
219 ars.

    Therefore it is considered by the Court that the plaintiff recover
of the defendant the debt aforesaid and the damages in form aforesaid
assessed by the jury together with his costs, by him about his suit in
this behalf expended and that he have his execution etc.

Needham Stevens   )
    vs.) No. 48 Case)
Raiford Crawford   )
    This day came the parties by their attornies and thereupon came a
Jury of good and lawful men To Wit William Truett, William Crane, Joseph Hicks, Daniel E. Harper, John Crain, Gessom Moss, Moore Henley,
Sampson Edward, Yancey Raney, James Elkins, Thomas Read & Allen Carroll
who being elected empannelled and sworn the truth to speak upon the issue
joined upon their oath do say they find the issues joined in f avor of
the plaintiff and that the defendant has not kept his several promises
and assumptions in the declaration mentioned and they assess the plaintiffs damages by reason of the defendants said promises to one hundred
Pg and seventy four dollars and ninety cents.
220   It is therefore considered by the Court that the plaintiff recover
of the defendant his damages aforesaid in favor aforesaid assessed by
the Jury together with his costs about his suit expended & that he have his
execution.

Samuel Harman   )
    vs.) Debt No. 50)Present James Ruffin, Edmund D. Tarver & Mertain
John Y. Cockeram   )   Taylor Esq.
    This day came the parties by their attornies and thereupon came a
Jury of good and lawful men To Wit Williams Truett, William Crain, Joseph
Hicks, Daniel E. Harper, John Crain, Gessom Moss, Moore Henley, Sampson
Edwards, Yancey Rany James Elkins, Thomas Read, A llan Carroll who being
elected empannelled and sworn the truth to speak upon the issues joined
upon their oath do say they find the issues joined in favor of the plaintiff
and that the said plaintiff hath not paid the said sum of two hundred &
fifty dollars in the plaintiffs declaration mentioned and they assess him
damages by reason of the detention thereof to seven dollars & fifty cents.
Therefore it is considered by the Court that the plaintiff recover of the
defendant the debt aforesaid and the damages in form aforesaid assessed by
the Jury together with his costs about his suit in this behalf expended
etc. from which said judgment the defendant prays and obtains, an appeal
to the next Circuit Court and gave bond with Roger B. Cockeram as his se-
Pg 221 curity.

Joseph A. Wallace, David Inland &   )
Joseph W. McKean from L. W. McKean   )
        vs.   )No. 51 Debt) Present same Justices
Thomas Hazlewoodk, Joshua Hazlewood)   as before.
& Wm. L. Land   )
    This day comes the parties by their attornies and thereupon came a
Jury of good & lawful men To Wit William Truett, William Crane, Joseph Hicks

Daniel E. Harper, John Crane, Gessom Moss, Moore Henley, Sampson Edward,
Yancey Raney, James Elkins, Thomas Read, & Allen Carroll, who being elected
empannelled and sworn the truth to speak upon the issues joined on their

Pg
221 oath do say they find the issues joined in favor of the plaintiffs and that
the defendants have not paid the debt of four hundred & twenty six dollars
the debt in the plaintiffs declaration mentioned and they assess their
damages by reason of the detention thereof to eighteen dollars & thirty four
cents. It is therefore considered by the Court that the plaintiffs recover
of the defendants the debt aforesaid and the damages aforesaid in form aforesaid assessed by the Jury as also their costs by them about their suit in this
behalf expended & that they have execution etc.

Joseph A. Wallace, David Inland, Joseph W. McKean firm of Jos.
W. McKean   vs.) Debt No. 52   ) Present same Justices
John H. McKinnie   ) as Before.

Pg
222   This day came the parties by their attornies and thereupon came a Jury
of good and lawful men to wit Williams Truett, Wm. Crain, Joseph Hicks,
Daniel E. Harper, John Crain, Cesson Moss, Moore Henley, Sampson Edward,
Yancey Rainey, James Elkins, Thomas Read, & Allen Carroll, who being elected
empannelled and sworn the truth to speak upon the issues joined upon their
oath do say they find the issues joined in favor of the plaintiffs and that
the defendant hath not paid the debt of two hundred & thiry eight dollars &
seven cents in the plaintiffs declaration mentioned and they assess their
damages by reason of the detention thereof to seven dollars and fourteen cents.
It is therefore considered by the Court that the plaintiff recover of the
defendant their debt aforesaid and his damages aforesaid in form aforesaid
assessed by the Jury as also their costs about their suit in this behalf expended & that the defendant be in mercy etc.

        The grand jury comes into open Court under the care of their officer and
presented a bill of presentment against John Warren for an assault endorses a
true bill signed by all of the Grand Jury. A deed of conveyance from Amos G.
Thompson to William A. Griffeth was produced in open Court and the execution
thereof was duly acknowledged by the said Amos G. Thompson to be his act &
deed and the execution of Eleanor Thompson was duly taken by E. Gossoth and
Lazerus Stewart as to hervoluntary act who had been appointed & commissioned
for that purpose ordered to be certified for registration.

Pg
223   And the Court adjourned to tomorrow morning 9 O'clock.
                                        Edmund D. Tarver
                                        James Ruffin Chm.
                                        J. M. McKean

Pg   Friday 11th July 1828
224 _____

        Court met according to adjournment present the worshipful
                                        James Ruffin   )
                                        Edmund D. Tarver   )
                                        Nathaniel Steel Esq.)
Thomas J. Hardeman Clerk, V. D. Barry, Solicitor, J. C. N. Robertson, Shff.

        Ordered by the Court that James Ruffin Robert A. Dandridge & James
Boguard be appointed commissioners to settle with Josiah Hatley administrator
of the estate of Lewis Dillahunty decd. & make report to next Court

C. T. & W. Howard   )
        vs.) Debt No. 54) Present James Ruffin, Edmund D. Tarver, Martain
Mark R. Roberts   ) Taylor Esq.
        This day comes the Justices by their attornies and thereupon came a
Jury of good and lawful men To Wit Williams Truett, Wm. Crane, Joseph
Hicks, Daniel E. Harper, John Crain, Gessom Moss, Moore Henley, Sampson Edward,

Yancey Rainey, James Elkins, Thomas Read & Allen Carroll who being elected
Pg empannelled and sworn the truth to speak upon the issues joined upon their
224 oath do say they find the issues joined in favor of the plaintiffs and they
assess their damages by reason of the detentin of the debt of one hundred
Pg and one dollars and seventy five cents in the plaintiffs declaration mention-
225 ed to two dollars. It is therefore considered by the Court that the plain-
tiffsrecover of the defendant the debt aforesaid and damages aforesaid in
form aforesaid assessed and the costs by them about their suit in this behalf
expended and the defendant in mercy.

John W. Burns   )
        vs.) Debt No. 55) Present same Justices as before.
Jeremiah Foote   )
        This day came the parties by their attornies and thereupon came a Jury
of good and lawful men To Wit William Truett, William Crane, Joseph Hicks,
Daniel E. Harper, John Crain Gessom Moss, Moore Henley, Sampson Edward,
Yancey Rainey. James Elkins, Thomas Read & Allen Carroll who being elected
empannelled and sworn the truth to speak upon the issues joined upon their
oath do say they find the issues joined in favor of the plaintiff and that
the said defendant hath not paid the debt of seventy five dollars eighty
seven cents in the plaintiffs declaration mentioned and they assess the
plaintiffs damages by reason thereof to one dollar seventy five cents. It
is therefore considered by the Court that the plaintiff recover of the defendant his debt & damages aforesaid in form aforesaid assessed and his costs
by him about his suit expended & that the defendant in mercy etc.

        Charles A. Huchinson served three days as a juror, Wm. Crane four days
as a Juror.

Joshua Hazlewood, Thomas Hazlewood & William T. Laird)
Pg firm of Hazlewood & Laird   )
226   vs.) Debt No. 56   ) Present James Ruffin
Mark R. Roberts   ) Edmund Tarver & John
Andrew Taylor   ) C. Cockeram, Esq.
) Justices.
        This day came the parties by their attornies & thereupon came a Jury
of good and lawful men Williams Truett, William Crane, Joseph Hicks, Daniel
E. Harper, John Crain, Gessom Moss, Moore Henley, S ampson Edward Yancey
Rainey, James Elkins Thomas Read & Allen Carroll who being elected empannelled
& sworn the truth to speak upon the issues joined upon their oath do say
they find the issues joined in favor of the plaintiffs and that the defendants
have not paid the debt of two hundred dollars in the plaintiffs declaration
mentioned and they do assess their damages for the detention thereof to three
dollars. It is therefore considered by the Court that the plaintiff recover
of the defendant the debt aforesaid & the damages aforesaid in form aforesaid
assessed by the Jury also their costs by them about their suit in this behalf
expended & they be in mercy etc.

John Foster   )
Hohn H. McKennie   )
        vs.   ) Debt No. 57) Present same Justices as Before.
George Read   )
        This day came the parties by their attornies and thereupon came a Jury
Pg of good and lawful men To Wit Williams Truett, William Crane, Joseph Hicks,
227 Daniel E. Harper, John Crane, Gessom Moss, Moore Henley, Sampson Edwards,
Yancey Rainy, James Elkins, Thomas Read & Allen Carroll who being elected
empannelled and sworn the truth to speak upon the issues joined upon their
oath do say they find the issues joined in favor of the plaintiff and that
the defendant has not paid the debt of one hundred & eighty five dollars

Pg
227 fifty cents in the plaintiffs declaration mentioned and they assess their
damage by reason thereof to two dollars seventy eight cents.

It is therefore considered by the Court that the plaintiffs recover
of the defendant the debt aforesaid and the damages aforesaid in form
aforesaid assessed & their costs by them about their suit in this behalf
expended from which judgment the defendant prays & obtains an appeal to
the next Circuit Court and gave bond with Wm. M. Crisp & Garrett Fitzgerald as his securities.

William Stoddent assigne)
of John Davis)
    vs.) Debt No. 59) Present same Justices as Before.
John Murray)

This day came the parties by their attornies and thereupon came a
Jury of good and lawful men To Wit William Truett, William Crane, Joseph
Hicks, Daniel E. Harper, John Crane, Cessom Moss, Moore Henley, Sampson
Edward, Yancey Rainey, James Elkins, Thomas Read & Allen Carroll, who being
empannelled & sworn the truth to speak upon the issues joined upon their
Pg oath do say they find the issues joined in favor of the plaintiff and that
228 the defendant hath not paid the debt of one hundred & twenty dollars in
the plaintiffs declaration mentioned and they assess his damages by reason
of the detention thereof to three dollars & sixty cents. It is therefore
considered by the Court that the plaintiff recover of the defendant his debt
aforesaid & his damages aforesaid in form aforesaid assessed as also his
costs about his suit in this behalf expended etc.

State)
    vs.) Extortion) Present same Justices as Before.
Walden Fuller)

This day came Solicitor General on the part of the State and the
defendant in proper person who being arraigned upon the Bill of Indictment
plead Not Guilty and for his trial puts himself on the Country and the
Soliciter General likewise and thereupon came a Jury of good and lawful
men To Wit, Joseph Rogers, Williams Truett, William Crain, Allen Carroll,
Joseph Hicks, Daniel E. Harper, John Crain, Cessom Moss, Wm. H. Tisdale,
Moore Henley, Yancey Rainey & William Ramsay who being elected empanneled
and sworn the truth to speak upon the issue of Traverse joined upon their
oath do say they find the defendant Guilty in manner and form as charged in
xthe Bill of Indictment.

It is therefore considered by the Court that the defendant be fined
the sum of fifty dollars and that the state recover against him his costs
in this behalf expended from which judgment the defendant prayed and obtain
an appeal to the next Circuit Court and with his security was recognized as
Pg follows.
229

State)
    vs.) Recognizance)
Walden Fuller)

This day came into open Court Walden Fuller and acknowledged himself to
be indebted to the State of Tennessee in the sum of two hundred fifty dollars
to be levied of his good and chattels, lands and tenements but to be void on
condition that he do make his personal appearance at the next Circuit Court
to be held for this County to answer said State on a Bill of Indictment for
extortion and not depart without leave first had and obtained.

State)
    vs.) Recognizance)
Walden Fuller)

This day came into open Court Charles T. Willman and acknowledged himself to be indebted to the State of Tennessee in the sum of one hundred

Pg And twenty five dollars to be levied of his goods and chattels land & tene-
229 ments but to be void on condition that Walden Fuller to make his personal
appearance at our next Circuit Court to be held for this County and answer the
State of Tennessee in a Bill of Indictment for Extortion and not depart
without leave first hadm and obtained.

```
State           )
  vs.   ) Estate No. 7 )
Walden Fuller        )
```
          This day came the Solicitor General on the part of the State and on
Pg motion and by assent of the Court a Nolli Prorequiis entered in this cause.
230 And thereupon came into open Court Walden Fuller and confesses judgment
for all costs. It is therefore considered by the Court that the State recover of the defendant his costs in this behalf & that he have her execution.

```
State         )
  vs.) No. 8  )
Walden Fuller )
```
          This day came the Solicitor General on the part of the State and on
motion and by assent of the Court a Nolli Prorequi is entered in this
cause and thereupon came xinto open Court W alden Fuller and confesses judgment for all costs. It is therefore considered by the Court that the State
 recover of the defendant her costs in this behalf & that she have execution etc.

```
State              )
  vs) Overseer No. 9 )
Walden Fuller      )
```
          This day came the Solicitor General on the part of the State and on
 motion and by consent of the Court a Nolli Prorequi is entered in this
case and the county pays the costs.

```
State                )
  vs.) Recognizances  )*Recognizances )
Jesse G. Grice       )
```
          This day came into open Court Jesse G. Grice and acknowledged himself
to be indebted to the State of Tennessee in the sum of two hundred dollars
Pg to be levied of his good and chattels, land and tenements, but to be void
231 on condition that he do make his personal appearance at our next County
Court to answer the State of Tennessee in a Bill of Indictment for an
Assault & Battery and not depart without leave first had and obtained.

```
State               )
  vs.                )
George E.  Graves    )
```
          This day came the Solicitor General on the part of the State and on
motion and by consent of the Court a Nolli Prorqui is entered in this cause,
and thereupon came Thornton Jones and confesses judgment for all costs.
Therefore it is considered by the Court that the State recover against said
Jones her costs expended etc.

```
State            )
  vs.  ) A & B    )
John E. Mayfield )
```
          On motion and it appearing to the satisfaction of the Court that a
Judgment taken last Court on a forfeiture against the defendant and upon
which execution final had issued from the Clerks office was erronious.
It is ordered by the Court that the same be set aside.

Pg
231
      The Grand Jury returned into open Court under charge of the sworn officer, two Bills of Presentments one against John Warren and one the State vs. Austin Miller both for assaults signed by the members of the Grand Jury. Also a Bill of Indictment the State vs. Champion Blythe for an assault & Battery indorsed not a True Bill Chesley D. Key, Foreman of the Grand Jury.

Pg
232
Robert W. Rivers   )
    vs.   ) Debt No. 22) Present same Justices as Before.
Nathan Avery   )
    This day came the parties by their attornies and motion having been made to the Court to dismiss this suit after argument heard. It is considered by the Court here that said suit be dismissed at costs of the plaintiff and that the that the defendant recover against the said Plaintiff his costs about his suit expended.

Walter Shineult   )
    vs.   ) Covenant No. 17) Present same Justices as Before.
James Hardin   )
    This day came the parties by their attornies and thereupon came a Jury of good and lawful men To Wit Williams Truett, William Crane, Daniel E. Harper, Allen Carroll, Joseph Hicks, Barney Skipper, John Robertson, William Overall, John Kelly, William Bogard, William Lambley & Moore Henly who being elected empannelled and sworn the truth to speak upon the issues joined upon their oath do say they find the issues joined in favor of the plaintiff and that the defendant has not kept and performed, his covenant as he has alleged in pleading and they assess the plaintiffs damages by reason thereof to one hundred and twelve dollars fifty cents. It is therefore considered by the Court that the plaintiff recover of the defendant his damages aforesaid in form aforesaid assessed his costs by him about his suit in this behalf expended & that he have mercy.

Pg
233

William Robinson   )
    vs) No. 23 Case) Present same Justices as Before.
John H. McKinnie   )
    This day came the parties by their attornies and thereupon came a Jury of good and lawful men To Wit William Truett, William Crane, Daniel E. Harper, Allen Carroll, Joseph Hicks, Barney Skipper, John Robertson, William Overall, Moore Henly, John Kelly, William Bougard, & William Lumbley who being elected empannelled and sworn the truth to speak upon the issues joined upon their oath do say they find the issues joined in favor of the Plaintiff and they assess his damages by reason of the several promises and assumptions in the declaration mentioned to one hundred and twenty dollars. It is therefore considered by the Court that the Plaintiff recover of the defendant his damages aforesaid in form aforesaid assessed by the Jury together with his costs about his suit in this behalf expended etc. From which said Judgment the defendant prayed and obtained an appeal to the next Circuit xCourt and gave bond with V. D. Barry as his security.

John Lea Lang   )
Parties given John Lea & Co.) Present same Justices as Before.
    vs.   )
Nathaniel Steele   )
    This day came the parties by their attornies and thereupon came a Jury of good & lawful men To Wit Williams Truett, William Crane, Daniel E. Harper, Allen Carroll, Joseph Hicks, Barry Skipper, John Robertson, William Overall Moore Henley, John Kelly, William Bogard & William Lambley, who being elected

empannelled and sworn the truth to speak upon the issue joined upon their oath do say they find the issues joined in favor of the plaintiff and they assess his damages by reason of the several promises and assumption in the declaration mentioned to one hundred and thirty one dollars and seventy five cents.

Therefore it is considered by the Court that the plaintiff recover of the defendant his damages aforesaid in form aforesaid assessed by the Jury as also his costs by him about his suit in this behalf expended the defendant in mercy etc.

James Walker Executor)
of the last will & testament of)
Saul Polk decd.)Present same Justices as Before.
     vs.) Debt No. 43)
Elisha W. Harris Adm. of)
the estate of M. C. Moorman decd.)

This day came the parties by their attornies and thereupon came a Jury of good and lawful men To Wit William Truett, Wm. Crane, Daniel E. Harper Allen Carroll, Joseph Hicks, Barney Skipper, John Robertson, William Overall, Moore Henley, John Kelly, William Bougard, William Lumbley, who being elected empannelled and sworn the truth to speak upon the issue joined upon their oaths do say they find the issue of fully administered in favor of the defendant & that he has fully administered all the goods & chattels rights & credits of the said M. C. Moorman an acct. which came to his hands to be administered
on. And further on do say on their oath that they find the issue joined of payment in favor of the plaintiff and that the defendant hath not paid the debt in the plaintiffs declaration mentioned of nineteen hundred and seventy one dollars and fifty cents and they assess his damages by reason to one hundred and sixty one dollars. It is therefore considered by the Court that the plaintiff recover of the defendant the debt aforesaid and the damages aforesadd in form aforesaid assessed by the Jury together with his costs about his suit in this behalf expended to be levied of the good and chattels rights and credits which were of the said M. C. Moorman due at the time of his death in the hand of the defendant to be administered of so much there be and if so much there be not then the costs of the proper goods & chattels land & tenements of the defendant to be levied etc. and it is agreed that execution shall be stayed until the 1st day of July 1829.

James Walker Ex. of the last)
will & testament of Saul Polk Decd.)
     vs.) Present same Justices as Before.
Elisha W. Harris Adm. etc. of the)
Estate of M. C. Moorman decd.)

This day came the parties by their attornies and thereupon came a Jury of good and lawful men To Wit Williams Truett, William Crane, Daniel E. Harper Allen Carroll, Joseph Hicks, Barney Ripper, John Robertson, William Overall, Moore Henly, John Kelly, William Bougard & William Lumbley who being elected empannelled and sworn the truth to speak upon the issues joined upon their oaths do say they find the issues joined of fully administered in favor of the defendant & that he has fully administered all the goods & chattels rights & credits of the said M. C. Moorman decd. which came to his hands to be administered on. And furtehermore do say on their oath that they find the
issues joined of payment in favor of the plaintiff and that the defendant hath not paid the debt of nineteen hundred & seventy one dollars, and they assess his damages by reason of the detention thereof to two hundred and

and seventy nine dollars. It is therefore considered by the Court that the plaintiff recover of the defendant the debt aforesaid & the damages aforesaid

in favor aforesaid assessed by the Jury together with his costs about his
suit in this behalf expemded tp be levied of the goods & chattels rights and
credits which were of the said M. C. Moorman at the time of his death in
the hand of the defendant to be administered if so much then be, and if so
much then be not then the costs of the proper good & chattels land & teneme
ent of the defendant to be levied on and it is agreed to stay execution
until the 1st day of Jany 1829. .

Nathaniel Steele)
    vs.) Debt No. 21) Present same Justices as Before.
Richard Saunders)
Carter C. Collins)

    This day came the parties by their attornies and on motion and by
leave of the Court this suit is dismissed as to Carter C. Collier and
thereupon came a jury of good and lawful men To Wit Williams Truett, Wm.
Crane, Daniel E. Harper, Allen Carroll, Joseph Hicks, Barney Skipper,
John Robertson, William Overall, Moore Henly, John Kelly, Wm. Bowgard, &
Pg
237 Wm. Lumbly who being elected empannelled and sworn the truth to speak upon
the issues joined between the plaintiff and Richard Saunders upon their
oath do say they the issues joined in favor of the plaintiff and that the
said defendant hath not paid the debt of four hundred dollars in the
plaintiffs declaration mentioned and they assess his damages by reason
thereof to fourteen dollars.
    Therefore it is considered by the Court that the Plaintiff recover
against said Richard Saunders the debt aforesaid in form aforesaid assessed also his costs about his suit in this behalf expended etc.

Duguid Mims)
    vs.) Debt No. 33) Present same Justices as Before.
Nathaniel Steele)
John B. Lacy)

    This day came the parties by their attornies and thereupon came a
Jury of good and lawful men To Wit Williams Truett, William Crane, Daniel
E. Harper, Allen Carroll, Joseph Hicks, Barney L. Ripper, John Robertson,
William Overall, Moore Henly, John Kelly, William Bougard & William Lumbley who being elected empannelled and sworn the truth to speak upon the
issues joined upon their oath do say they find the issues joining between
the plaintiff and the defendant Lacy in favor of the defendant and further-
more on the oath do say they find the issues joined between the Plaintiff
& Steele in favor of the Plaintiff and that the said Plaintiff hath not
paid the debt of one hundred & forty five dollars in the plaintiffs declar-
Pg
238 ation mentioned & they assess his damages by reason of the detention thereof to four dollars thirty five cents.
    Therefore it is considered by the Court that the plaintiff recover
of the defendant Steele the debt aforesaid assessed & also his costs by
him about his suit in this behalf expended & that he have execution.

James Alexander)
    vs.) Certiovari No. 61)
William Lumbley)

    An affadavit of the defendant this cause is continued an affadatt of
the defendant and it is ordered by the Court that the said defendant have
leave to take the deposition of Turner Lumbly live in the state of Miss-
issippi on giving 30 days notice.

Hazlewood & Land)
    vs.) Appeal No. 62)
Mark R. Roberts)

Pg
238   This day came the Plaintiff and dismisses this suit at their costs.
       Therefore it is considered by the Court that the said Mark R. Roberts
do secure of said Hazlewood & Land his costs about his appeal in this behalf expended etc.

An   An additional inventory of the Estate of Lewis Dillahunty deceased was
returned into Court and ordered to be recorded.

       An additional Inventory of the Estate of Thos. Alsup decd. was returned
into Court & ordered to be recorded.

Pg   Valentine D. Barry   ) Present James Ruffin, Edward D. Tarver,
239   vs.   ) No. 63 Appeal) Martain Taylor Esq.
      John Murray   )
       This day came the parties by their attornies and thereupon came a Jury
of good & lawful men To Wit, Williams Truett, William Crain, Daniel E. Harper, Allen Carroll, Joseph Hicks, Barney L. Kipper, John Robertson, William
Overall, Moore Henley, John Kelly, William Bougard William Lambly who being
elected empannelled and sworn the truth to speak upon the matters in controversy, upon their oath do say they find in favor of the plaintiff the
sum of eighteen dollars and twenty five cents. Therefore it is considered
by the Court that the Plaintiff recover of the defendant the said sum of
eighteen dollars & twenty five cents as also his costs about his appeal
in this behalf expended etc.

      Josiah Hatley &   )
      Wm. Bougard adm.   )
           vs.   ) Debt No. 42   )Present same Justices as above.
      William Crane   )
       This day came the Justices by their attornies and thereupon came a
Jury of good and lawful men To Wit Peter Rogers, William Steelman, David
C. Powell, William Truett, Daniel E. Harper, Allan Carroll, Joseph Hicks, &
Barney Kipper, John Robertson, William Overall, Michial Read & John Kelly
who being elected tried and sworn the truth to speak upon the issues joined
upon their oath do say they find the issues joined in favor of the defend-
Pg   ant. Therefore it is considered by the Court that the defendant go hence
240   without day and recover his costs about this suit in this behalf expended
etc.
       This day came the defendants by attorney and moves the Court to
dismiss this cause at the Plaintiffs costs which after argument is done.
Therefore it is considered by the Court that the defendants Rebran & De-
priest recover of said Crawford their costs expended etc.

      John McKinnie   )
           vs.   ) Certiovari No. 65) Present same magistrates as before.
      William Cone   )
       This day came the parties by their attornies and thereupon came a
Jury of good and lawful men To Wit Peter Rogers, William Steelman, Daniel
E. Harper,   Allen Carroll, Joseph Hicks, Barney Skipper, John Robertson,
William Overall, Michial Read & John Kelly who being elected empannelled
and sworn the   truth to speak upon the matters in controversy upon their
oath do say   find in favor of the defendant William Cone the sum of seventy
seven dollars and   sixty two cents debt principal & costs the amount of the
judgment of the   justice below.
       Therefore it is considered by the Court that sd. William Cane re-
cover of said John McKinnie the said sum of seventy seven dollars sixty two
cents and on   motion also against his securities Samuel W. Eclog, Wm. B.

Pg 240
Pg 241

Robinson & Richard Lamb together with 12 pr. cpt. interest p. annum from the rendition of the judgment below up to this time also his costs about his suit in this behalf expended etc.

Thomas Simmons)
vs.) Attachment)
Charles W. Shuffer)

This day came the plaintiff by his attorney and the defendant being solemnly called to come into Court and replevy of his property attached came not but made default. Therefore it is considered by the Court that Judgment be entered up against the said defendant but because it appears here to the Court that the said attachment is in damages. Therefore it is ordered that a writ of Inquiry of Damages issue returnable to the next term of the Court.

Richard Lamb)
vs.) Certiovari) Motion to dismiss Present James Ruffin, E. D.
Daniel Shaw) Tarver, & Martain Taylo, Esquires.

This day came the parties by their attornies and the said Daniel Shaw by his attorney moved the Court to dismiss said Certiovari and upon solemn argument had thereon, it is ordered that the said motion be sustained & that the same be dismissed.

It is therefore considered by the Court that the said Shaw recover of the said Lamb and John C. McKean his security the sum of forty dollars the judgment of the magistrate below together with costs also the sum of two dollars & 52 cts & interest thereon at the rate of 12 pr. pc. pr. annum for the rendition of the Judgment below up to this time & his costs about his suit in this behalf expended etc.

Pg 242

Thomas James)
vs.) Motion No. 1)Present same Justices as Before.
Gideon Pillow)
Nathaniel Steele)

On motion and it appearing to the satisfaction of the Court that an execution had issued against the defendants by Joseph W. McKean Esq. a Justice of the Peace for this county on behalf of the Plaintiff. For the sum of sixteen dollars seventy five cents debt & costs and which said execution had come to the hands of Philip I. Kearney, a constable of said County and by him for want of personal property to by on had been levied on Gideon Pillow interest in a 500 acre tract of land in range 5 , Section 3 No. of Entry 693 the 11th day of July 1828.

It is therefore ordered adjudged and decreed that the said tract of land be exposed to sale as required by Law to satisfy the said debt together with the costs & also the costs of this motion and that Venditiona Exponas issue accordingly.

Samuel C. Brooks)
vs.) No. 2 Motion) Present same Justices as Before.
Duguid Mims)

On motion and it appearing to the satisfaction of the Court, that an execution had issued against the defendant by Francis Shoemake Esquire a Justice of the Peace for this County on behalf of the plaintiff for the sum of nineteen dollars & sixty cents, debt & costs and which said execution had come to the hands of Philip L. Kearney a Constable of said County and by him for want of personal property levied on one Town Lot in the Town of Bolivar it being Lot No. 6 in Square No. 14 the 11th day of July 1828 . It is therefore ordered adjudged and decreed that the said Lot be exposed to sale as required by Law to satisfy the said debt together with the costs & also their costs of the motion and that a venditiona exponas issue accordingly.

Pg 243

243 Needham Stevens   )

      vs.   ) No. 3 Motion)Present same Justices as Before.

Duguid Mims   )

      This day came the plaintiff by attorney and on motion and it appearing to the satisfaction of the Court that an execution had issued from Joseph W. McKean Esquire Justice of the Peace for this County in behalf of the Plaintiff against the defendant for the sum of thirteen dollars thirty one cents debt with 50 cents costs and which said execution had come to the hand of Philip L. Kearney a constable of this county and by him for want of personal property levied on one town lot in the town of Bolivar known as Lot No. 6 in Square No. 14 the 14th July 1828. It is therefore ordered adjudged and decreed that the said Town Lot be exposed to sale as required by law to satisfy the said debt together with the costs & also the costs of this motion and that a venditiona Exponas issue accordingly.

James Elkins   )

      vs.)Debt   )

Walden Fuller   )

      On motion it is ordered by the Court that the Plaintiff have leave to take the deposition of Levi H. Coe on giving 30 days notice to the opposite party.

Pg
244 Jos. P. & W. W. Atwood   )

        vs.   ) Motion No. 4   )Present same Justices as Before.

Nathaniel Steele   )

Wm. W. Lennard   )

      On motion and it appearing to the satisfaction of the Court that an execution had issued from Joseph W. McKean Esq. a Justice of the Peace for this County on behalf of the Plaintiffs against the defendants for the sum of thirty dollars & fifty cents debt & costs and which said execution had come to the hands of Philip L. Kearney a Constable of said County and by him for want of personal property to lev upon had been levied on it Steele interest in a 100 acres of land in R. 2 L. 4 entered in the name of Thos. H. Williams by entry No. 2382 11th July 1828.

      It is therefore ordered adjudged and decreed that the said tract of land be exposed to sale as the law directs to satisfy said execution together with the costs also the costs of this motion and that a venditiona exponas issue accordingly.

James Cox & Thos. Jameson   )

        vs.) No. 5 Motion   )Present same Justices as Before.

Joseph & Rowley Gray   )

      On motion and it appearing to the satisfaction of the Court that an execution had issued from Joseph W. McKean a Justice of the Peace for this County in behalf of the plaintiffs against the defendants for the sum of thirty nine dollars, ninety six cents debt & costs and which said execution had come to the hands of Philip L. Kearney a constable of said

Pg
245 County and by him for want of personal property levied on 100 acres of land No. of entry 2365 in Range 34 S 4 as the property of Rowley Gray this 11th July 1828.

      Therefore it is ordered decreed and adjudged that the said tract of land be exposed for sale as required by law to satisfy said debt together with the costs also the costs of this motion and that venditiona exponas issue accordingly.

Pg
245 Jos. P. & Wm. W. Atwood)
         vs.) No. 6 Motion) Present same Justices as Before.
Nathaniel Steele)
W. W. Lennard)

On motion and it appearing to the satisfaction of the Court that an execution had been issued by Jos. W. McKean Esq. Justice of the Peace for this County on behalf of the Plaintiff against the defendants for the sum of thirty dollars & fifty cents debt & costs and which said execution had come to the hand of Philip L. Kearney a Constable of said county and by him for want of personal property levied on 100 acres of land No. Entry 2382 in Range 2 S. 4 entered in the name of Tho. H. Williams the 11th of July 1828. It is therefore ordered adjudged and decreed that said Tract of Land be reopened for sale as required by Law to satisfy said debt together with the costs of this motion and that a vanditiona exponas issue accordingly.

Adjourned to tomorrow morning 8 O'clock.

                           E. D. Tarver J. P.
                           Jas. Ruffin J. P.
                           N. Steele J. P.

Pg
246   The Court met according to adjournment Present the whoshipful James Ruffin, Edmund D. Tarver, Nathl. Steele, Esquires Justices, J. C. N. Robertson, Shff, Tho. J. Hardeman, Clerk.

State)
   vs.) A & B)
Robert Hays Jr.)

This day came the Solicitor General on the part of the State and the defendant in proper person who being arraigned upon the Bill of Indictment plead Not Guilty and for his trial puts himself on the Country and the Solicitor General likewise and thereupon came a Jury of good and lawful men To Wit Thomas Read, Richard Lamb, Robert D. Jackson, Hardins Adams, John Hill, John E. Mayfield, Needham Stevens, William Truett, Allan Carroll, Daniel E. Harper, Joseph Hicks, & Robert C. Moore who being elected tried and sworn the truth to speak upon the issue of Traverse joined upon their oath do say the defendant is guilty in manner and form as charges in the Bill of Indictment. Therefore it is considered by the Court that the said defendant be fined six c/p cents to be imprisoned four hours and then to remain in the custody of the Sheriff until the fine and cents are paid or secured from which said Judgment the defendant prayed and obtained an appeal to the next Circuit Court & was recognized accordingly.

State)
   vs.) Recognizance)
Robert Hays Jr.)

This day came into open Court Robert Hays & acknowledged himself to
Pg be indebted to the State of Tennessee in the sum of two hundred dollars
247 to be levied of his goods & chattels land & tenements but to be void on condition that he do make his personal appearance before the next Circuit Court to be held for this County and then and there to answer the State of Tennessee for an Assault & Battery and not depart without leave first had.

State)
   vs.) Recognizance)
Robert Hays Jr.)

This day came into open Court Robert Kelly & Jesse Henson who acknowledged themselves to be indebted to the State of Tennessee in the sum of one hundred dollars each to be levied of their goods and chattels land &

Pg
247 tenements but to be void on condition that the said Robert Hays do make
his personal appearance at the next Circuit Court to be held for this
County to answer the State of Tennessee on an indictment for an assault
& Battery and not depart without leave first had & obtained.

```
James H. Sheppard          )
        vs. ) Covenant    )
Joseph Morman              )
Levy Crow                  )
```

This day came the plaintiff by his attorney and it being the last
day of the term & appearing to the satisfaction of the Court that the
defendant had fixed no sufficient plea or pleas or demeaner to the
plaintiffs declaration, and the defendant being solemnly called to come
into Court & file his plea or pleas or demur came not but made default
Pg and it appearing to the Court that the plaintiffs demand sound in
248 damages and that final judgment cannot be rendered at this term.

It is ordered by the Court that a Writ of Inquiry be awarded to the
next term of this Court and that a Jury come to inquire of the damages
the Plaintiff has sustained.

The Grand Jury returned into open Court and in the case of the
proper officer a Bill of Indictment for an assault & Battery indorsed
a True Bill Chesley D. Key foreman of the Grand Jury.

```
Thomas Henderson                )
for the use of Atlas Jones      )
        vs.) Debt No. 45        )      Present J    ames Ruffin, Edmund D.
Hiram Casey                     )      Tarver, Nath Steel Esq.
```

This day came the parties by their attornies and thereupon came a Jury
of good and lawful men To Wit Thomas Read, Richard Lumbley, Richard D. Jackson, Hardin S. Adams, John Hill, John E. Mayfield, Needham Stevens, Williams
Truett, Allen Carroll, Daniel E. Harper, Joseph Hicks & Robt. C. Moore,
who being elected empannelled and sworn the truth to speak upon the
issues joined upon their oath do say they find the issues joined in favor
of the Plaintiff and that the defendant hath not paid the debt of two
hundred & forty dollars debt in the plaintiffs declaration mentioned and they
assess his damages by reason of the detention thereof to twenty four doll-
xars & thirty cents. Therefore it is considered by the Court that the
Pg plaintiff recover of the defendant the said debt aforesaid & the damages
249 aforesaid in form aforesaid assessed by the Jury as also his costs by him
about his suit in this behalf expended etc. and execution.

Stayed till next term.

```
John Lea  Suing                          )
Partner firm of J. Lea & Co.             )
        vs.                              ) Present same Justices as Before.
Thos. J. Hardeman &                      )
John H. Bills last                       )
will & testament of E. Polk decd.        )
```

This day came the parties by their attornies and thereupon came a
Jury of good and lawful men To Wit Thomas Read, Richard Lumbley, Richard
D. Jackson, Hardin S. Adams, John Hill, John E. Mayfield, Needham Stevens,
Williams Truett, Allen Carroll, Daniel E. Harper, Joseph Hicks, & Robert
C. Moore, who being elected empannelled and sworn the truth to speak upon
the issues joined upon their oath do say they find the issues joined in
favor of the Plaintiff and they assess his damages by reason of the several
promises and assumptions in the plaintiffs declaration mentioned to one

Pg
249 hundred and twenty seven dollars & forty cents. Therefore it is considered by the Court that the plaintiff recover of the defendants the damages aforesaid in form aforesaid assessed by the Jury also his costs by him about his suit in this behalf expended to be levied of the goods & chattels rights and credits of the said Ezekial Polk decd. at the time of his death in the hand of the defendants if so much there be and if so much there be not then the costs of the goods & chattels land & tenements of the defendants.

Pg
250

Franklin Sharker)
    vs.   )   Present the same Justices as Before.
John McKinnie)

This day came the plaintiff by his attorney and the defendant being solemnly called to come into Court and replevy his property attached came not but made default. Therefore it is considered by the Court that judgment final be given in this case for the sum of one hundred & eighty dollars debt the sum in the plaintiffs declaration mentioned and the interest thereon amounting to fifty seven dollars & sixty cents together with the costs on the same accruing & that he have his execution.

Roderick Williams   )
    vs.) Certiovari, Motion to dismiss)
Charles L. Howard   )
Willie L. Riddle   )

This day came the parties by their attornies and thereupon all the matters and things arising in said defendants motion to dismiss the same being heard and by the Court here understood & after solemn argument had thereon. It is considered by the Court that the said defendant take nothing by their said motion, that the same be over ruled and said suit set down for trial at the next term of this Court.

Grand Jury dismissed the 5th day, William Truett, Allen Carroll, Joseph Hicks, & Daniel E. Harper and entitled to 5 days- H. W. Bram, Jesse Pipkin 5 days such as Constable.

Pg
251 State   )
  vs.) Sci Facias)
Shirley Goodwin   )

This day came the defendant as will as the Solicitor General on the part of the state. Whereupon the defendant moved the Court to quash the Sciri facias in this case and after argument being had thereon it is considered that the motion be guarded and that the defendant go hence without and that the costs in this case be paid by the County etc. from which said Judgment the Solicitor General prays and obtains an appeal to the Next Circuit Court.

State   )
  vs.) Sci Facias   )
James W. Townsend   )

This day came the defendant as well as the Solicitor General on the part of the state whereupon the defendant moved the Court to quash the Sciri Facias in this case and after argument being had thereon it is considered that the motion be sustained and that that the same be quashed and that the defendant go hence without day and that the costs in this case be paid by the County etc. upon which this judgment the Soliciter General prays and obtains an appeal to the next Circuit Court.

Pg Robert Glenn   )
251   vs.) Sci Fia   )
    David Leffland   )
        This day came the Plaintiff by his attorney and the defendant being
solemnly called to come into Court and plead to the Sci Facias served on
him came not but made default. Therefore it is considered by the Court
Pg that the plaintiff recover of the defendant the sum of twenty five dollars
252 and seventy three cents costs as stated in the said Sciri Facias together
with his costs in their behalf expended and that execution issue accordingly.

    Joshua Hazlewood & Thomas Hazlewood)
    & Wm. T. Land   )
        vs.   ) Debt   )
    Mark RoRoberts   )
    Abner Taylor   )
        This day came the defendants into open Court and prayed and obtained
an appeal in the case to the next Circuit Court for the County and gave
bond with Julius C. N. Robertson as security.

    Joseph W. McKean Joseph A. Wallace   )
    & David Ireland   )
            vs.   )
    Joshua Hazlewood Thomas Hazlewood   )
    & Wm. T. Land   )
        This day came the defendants into open Court and prayed and obtained
an appeal to the next Circuit Court in this case to be held for this County
and gave bond with W. W. Bomar & T. W. Pinckard as their security.

    Daniel Davis   )
        vs.) Debt   )
    Wilie L. Riddle   )
        This day came the defendant into open Court and prayed and obtained
an appeal to the next Circuit Court for this County and gave bond with
L. Davis & John Crane as his securities.

        A deed of conveyance from Daniel Puryear to James H. McReynolds for
144 acres of land was exhibited in open Court and proved by the oath of
R. C. Friar & T. W. McKean two 66 the witnesses thereto etc.

Pg Wm. Justice   )
253   vs.   )
    Josiah Hatley adm. etc.   )
        This day came the defendant in proper person and prayed and obtained
an appeal to the next Circuit Court for this County and gave bond with
James Bogard as his securities.

    Wm. Justice   )
        vs.) Covenant)
    Josiah Hatley Adm.)
        This day came the defendants in proper person and prayed and obtained
an appeal to the next Circuit Court to be held for this County and gave
bond with Allen A. Carroll & George Read as his securities.

        A deed of conveyance from Duguid Mims to John B. Lacy was exhibited
in open Court and the execution thereof duly acknowledged by said Mims
to be his act and deed and it was ordered to be certified for registration.

        A plot & certificate for 50 acres of land with the transfer thereon from Samuel Givens to John B. Lacy was produced in open Court and proven by the oaths of E. C. Crisp & D. Mims subscribing witnesses and ordered to be certified.

The Grand Jury returned into open Court under charge of their sworn officer a Bill of Indictment. The State vs. William Lanham for an assault
& battery ordered a True Bill. C hesley D. Key foreman of the Grand Jury.

A plot & certificate for 40 acres of land with the transfer thereon from Duguid Mims to E. R. Belcher was produced in open Court and acknowledged by the said Mims to be his act and deed and ordered to be certified.

A deed of gift from William Barnett to Samuel Lambert of a negro woman & child named Kitty and Avelin in trust for the one of Alfred M. Shelby was produced in open Court & the execution thereof duly proven by the oath of James N. McReynolds one of the witnesses thereto and ordered to be certified for registration.

Hazlewood & Land)
    vs.) Forfeiture)
Michial Read)
    This day came the Plaintiffs by their attorney and John C. Cherry a witness summoned on behalf of the plaintiff being solemnly called to come into Court and give evidence on behalf of said plaintiffs came not, but made default. It is therefore considered by the Court that the plaintiffs recover of said John C . Cherry the sum of one hundred & twenty five dollars unless he appear at the next term of this Court and show cause if any he has or can why judgment final & execution thereof against him should not be had and that Sci Facias issue accordingly.

A deed of conveyance from Andrew Cavett to James T. Scott for pr. of a town lot was exhibited in open Court and the execution thereof acknowledged by said Cavett to be his act and deed and ordered to be certified for registration.

Joseph M. McKean et al)
    vs.) Debt)
John A. McKennie)
    This day came the defendant in open Court and prayed an appeal in this case to the next Circuit Court for this County which was granted and who gave bond with John B. Lucy & Thomas L. Oliver as his securities.

State)
    vs.) Sci Fa)
Barnaby Skipper)
    This day came the Solicitor General on the part of the State and the defendant in proper person whereupon the defendant moved to quash the Sci Facias in this case and after argument had thereon, it is considered that the motion be sustained and that said Sci Facias be quashed and that the defendant go hence without day & that the costs of this case be paid by the County from which judgment the Solicitor General prays and obtains an appeal to the next Circuit Court.

Valentine D. Barry)
    vs.) Appeal)
John Murray)
    This day came the defendant in open Court and prayed an appeal to the Circuit Court which was granted who gave bond with John Read H. L. Adams

Pg
255 and James Murray as securities.

Pg
256 Armour & Lake   )
           vs.   ) Court as before.
      Chesley D. Key Adm.   )
          This day came the plaintiff by his attorney and thereupon it appear-
ing to the satisfaction of the Court that an execution had issued from a
Justice of the Peace against said defendant in behalf of said Plaintiff for
the sum of fourteen dollars & eighty two cents debt with interest from
the 5th day of February 1828 & lawful costs which said execution for want
of personal state is levied upon one hundred and twelve acres of land in
the 10th District 4th Range 4th Section. It is therefore ordered by the
Court that a Sci Facias issue requiring the heirs of Jefferson Key deceased to appear at the next term of this Court to show cause if any they
have why said land should not be ordered for sale to satisfy said Plaintiffs
debts & costs.

      John L. Rogers   )
           vs.   )   Court as Before.
      Chesley D. Key Adm.   )
          This day came the plaintiffs by their attorney and thereupon it
appearing to the satisfaction of the Court that an execution had issued
from a Justice of the Peace against the defendant in behalf of said
Plaintiff for the sum of twenty dollars & twenty five cents debt with
interest and costs from the 5th day of February 1828 which said execution
for want of person estate is levied on one hundred & twelve for acres
Pg of land in the 10th District 4th Range & 4 Section. It is therefore or-
257 dered by the Court that a Sci Facias issue requiring the heirs of Jefferson Key deceased to appear at the next term of this Court to show cause
if any they have why said land should not be ordered for sale to satisfy
said plaintiffs debt & costs.

      John Trimble   )
         vs.) Motion   ) Court as Before.
      Chesley D. Key Adm.   )
          This day came the plaintiff by his attorney and thereupon it appear-
ing to the satisfaction of the Court that an execution had issued from
a Justice of the Peace against said defendant in behalf of said Plaintiff
for the sum of twenty five dollars twelve and a half cents with interest
from the 27th day of October 1827 together with costs which said execution
for want of personal estate is levied upon one hundred & twelve acres of
land in the 10th District 4th Range & 4th Section. It is therefore ordered
by the Court that a Sciri Facias issue requiring the heirs of Jefferson
Key deceased to appear at the next term of this Court to show cause if any
they have why said land should not be ordered for sale to satisfy said
plaintiffs debt & costs.

      State   )
         vs.) Execution)
      Walden Fuller   )
      the defendant   )
          This day came into open Court Walden Fuller and by attorney moved the
Pg Court to reconsider the judgment of fifty dollars entered against him on
258 yesterday and which was done, and thereupon be the said Walden Fuller
remaked the order of appeal to the Circuit Court. It is therefore considered
by the Court that the Judgment of yesterday be reconsidered as to the sum

of fifty dollars and that the said defendant be fined ten dollars & the costs

Pg
258
of this prosecution, and thereupon the said Walden Fuller and D. W. Love came forward in open Court and confessed judgment for the whole. Therefore be it considered by the Court that the State recover the said fine of ten dollars & costs against said defendant and Daniel W. Love and that she have her execution.

And the Court adjourned to Court in Course.

N. Steele J. P.

J. W. McKean J. P.

F. Shoemake

Pg
259

Monday   6th October 1828

_____

At a Court of Pleas & Quarter Sessions begun and held for the County of Hardeman & State of Tennessee at the Court House in the Town of Bolivar on the 1st Monday in October A. D. 1828. Present the worshipful James Ruffin, James W. McKean, Edward Owens, Lazarus Stewart, Elijah Cossett, Caleb Brock, Francis Shoemake, Gabrial Bumpass, Thornton Jones, John Rosson, Edmund D. Tarver, Elihu W. Boyte, Martain Taylor, Walter Scott, Wm. L. Duncan, J. C. N. Robertson Shff. Thos. J. Hardeman Clk.

Proclamation having been made by the Sheriff in due form of law.

This day came into open Court Polly Martindale & Thomas Martindale and prayed the Court that they be permitted to administer on the Estate of William Martindale decd. and thereupon it appearing to the satisfaction of the Court here that the said William Martindale died without making a will. It is therefore ordered by the Court that the said Polly & Thomas Martindale be permitted to administer in said Estate and thereupon came forward the said Polly & Thomas and executed a Bond in the sum of four hundred dollars with John Wright & William Lumbly as their securities, and were qualified as the law directs and received letters of administration.

Pg
260
Ordered by the Court that Robat C. Friar E. C. Hill & John Goodman be appointed commissioners to lay off and set apart one years provision to Polly Martindale widow of William Martindale deceased and make report to next Court.

Burtis Alford produced in open Court one wolf scalp adjudged to be over four months old, and being qualified. Ordered that he have a certificate for the same.

Ordered by the Court that George Seaton be released from the payment of taxes on four negroes for the year 1828. It appearing to the satisfaction of the Court that they were not liable for taxation.

A deed of conveyance from William Chapman to West Harris for 25 acres of land was exhibited in open Court and the execution thereof duly proven by the oaths of Thomas J. Hardeman & Roger Barton subscribing witnesses thereto. Ordered to be certified for registration.

This day came into open Court Gabrial Bumpass and moved the Court that he be appointed a guardian to his two children Alfred&Gabrial&Bumpass and the Court having considered of the same. It is ordered that he be appointed guardian aforesaid, and thereupon came the said Gabrial and gave bond as the law directs with Moses Bumpass as his security in this sum of two hundred dollars.

Pg
261
A deed of conveyance from Nathaniel Steele to William Rose for 49 152/160 acres of land was produced in open Court and the execution thereof

Pg
261 proven by John H. McKennie & Wm. G. Steele subscribing witnesses thereto and ordered to be certified for registration.

A deed of conveyance from Jonas Musgrove to John L. Goodman was produced in open Court the same being for land, and acknowledged by the said James Musgrove to be his act and deed. Ordered to be certified for registration.

A deed of conveyance from John L. Goodman to John D. Davidson for land was produced in open Court and the execution thereof duly proven by the oaths of F. C. Hill & William O. Mohundro subscribing witnesses thereto. Ordered to be certified for registration.

A deed of conveyance from John D. Davidson to John L. Goodman for 200 acres of land was exhibited in open Court, and the execution thereof proven by the oaths of R. R. Hill & William O. Mohundro subscribing witnesses thereto. Ordered to be certified for registration.

The will and testament of Archer Nail was produced in open Court and the execution thereof by James H. Sheppard in the presence & by the direction of the said Archie Nail duly proven by the oaths of John Prewett and
Pg Hugh Davis two of the subscribing witnesses thereto and thereupon on appli-
262 cation of Rebecca Nail widow of said Archie that she be permitted to have letters of administration with the will annexed. It is ordered by the Court that she have the same on giving bond as the law directs and thereupon came the said Rebecca and gave bond in the sum of two thousand dollars with Robert Robson & Albert G. Harper as her securities and qualified accordingly and received letters etc.

This day came into open Court John Teague and prayed the Court to be permitted to administer on the estate of Eli Donald and it appearing to the satisfaction of the Court that the said Eli Donald died without making a will. It is therefore ordered by the Court in consideration of said petition that the said John Teague be admitted to administer on said Estate and thereupon came the said John Teague and gave bond in the sum of four hundred dollars with Henry Marsh & Alsey Deen as his securities was qualified as the law directs and received letters of administration.

A power of attorney from Thomas Vaughan & Martha P. Vaughan to John W. Vaughn was exhibited in open Court and duly acknowledged by the said Thomas & Martha Vaughn to be their act and deed for the purposes therein expressed & ordered to be certified.

Pg
263 An account sales additional of former ones of the estate of Michial Pirtle deceased was produced in open Court by the administrator of said estate & ordered to be recorded .

This day came into open Court William W. Shackleford and prays the Court to be permitted to administer on the estate of Pattrick Dawson deceased and on consideration it is ordered by the Court that said Wm. W. Shackelford be permitted to administer on said estate by giving bond as the law directs. And thereupon came the said Shackleford and executed his bond with George Martin as his security in the sum of one hundred dollars and was qualified as the law directs.

A deed of conveyance from William Rose to Alfred M. Rose for 49 156/160 acres of land was produced in open Court and acknowledged by the said William

Pg to be his act and deed. Ordered that said deed be certified for regis-
263 tration.

A power of attorney from Moses Bumpass, T homas Clayton & Gabrial
Bumpass to Jonathan Cruse was produced in open Court and akknowledged by
said Moses Thomas Gabrial to be their act & deed for the purposes therein
expressed. Ordered to be certified.

A deed of conveyance from Simon Huddlestone by his atto. in fact
Pg Simon Huddlestone go to Adm. R. Alexander for 500 acres of land was ex-
264hibited in open Court and proven by the oaths of John Murray E. Alexander
& James N. Murray subscribing witnesses thereto. Ordered to be certified
for registration.

A power of attorney from Edward B. Bass to Soloman Pope was produced in open Court andx the same duly acknowledged by said Bass to be his
act and deed for the purposes therein expressed. Ordered to be certified
etc.

A deed of conveyance from John Simms to Parish S imms for fity acres
of land was produced in open Court and acknowledged by the said John
Simms to be his act & deed. Ordered to be certified.

Two plats & ce rtificates with the transfers thereon one of 5 acres
& the other for 30 acres from John Smithey to Cumberland Robinson were
produced in open Court and the execution thereof duly proven by the oaths
of Walter Robinson & Walter Scott subscribing witnesses thereto. Ordered
so to be certified.

A plat & certificate with the transfer thereon from Eli D. Hanky
by his agent Geo.Hanks to Michial Beavers was produced in open Court and
acknowledged by the said Eli to be his act & deed. Ordered to be certified.

Pg   An account sales of the estate of Levi Moore decd. was returned into
265 open Court by the administrator and ordered to be recorded.

This day came into open Court John Burns as constable of this County
and moved the Court that he be permitted to give new security in his said
office which application was granted by the Court and thereupon he came
forward and gave bond with Charles McDaniel Jones Musgrove, Thomas A.
Neely, John Foster & Robert Thompson as his securities.

Proclamation having been made in due form of law the Court proceeded
to ballot for constable in Capt. Hazlewood Company and thereupon on counting
the votes Philip I. Kearney was included and gave bond with Joseph W. Mc-
Kean & John C . McKean as his securities. The Court then next proceeded
to choose a constable in Capt. Buchers Company and on balloting Samuel
Howell was duly elected and who came forward was qualified and gave bond
with Franklin Thrasher & Charles Cook as his securities. The Court then
proceeded to elect a Constable in a new Company and on balloting John T.
Jones was declared elected and was qualified & gave bond with Wm. L.
A. Tisdale & Thornton Jones as his security.

Pg   Ordered by the Court that Joseph Watson have ordinary license to
266 keep publick house in this county, and who being duly qualified as the
law directs gave bond with P. Matheny Walden Fuller, & F. Shoemake as
his securities and received license.

Pg
266   An inventory of the Estate of Joseph Murphy deceased was returned into Court by the administrator of said Estate and ordered to be recorded. Also an account sales of said property & a settlement of John Murphy with said estate ordered by the Court that they be recorded.

    Ordered by the Court that the County Trustee (a majority of the Justices being present and voting for the same) pay Valentine D. Barry Solicitor General the sum of forty five dollars for his ex- officio services for the year 1828.

    Ordered by the Court a majority of parties being present and voting for the same that Julius C. N. Robertson Sheriff be paid Byx the County Trustee the sum of fifty dollars for his Ex Officio services for year 1828.

    Ordered by the Court that the County Trustee (a majority of the Justices being present and voting for the same) pay Thomas J. Hardeman Clerk of this Court the sum of forty dollars for his Ex Officio services for the year 1828.

Pg
267   Ordered by the Court that Jesse Storey oversee the clearing out and keep in repair the road from the mouth of Clover Creek through the bottom to the foot of the hill near John Pirtle's and that in addition to the hand alread designated to work under him, he have all & theirs within his bound not specified by name.

    Ordered that Edmund D. Tarver, Frances Shoemake and John Y. Cockeram, Thos. James C. C. Collier & any two of them administrtor & administrator of the estate of John C. Old decd & report to this Court.

    Ordered that Joseph W. McKean, Francis Shoemake, Nath Steele, William Ramsey, Needham Stevens, Wm. W. Lennard Thomas James, Allen Hill, R. C. Friar , Wm. C. Steele, I. P. McNeal & John C. McKean or any five of them view out and mark a road from the north end of the Main Street in the town of Bolivar to the Bridge on Hatchie River, the nearest & best way and report to this Court.

    Ordered that Martin Lorance Thomas Stevenson and Alsey Deen be appointed to lay off one year provis. for Margaret Donald widow of Eli Donald decd.

    Ordered by the Court that John V. Davidson, Edward B. Hill, John Burns, John L. Goodman & Wm. Mohandro be appointed a Jury of view to mark out a
Pg road from John Burns by Davis Mill on Porters Creek the nearest and best
268 way on to Bolivar & report to next Court.
    Ordered that Daniel Cutbirth & Joseph L. Rosson be appointed Commissioners to settle with the administrator of the estate of John Duncan dedd. and report to next Court.

    Ordered by the Court that William Davis be appointed overseer of the State line road from Lumbleys Grocery to the east fork of Spring Creek & the following hands work under his directions; John Wortham, Wm. Stewart, Amos Foster, Joseph Stewart, Lazarus Stewart, Robert Willson, Thomas Parker , John Parker, Samuel Parker, Thos. Robinson & all others between the road on the State line & west of Porters Creek.

    Ordered that Solomon W illoughby, Vincent Willeby, Harris Wiggins, James Smith, Charles Childrop & Matthew Willey do view and straighten the road

Pg
268 leading to Jackson from Loftons bridge so far as Grays Creek was to have
the same as straight as practicable .

Ordered that the County Trustee pay Richard T. Bailey two hundred
and seventy one dollars and fifty cents for building a bridge on Spring
Creek so soon as said bridge shall be rec'd by the Commissioners and that
fact certified by said Commissioners to him out of any monies not other-
Pg   wise appropriated.
269

Ordered by the Court that Andrew Taylor & Mark R . Roberts be appointed
Commissioners to settle with John Crane guardian of Kelly Hopper & Jeremia
Hopper and report to next Court.

Ordered by the Court that John Burns, James Rutherford, James Walden,
Abner Vaughan, Elijah Chisam, Robert Box, Moses Ayes, & Thomas Johnson
or any five of them be a Jury of view to view and mark out a road from
Waldems bridge on Hatchie River in a direction for La Grange to extend
as far as the County line and report to next Court.

Ordered that Robert Kelly be appointed overseer of that part of the
road leading from Bolivar to Purdy, that lies between Bolivar & Hays ferry
& that he have all the hands that live within one half of a mile of said
road on the East of Spring Creek, also all the hands that live East of the
town of Bolivar & West of Spring Creek including William Steelman & Majr.
Ramsays hands and those hands belonging to Joseph Coe that live out of
town to work under him.
Ordered that Richmond Baker be appointed overseer over that part of the
road leading from Bolivar toward Purdy beginning at the first branch East of
Pg   Robt. Hays field and continuing East to the McNairy County line & that
270   he have all the hands that live in two miles of said road to work on said
road under his directions.

Ordered that Wm. B. Robertson, Wm. L. Duncan William L. Duncan, William
Jacobs, Eli Cox, Washington Lumbley, Wm. McBee, Robert C. Friar, or any five
of them be a jury of view to mark out a road from Michial Reed by Lionel
to the County line in a direction for Purdy Crossing Hatchie at the West
point and report to next Court.

Ordered by the Court that Robert Murray propritor of the land west
of Bolivar have leave to open La Foyette, Market & Jackson Streets a due
west course through his land provided he continues the same at least forty
feet wide & in the same direction of said streets. It is further ordered
(that after his so doing) he have leave to close up the present road through
his land.
Ordered that Nathan Ragon, Miles Philly, Michial Rook, Jarvis,Sweeton,
Samuel Newsom, Aaron Sweeton, Samuel Newsom, Aaron Stinson, Wm. McGlothlin,
& Jacob Hatterfield be a jury of view to mark out a road from the East end
of the Hatchie causeway to Nuckolls Mill & thence to the County line to
meet the road from Purdy to Bolivar by Jacob Bradfords and report to next
Court.

Pg   Ordered that the Commissioners heretofore appointed to settle with J.
271   Hatley adm. of L. Dillahunty have until next Court to settle report.

Ordered by the Cour t that Joseph W. McKean & William Ramsay be appointed to settle with Thomas J. Hardeman and John H. Bills executors of the
last will and testament of Ezekial Polk decd. from the state of their last
settle ment until the end of the present year, and make them such reasonable allowance for services rendered as may be right & proper and that they
make report to next term of this Court if practicable if not then to the
term next ensuing.

Pg
271   Ordered by the Court that that part of the Sommerville road that is
opened round Rivers field shall be established and known as a publick
road.

            Ordered by the Court that Joseph Taylor overseer and keep in repair
that part of the road leading from Willeby field to Isaac Johnson and that
he have Killom Conner all the hands on the north side of Piney Creek and as
far as Jesse Henson then a north direction to Isaac Johnsons from thence
to the dividing ridge between Piney & Greys Creek to Sol Willoughbys field
to work under his direction.

            Ordered by the Court that Abraham Breeding oversee and keep in repair
Pg   that part of the road leading from Isaac Johnsons to Saml. Jones and
272   have all the hands beginning at said Johnsons from thence to Jesse Hensons
and all the hands north & east that formerly worked under Robert Harris to
work under his directions.

            Ordered that William Ramsay John Y. Cockeram, John Molay, James Mc-
Dowel, Isaac L. Moody, George M. Pirtle, Edmund D. Tarver, and Chesley D.
Key or any five of them be a jury to lay off and set apart the dower of
the widow of the late Samuel Steele decd. in all the land of which the
decd. seized expossessed and report to next Court.

            Ordered that George M. Pirtle Chesley D. Key Edmund D. Tarver and
John Molay or any three of them be commissioners to divide and allot the
negroes belonging to the estate of Sam Steele decd. between the heirs
of said estate and report to next Court.

            Ordered that Amos Warner oversee the clearing out & keeping in
repair the Fowler Ferry road from Michial Read to Mr. McBees and that
John Sarcer, James Benton, Edmd. Ross, N. Cartwright, Will Copeland
John Crawford, Arthur Fulghum Will Jacobs, John Jacobs, Thos. Grantham,
Richard Holloman, Berry Hamlin, N. B. Robinson, John Hamlin, Rob Cagle
& G. R. Stokes work thereon under his direction.

Pg   Ordered that Howell Boyte oversee the clearing out & keeping in re-
273   pair the road from Mr. McBees to the McNairy County line and that Robt.
Beard, Thos. Beard, Moses Bishop, Ichabod Flower, John N. Jenkins, James
Gage, Will Talen, Rigdon Howell, Stephen Rogers, David Ammons, Bankly
Donnelson, Burney Skipper, Beavers, Thos. Boyte Jesse Coer, Willy Coer,
Sampson Edwards J. Cherry, Russell& Newell Graves hands work thereon under
his directions.

            Ordered by the Court that Howell Myrick, D. W. Hallum, Thomas Tombs,
Wm. Mynick, Elisha W. Harris, H. M. Simpson & John D. Carroll, be appointed
a Jury of view to lay out and mark a road from Rennicks to intersect the
line road at A. McKenzies and thence to the County line the nearest and
best way and make report to next Court.

            Ordered that Berkly Donnelson oversee the clearing out and keep in
repair that part of the road from Simpsons Ferry to the County line, and
that all the hands that formerly worked under Wm. Simpson work thereon
under his direction.

            Walden Fuller tendered his resignation as overseer of the road from
Bolivar to the Hatchie ferry. Ordered that the same be accepted.

Pg   Ordered that Joseph Dobbs, Amer. G. Thompson, John Allison, James Brown,
274

Pg
274 & Charles Cock be appointed a jury of view to lay out & mark a road from Thomas Washburns on the Memphis road to Charles Cock's mill in Spring Creek the nearest & best way and make report to next term.

Ordered by the Court that Henry W. Duncan oversee & keep in repair the road leading from Duncan landing on Hatchie to intersect the road leading from Bolivar to Brownsville and that all the hands living within one mile of said road to work thereon to open said road and report to next Court.

Ordered that Thomas Grantham be appointed overseer of the road in the place of William Fulghum and that he have all the hands that worked under said Fulgham To Wit John Robertson, Thos. & Joel Grantham, John & Berry Hamlin Wm. Pain, Raiford, Arthur & Wm. Fulgham, Jacob Chambers, Cagle, Avery Clark, Thornton, and Johnson to work under his directions.

Ordered that Wilkins L. Hunt & Andrew Taylor be appointed to aportion the hands to work on the road under James Cody overseer etc.

Ordered that Friday next be set apart to do County business.

Pg
275 Ordered that Walter Scott, Obodiah May, Daniel Munty, William Deeson Jr., Wm. Deeson Sr. Abram Deeson, Isaac Deeson, John Deeson , Edward Henson, Joseph P. Stockton, Thomas T. Cooper & Samuel P. Hall, do work on the road leading from Bolivar to Brownsville under George Taylor overseer thereof.

Francis Shoemake   )
     vs.) Copias ad Satis.)
William A. Allen   )

This day came the aforesaid William A. Allen in custody of the Sheriff and prays the Court to be permitted to take the benefit of the insolvent oath of this state as regulated by law, and the said Allen having filed with the Clerk a schedule of property he possesses, and the Court having examined him touching his condition, and been satisfied therewith. It was ordered that the oath of Insolvency be administered to him and which was done accordingly by the Clerk as the law directs and the said Allen was discharged from custody by warrant etc.

A deed of conveyance from Zachariah Chandler & Polly Chandler his wife to James Tull for 200 acres of land was exhibited in open Court and the said Polly Chandler having been just privity examined apart from her husband as to her voluntary consent thereto and West Harris & Edward Owens, Esq. Justices having performed that duty and repeated to Court her consent thereto without the concion of her said husband the said deed Pg 276 was acknowledged by the said Zachariah Chandler and Polly his wife. Ordered by the Court that the same be certified for registration.

Ordered that the County Trustee pay William Shackelford the sum of two dollars & fifty cents for the board & imprisonment of Francis Beoby four days. Also the further sum of one dollar & seventy five cents for boarding and imprisoning Samuel Boyd two days. A majority of Justices being present and voting therefore.

The will of Aaron Burleson was produced in open Court by the execution appointed therein to wit A. R. Alexander & Wm. Bryant, and proven by the oath of one of the subscribing witnesses thereto, and it is ordered by the Court that on the coming in of one of the other witnesses and proving the execution of said will that letters testamentory do issue to said executors by their giving bond and security in the sum of five thousand dollars.

Pg
276
Ordered by the Court that the following persons be summoned to attend by the Sheriff at the next Circuit Court to serve as jurors To Wit Samuel Montgomery, Robert Robson, Richard T. Bailey, William B. Robinson, John D. Davidson, Robert Parks, Peter Hunnel, Solomon Cooper, Uriah Davis, Samuel Jones, William Love, Stephen Jarmon, David B. Carnes, Thomas L. Duncan, Edward B. Hill, Justice Lake, William Orr, William E. Williams, William

Pg
277
Todd, Major William Ramsay, James McReynolds, Robert Warren, Adam R. Alexander, James Read, Elisha W. Boyte & William Fellow, & Philip I. Kearney & Jesse Pipkin as Constables and that Venni Facias issue accordingly.

m   Ordered by the Court that the following persons be summoned to attend at our next County Court to serve as jurors To Wit Josiah Wammack, Robert Box (Major) Andrew Cain, John Fortnes, Booker Foster, Eli Sweeton, Kincher Basden, Charles McDaniel, Michial Beavers, Wm. H. Duberry, Peter C. Reeves, Samuel Lambert, Charles T. Howard, Robert Kelly, James Elkins, James Slaughter, William Ramsay, James B. Smith, William W. Lennard, William Kelly, William Taylor, Lewis Johnson, Newell Crane, George Kirk, Daniel Minner & Jacob Pirtle & Henry W. Brown as Constables to serve and that a Venni Facias issue accordingly.

Ordered that John B. Lacey be released as overseer of the road leading from Bolivar to Memphis and that Isaac Scott be overseer in his room with the same hands.

And the Court adjourned to tomorrow morning 9 O'clock.

Edmund D. Tarver
John R. Cockeram
West Harris

Pg
278
Tuesday 7th October 1828

Court met according to adjournment. Present the worshipful James Ruffin Edmund D. Tarver and John Y. Cockeram Esquires Justices, Thomas J. Hardeman, Clerk, J. C. N. Robertson, Sheriff, V. D. Barry, Solicitor.

Procaamation being made as the form is the Sheriff returned into open Court a Venira facias in the following words & figures viz; The State of Tennessee

To the Sheriff of Hardeman County Greeting, You are hereby commanded to summons the following persons to attend at our next Court of pleas & quarter sessions to be held for the County of Hardeman at the Court House in the town of Bolivar on the first Tuesday after the first Monday in October next to serve as jurors for said term (to wit) Coleman Draper, Isaac Sanders, Eli Ammons, Robert Jones, Joel Grantham, Thomas Grantham, James Elkins, I. Ricks, Joel Rainer, Humphrey C. Warren, Henry T. Rucker Andrew Blackwood William, Wm. Swan Duncan George Flaid Allison Cox, Isaac L. Moody, Wm. H. Moers, James Marsh, Wm. Owen Jesse Carley, Daniel Muntz, William Pirtle, James Wood, W illiam Whitaker Alexander Kirkpatrick Randolph Mott & John Polk also Jesse Pipkin, to serve as constable. Herein fail not and have you then and there this writ witness , Thomas J. Hardeman , Clerk of said Court of Pleas & Quarter Sessions at office the first Monday in July A. D. 1828. T hos. J. Hardeman, Clerk.

Pg
279
And on the back of which was State of Tennessee Venira Facias to October term To the Sheriff of Hardeman County Greeting Issd. July 23'd 1828. Come to hand same day issued and thereby certify that I have summoned   all of the within named jurors except Eli Ammons & George Floid and that they are all free

Pg
279 holders or home holders over the age of twenty one years & inhabitants of Hardeman County given under my hand this 7th October 1828 J. C. N. Robertson Shff. Of whom the following persons being duly elected empannelled sworn & charged to enquire for the body of Hardeman County retired to consider of Presentments under the care of Jesse Pipkin an officer sworn to attend them to wit Alexander Kirkpatrick foreman appointed by the Court Daniel Mountz James Wood, John Polk, Jesse Kesley, Robert Jones William Owen, Randolph Mott, Coleman Draper, Isaac Ricks, William Duncan, Joel Rayner and Henry T. Rucker.

Joseph P. Stockton)
    vs.) Appeal)
Elijah C. Hull)

    This day came the parties by their attornies and thereupon came a Jury of good & lawful men to wit, Humphrey C . Warren, Isaac L. Moody, Thomas Grantham, James Elkins, James Marsh, William Pirtle, William H. Moores, Benjamin Gates, William Fillow, John Mills, Jacob Arnold and Hiram Willoughby who being elected tried & sworn the truth to speak upon the matter in dispute on their oath do say they find a favour of the plaintiff the sum of ten dollars sixteen and three fourth cents& the further sum of seventy cents costs the amount of the judgment below. It is therefore considered by the Court that the plaintiff recover of the defendant the said sum of ten doll-

Pg ars sixteen 3/4 damages and seventy cents costs in manner and form found by
280 the Jury and also his costs in this Court on account of his said Appeal expended etc. From which said judgment the said Elijah C. Hull prays and obtains an appeal to the next Circuit Court and gave bond with security etc.

Peter a man of color) Present James Ruffin, Edmund D. Tarver & John
    vs.)) Y. Cockeram, Esq.
John Saunders)

    This day came the parties by their attornies and thereupon came a Jury of good and lawful men To Wit G. W. Adams, Michial McKinnie Albert B. Harper, Hugn P. Reed, Walden Fuller, John Wells, James Hardie, W. P. Haden, John F. Robinson, James Little Archibald Chaffin & Jeremiah Williams who being elected empannelled & sworn the truth to speak upon the issue joined upon their oath do say they find the defendant guilty in manner and form as complained of in the plaintiffs damages to fifteen dollars.

    It is therefore considered by the Court that the plaintiff recover of the defendant his damages aforesaid in form aforesaid assessed by the Jury as also his costs about his suit in this behalf expended, and therefore came into open Court Thomas W. Daniel and confesses judgment for said damages & all costs of suit. Ordered that execution issue accordingly.

Pg James Caruthers)
281   vs.) Debt No. 36) Present same Justices as Before.
Nincan Steele)

    This day came into open Court the defendant Nincan Steele and says he cannot gainsay the Plaintiffs right of action and thereupon confesses judgment for two hundred & sixteen dollars & costs of suit . It is therefore considered by the Court that the Plaintiff recover of the defendant the said sum of two hundred & sixteen dollars debt & costs of suit as confessed aforesaid, and thereupon the said plaintiff agrees to stay execution on said judgment for the space of two months & fifteen days.

James H. Wilson)
    vs.) No. 54 Debt)Present same Justices as before.
James Wright)

Pg
281
    This day came into open Court the defendant James Wright and says he cannot gainsay the Plaintiffs right of action and thereupon confesses judgment for the sum of two hundred & thirty three dollars debt and sixteen dollars & thirty one cents interest thereon also the costs of this suit.

    It is therefore considered by the Court that the Plaintiff recover of the said defendant the said debt of two hundred thirty three dollars debt & sixteen dollars & thirty one cents & interest & costs of suit as confessed aforesaid and thereupon the said plaintiff by his attorney agrees to stay execution on said judgment until the 1st day of March next.

Pg
282
Willie L. Riddle   )
      vs.) Debt   )
Robert Hancock   )
    This day came into open Court the Plaintiff and says he will no further prosecute his suit against the defendant but takes a non suit. It is therefore considered by the Court that the defendant recover of the Plaintiff his costs about his defence in this behalf expended etc.

    A plat & certificate with the transfer thereon from James Bond to John M. Davis and transferred by said Davis to Charles T. Howard was produced in open Court and said transfer acknowledged by the said John M. Davis & James Bond & ordered to to so to be certified.

John N. McKennie   )
    vs.) Petition for Certiovari)
C. T. & W. Howard   )
    This day came into open Court John H. McKennie and prays the Court for writs of Certiovari & Supercedias directed to Caleb Brock Esq. a Justice of the Peace for this County to send up a transcript in this case & in supercedias to all Sheriff & constables to stop all further proceedings etc. & on hearing said petition it is ordered that writs issue accordingly on said McKennie's giving bond & security as the law directs.

John B. Lacey   )
    vs.) Petition for Certiovari)
Pg
283
Culpepper Matheny   )
    This day came into open Court John B. Lacey and prays the Court for writ of certiovari directed to Francis Shoemake Esq. a Justice of the Peace for said County to send issue a transcript in this case, & also a supersedas to all Sheriff & Constable to stop all further proceedings etc. & on hearing said petition it is ordered that writs of certiovari & Supercedas issue accordingly on said Laceys giving bond and security as required by law.

    A power of attorney from Alexander Aiken to William D. Aiken was exhibited in open Court and duly acknowledged by said Alexander to be his act & deed ordered to be certified etc.

    The last will & testament of William N. Fleming decd. was produced in open Court and the execution thereof proven by the oaths of Wm. W. Bomar & N. Thompson two of the subscribing witnesses thereto & the codical of said will proven by the oath of N. Thompson & S. H. Doxer the subscribing witnesses thereto and thereupon came James Ruffin one of the executors named in said will and entered on bond in the sum of ten thousand dollars with R. A. Dandridge as his security, and received letters testamentary

Pg
283   on being qualified according to law & the same was ordered to be recorded.

       A deed of conveyance from Thomas J. Hardeman to V. D. Barry for two
       town lots was exhibited in open Court and the execution thereof duly ac-
Pg   knowledged by said Hardeman to be his act & deed. Ordered to be certified
284   for registration.

       A deed of conveyance from Wm. Henson to John Crane for 42 acres of land
       was produced in open Court and proven by the oaths of Miles Birdsong&
       Ichabod Wadkins subscribing witnesses thereto. Ordered to be certified for
       registration.

       A Bill of Sale from Richard Saunders to William Saunders for a negro
       woman & child was produced in open Court and acknowledged by the said
       Richard Saunders to be his act & deed. Ordered to be certified for regis-
       tration.

       A deed of conveyance from Alexander, his wife, McClanahan and Leaner
       McClanahan to Elisha Moore was exhibited in open Court and the said
       Leaner being first privily examined by the Court separate and apart from
       her said husband touching her voluntary consent thereto and she having
       consented over her own free will without the influence or coercion of
       her said husband, the said deed was duly acknowledged in open Court by
       said Alexander & Leaner to better act & deed. Ordered to be certified
       for registration.

       This day came Sinia Scott Andrew Scott Joseph Scott and Sarah Scott
       minor heirs of   deceased and chose Richard S. Powell Guardian to said
       Sinia Andrew, Joseph and Sarah Scott and said Powell entered into bond
       and security as the law directs etc.
Pg
285
       Court adjourned until tomorrow morning nine o'clock.
                                            James Ruffin Chm. C. C.
                                            Edmund D. Tarver
                                            West Harris

Pg   Wednesday 8th Oct. 1828
286
       The Court met agreeable to adjournment. Present the worshipful James
       Ruffin Edmund D. Tarver & John Y. Cockeram Esq. Tho. J. Hardeman Clk.
       J. C. N. Robertson, Shff. John Fitzgerald

John Fitzgerald   )
       vs.) No. 7 Case) Present as above.
Garret Ford   )
       This day came the parties by their attornies and thereupon came a
Jury of good & lawful men to wit H. C. Warren, Isaac L. Moody, Thomas
Grantham, James Elkins, James March, Wm. Pirtle, Wm. H. Moore, Benjamin
Oates, John Mills, Jacob Arnold & Hiriam Willoughby who being elected empannelled & sworn the truth to speak upon the issue joined upon their oath
do say they find in favor of the Plaintiff and they do assess the Plaintiff
damages by reason of them assumption and undertakings of the said defendant
in the Plaintiffs declaration alleged to one hundred & sixty dollars & twenty
cents.   It is therefore considered by the Court that the Plaintiff recover
of the defendant the said sum of one hundred & sixty dollars & twenty cents

Pg
286
damage in form aforesaid assessed by the Jury as all his costs in behalf of his said suit expended etc. and thereupon the said defendant by his attorney moved for a rule upon the plaintiff to show cause why a new trial should not be granted, and which said rule was granted by the Court accordingly.

Benjamin Gates proved two days a juror.

Pg
287

John Lea   )
   vs.) No. 3 Trover) Present the same Justices as before.
Archibald L. Lockman)

This day came the parties by their attornies and thereupon came a Jury of good and lawful men To Wit Nicholas Nail, Robert Box, Wm. Wilson, Geo. W. Adams, Wm. Bell, Arthur Mowrow, Hardin S. Adams, Thomas Newland, John E. Mayfield, Abram Shipman, Jesse G. Grice & Walden Fuller who being elected empannelled and sworn the truth to speak upon the issues joined upon their oath do say they find the defendant Not Guilty in manner and form as complained of in the Plaintiffs declaration. It is therefore considered by the Court that the defendant go hence without day and recover of the Plaintiff his costs about his suit in this behalf expended etc.

Arthur Jones   )
   vs.) No. 8 Case)
William Rennick   )

This day came the Plaintiff by his attorney and says he will no further prosecute his said suit but takes a non suit. It is therefore considered by the Court that the defendant recover of the plaintiff his costs about his suit in this behalf expended etc.

Pleasant W. Miller   )
Wm. A. Cook   )
   vs.) Debt No. 5) Present same Justices as before.
Jesse Ward   )
John N. McKennie

Pg
288
This day came the Plaintiffs by their attorney, and the said John H. McKennie one of the defendants being solemnly called to come into Court and plead to the plaintiff declaration filed against him came not but made default. It is therefore considered by the Court that the Plaintiffs recover of said McKennie the sum of one hundred & fifty dollars in the said plaintiffs declaration mentioned & then costs in this behalf expended etc. And thereupon came a Jury of good and lawful men To Wit Humphrey C. Warren, Isaac L. Moody, Thomas Grantham, James Elkins, James March, William Pirtle, Wm. H. Moore, Benjamin Gates, John Mills, Jacob Herald, John L. Goodman, & Thornton W. Pinchard who being elected empannelled & sworn the truth to speak upon the issues joined between the plaintiff & the said Jesse Ward the other defendant upon their oath do say they find the issues joined in favor the plaintiffs that said using obligatory has not been uttered or added to since the delivery and that the said defendant has not paid the said debt of one hundred & fifty dollars in the Plaintiffs declaration mentioned as the plaintiffs in replying to the defendant in that behalf hath alledged. It is therefore considered by the Court that the Plaintiff recover of said Jesse Ward the said sum of one hundred fifty dollars debt as found by the Jury aforesaid & also their costs by them about their suit in this behalf expended. Whereupon the said John H. McKennie by his attorney moved the Court to set aside the judgment by default as to him, and an argument heard it is

Pg
289
so ordered by the Court, by the said McKennie paying the costs of this term & pleading to the Plaintiffs declaration. So that a trial can be had during this term.

Pg
288 Goodall & Caruthers   )
                vs.   ) Appeal   )
Wm. Whitaker   )

In this case it is ordered that the defendant Whitaker have leave to take the deposition of Owen Williams Davis Goodall in Smith County also John N. McKinnie on giving the opposite party legal notice.

The Grand Jury returned into open Court under the charge of their proper officer sworn for that purpose a Bill of Presentment the state of Tennessee vs. Joseph C. Teague for an assault also a Bill of Presentment. The State vs. Nathan McAfer Michard Rogers for an affray severally indorsed a True Bill A Kirkpatrick foreman of the Grand Jury and the rest of the Jury.

Valentine D. Barry   )
            vs.) alias Sci Fa 17   )   Present same Justices as before.
The Heirs of Jefferson Key, decd.)

This day came the Plaintiff by his attorney and it appearing to the satisfaction of the Court that there has been two Sci Facias issued against the defendants and upon which there has been two returns that they are not inhabitants of this state.

Therefore it is considered by the Court that the Plaintiff recover against the defendants the sum of ten dollars the debt in the Scive facias mentioned together with the further sum of sixty cents interest to this

Pg
290

time and his costs by him in this behalf expended to be levied of the land tennents & hired tennants in their hand by discent from said Jefferson Key decd. and that execution issue etc.

Valentine D. Barry   )
            vs.) Alias Sci Fa 18)Present same Justices as Before.
The Heirs of Jefferson Key decd.)

This day came the Plaintiff by his attorney, and it appearing to the satisfaction of the Court that there has been two Sdive Facias issued against the defendants and upon which there has been two witnesses that they are not inhabitants of this state.

Therefore it is considered by the Court that the Plaintiff recover against the defendant the sum of twenty dollars the debt in the Sciri facias mentioned, together with the further sum of one dollar & ten cents interest to this time and his costs by him in this behalf expended to be levied of the land tenements & hired permanently in their hand by descent from said Jefferson Key decd. that execution issue etc.

John Lea & James Lea   )
firm of J. Lea   )   Present same Justices as Before.
            vs.) Alias Sci Fa 19)
The Heirs of Jefferson Key decd.)

This day came the Plaintiffs by their attorney and it appearing to the satisfaction of the Court that there has been two Scivi Facias issued against the defendants, and upon which there has been two returns that they are not inhabitants of this state. Therefore it is considered by

Pg
291

the Court that the Plaintiffs recover against the defendants the sum of eighty three dollars and thirty two cents the judgment in the Scire Facias mentioned together with the further sum of two dollars & forty centxs interest to this term and his costs by him in this behalf expended to be levied of the lands tenements & hired tennants in their hands by discent from said Jefferson Key decd2 and that execution issue accordingly.

Pg
291 David W. Wood for)
the case of Wm. Todd)
vs.) Alias Sci Fa 20) Present same Justices as before.
The Heirs of Jefferson)
Key decd.)

This day came the plaintiff by his attorney, and it appearing to
the satisfaction of the Court that there has been two Scive Facias issued
against the defendants and upon which there has been two returns that
they are not inhabitants of this state.

Therefore it is considered by the Court that the Plaintiff recover
against the defendants the sum of eighty four dollars & sixty seven
cents debt, interest & costs from the rendition of the Judgt. before the
magistrate to the present time and the costs in this Court in this behalf expended to be levied of the land tenements hired tenants in their
hand by descent from said Jefferson Key deceased and the executors
issue accordingly.

Pg
292

A deed of conveyance a s appears signed by Oney Harvey and produced
in open Court by Nicholas Nail purporting to be a deed from Oney Harvy
to Nicholas Nail for eighty acres of land and E. C. Crisp & J. R.
Craddock the witnesses thereto subscribed after herein duly sworn say
they did not see said Harvey deliver the same but saw him in the said
they saw Oney Harvey sign the same but kept it in his own possession the
probate of the said deed was objected to by Harveys Connal the same
was ordered to be certified for registration.

A deed of conveyance from Adam R. Alexander to Arthur Fulgham for
500 acres produced in open Court & the execution thereof was duly
acknowledged by said Adam R. Alexander the same was ordered to be certified for registration.

The last will and testament of Aron Burlesson Deceased was exhibited in open Court and the execution thereof was duly proven by the
oaths of Peter G. Rives and Thomas Crawford the subscribing winess
thereto Crawford having proven the same on Monday of this term the same
was ordered to be recorded and thereupon came forward A. R. Alexander
& William Bryan who were named in the will as executors and with
approbation of the Court was qualified as such and gave bond of five
thousand dollars with Peter G. Rives & W. W. Crain as their securities.

Pg
293
A deed of conveyance from Duguid Mims to Daniel W. Love for half
of a town lot was exhibited in open Court & duly acknowledged by said
D. Mims the same was ordered to be certified for registration.

A settlement with the administrators of Hamilton Cockburn decd.
was produced in open Court by V. D. Barry & N. Steel the commissioners
appointed by Court for that purpose ordered to be recorded.

Sampson Edwards)
vs.)
Jesse Grice)

This day came Sampson Edwards into open Court and the Elihu Cornelius
being solemnly called to come into Court and give evidence on the behalf
of said Edward in a certain action depending in this Court where the said
Sampson Edward is plaintiff and Jesse C. Grice and Silas Hart are defendants came not and it appearing to the Court here that the said Eli
Cornelius had been regularly subpoened to appear here at this Court and

Pg
293
testify in behalf of the said Edward in said suit which was then & there
called to be tried.

It is therefore considered bhat the said Edward recover of the said
Elihu Cornelius the sum of one hundred & twenty five dollars unless he
the said Cornelius be and appear before this Court at our next term and show
cause why execution thereof should not be awarded against him etc. And

Pg
294
it is ordered that a writ of Sci Facias issue accordingly etc.

David W. Wood)
for the use of Wm. Todd)
      vs.) Alias Sci Fa No. 22) Present same Justices as Before.
The Heirs of Jefferson Key decd.)

This day came the plaintiff by his attorney and it appearing to the
satisfaction of the Court that there has been two Scive Facias issued
against the defendants and upon which there had been two returns that they
are not inhabitants of this state.

Therefore it is considered by the Court that the Plaintiff recover
against the defendants the sum of eighty four dollars sixty seven cents
debt & interest and costs of the judgment of the magistrate below up to
this term & the costs in this Court in this behalf expended to be levied
of the land tenenents & the ditanents in their hand by drtcent from said
Jefferson Key deceased & that execution issue accordingly.

David Journegan)
      vs.) Present same Justices as Before.
The Heirs of Thomas B.)
Hughes decd.)

This day came the Plaintiff by his attorney and it appearing to the
satisfaction of the Court that there has been two Scivi Facias issued
against the defendants and upon which then has been two returns not found
in this County. Therefore it is considered by the Court that the Plaintiff recover against the defendants the sum of five hundred & four dollars

Pg
295
& twenty cents the damages in the said Sci Facias mentioned, together with
the farther sum of fifteen dollars and seventy two cents interest up to
this time and his costs by him in this behalf expended to be levied of the
land tenements heir ditamints in their hand by descent from said Thomas
B. Hughes decd. & that execution etc.

Sampson Edward)
      vs.) Trover No. 11)
Jesse G. Grice &)
Silas Hart)

In this case on motion of counsel it is ordered that both parties
be permitted to take depositions in and out of the state on giving due
legal notice.

And the Court adjourned to meet tomorrow morning 9 O'clock.
                                    E. D. Tarver J. P.
                                    West Harris J. P.
                                    James Ruffin J. P.

Pg
296
_____ Thursday Octobber 9th 1828 _____

The Court met according to adjournment. Present the worshipful
James Ruffin, Edmund D . Tarver & Thomas James Esquire Justices, Thos.
Hardeman, Clk. V. D. Barry, Sol. Genl., J. O. N. Robertson Shff.

On motion Alfred W. G. Davis & Powhatan May Esq. was admitted to prac-

Pg
296 tice as attornies in this Court and qualified accordingly as the law
directs.

```
State x              )
   vs. ) Obstrucing Road  )
Wm. N. Fleming          )
```

This day came the Solicitor General on the part of the State and
suggests the death of the defendant in this returning. And thereupon it
is considered by the Court that the said cause be dismissed and that the
said cause be dismissed and that the County pay the costs.

```
John Fitzgerald                    )
      vs. ) Case Motion for new trial  )
John Ford                          )
```

This day came the parties by their attorneys and therefrom the motion
of the defendants counsel for a new trial coming on to be argued, and the
same being fully argued by counsel and herefully understood by the Court.
It is the opinion of the Court that said defendant take nothing by his said
motion and a new trial is refused. And therefrom came the said defendant
and prays an appeal to the next Circuit Court for this County which is
granted and gave bond with William Davis & John Brown as his security.

Pg   Ordered that Thomas James & C. Collier be added to the order to settle
297 with the administrator & administratix of John E. Old de'cd. and make
report to this court if possible.

```
State           )
   vs.  ) A & B  )
James Gunter    )
```

This day came into open Court James Brown and acknowledged himself to
be indebted to the State of Tennessee the sum of one hundred & twenty
five dollars to be levied of his good & chattels law and tanements, but
to be void on condition that the said James Brown do make his personal
appearance at our next County Court to be held for this County at the
Court House in Bolivar on the first Thursday after the first Monday in
January next then and there to give evidence on behalf of the State in a
Bill of Indictment against said James Gunter for an assault & Battery etc.

```
State       )
   vs. )     )
John Foster )
```

This day came the Solicitor General on the part of the state and
Thomas J. Oliver the prosecutor in this cause being solemnly called to
come into Court and prosecute in behalf of the State came not but made
default. A nd it appearing to the Court here that said Thomas J. Oliver
had been duly subpoened to appear here at this Court and testify on behalf
the said state when the said cause was called to be tried. Therefore it
Pg is considered by the Court that the said Thomas J. Oliver be taxed with
298 the costs of this prosecution and that the clerk do issue execution for the
same and that the State do further recover of him the said Thomas J.
Oliver the sum of one hundred & twenty five dollars unless he the said
Oliver do make his personal appearance before this Court at our next term
and show cause why execution final should not be awarded against him etc.
And it is ordered that a Writ of Sciri Facias issue accordingly.

```
State                          )
   vs. ) Indictment, Malicious Mischief.)
John Foster                    )
```

Pg
298   This day came the Soliciter General on the part of the State and
Willie L. Riddle & James Bond being solemnly called to come into Court
and give evidence on behalf of the State in a certain matter where the
said State is Plaintiff and John Foster defendant came not and it appearing to the satisfaction of the Court that the said Willie L. Riddle &
James Bond had been regularly subpoened to appear here at this Court and
testify on behalf of said state in said suit when called. It is therefore
considered by the Court that the state recover of the said Willie L.
Riddle & James Bond the sum of one hundred & twenty five dollars each,
unless they appear at our next term of this Court and show cause why execution thereof should not be awarded against them. And that Sci Facias
issue accordingly.

Pg   State   )
299   vs.) Affray   )
      Thomas Newland   )
          This day came the Solicitor General on the part of the state, and says
he will no further prosecute this suit and moves the Court that a Nolli
Prosequi be entered thereto. And it is thereupon considered by the Court
that a Nolli Prosequi be entered & the County pay the costs.

      State   )
        vs.) Affray   )
      Thomas Newland   )
          This day came the Solicitor General on the part of the State and
give evidence called to come into Court and give evidence on behalf of
the state in the case wherein the said State is Plaintiff and Thomas Newland is defendant came not. And it appearing to the satisfaction of the
Court that the said Charles Jones had been regularly subpoened to appear
here at this Court and testify on behalf of said state in said suit when
called. It is therefore considered by the Court that the sd. state recover of the said Charles Jones the sum of one hundred & twenty five dollars
unless he appear at our next Court and show cause why execution thereof should
not be awarded against him and that Sci Facias issue accordingly.

      State   )
        vs.) Indict. for Mal. Mischief.)
      John Foster   )
          This day came the Soliciter General on the part of the State & the defend-
ant in proper person who being arraigned and charged upon the Bill of Indict-
Pg   ment plead Not Guilty and for his trial puts himself on the County and the
300   Soliciter General likewise and thereupon came a Jury of good and lawful men
To Wit Humphry C. Warren, Isaac L. Moody, T homas Grantham, Wm. Fellow, James
Elkins, James Marsh, Wm. Pirtle, Wm. H. Moore, John Mills, Michial Read, Newel
W. Crain & Thos. Newland who being elec ed empannelled and sworn the truth to
speak upon the issue of Traverse joined upon their oath do say they find the
defendant Not Guilty in manner and form as charged in the Bill of Indictment.
Therefore it is considered by the Court that the defendant go hence without
day and recover of the state his costs etc.

          A power of attorney from James Mayfield to Sutherland Mayfield was pro-
duced in open Court and the execution thereof duly proven by the oaths of
Andy Kirk & Wm. Mayfield subscribing witnesses thereto and ordered to be
certified.

      State   )
        vs.) A & B)
      Jesse G. Grice)
          This day came the Solicitor General on the part of the State and the

Pg
300 defendant in proper person who being arraigned and charged upon the Bill
of Indictment plead Not Guilty and for his trial puts himself on the
Pg Country and the Soliciter General likewise and thereupon came a Jury of
301 good and lawful men to wit Humphy C. Warren, Isaac L. Moody, Thomas Grantham, James Elkins, James Marsh, Wm. Pirtle, William U. Moore, John Mills,
Michial Read, Wm. Lumbley, N. W. Crane & Thomas Newland who being elected
empannelled & sworn the truth to speak upon the issue of traverse joined
upon their oath do say they find the defendant Not Guilty in manner and
form as charged in the Bill of Indictment. Therefore it is considered by
the Court that the defendant go hence without day and recove of the State
his costs etc. And thereupon on motion of the Solicitor General and the
concurrence of the Court, Sampson Edward the prosecutor was taxed with said
costs, it appearing to the satisfaction of the Court that said prosecution was
groundless and trivial.

State)
vs.) Riot)
Edward Burleson &)
Alexander Aiken)

This day came the Soliciter General on the part of the State and the defendants in proper person who being arraigned and charged upon the Bill of Indictment plead Not Guilty and for their trial put themselves on the country and the
Soliciter General likewise and thereupon came a Jury of good and lawful men
To Wit Humphy C. Warren Isaac L. Moody, Thomas Grantham, Wm. Fellow, James
Pg Marsh, William Pirtle, William H. Moors, John Mills, Michial Read, Wm.
302 Lumbley, N. W. Crain & Thomas Newland who being elected empannelled & sworn
the truth to speak upon the issue of Traverse joined upon their oath do say they
find the defendants Edward Burleson & Joseph Burleson Guilty in manner and form
as charged in the Bill of Indictment and they do find the defendant Alexander
Aiken Not Guilty in manner and form as charged in the Bill of Indictment
and thereupon the said defendants Edward & Joseph Burleson moved the Court to
grant a new trial, and a rule was made for cause to be shown why not to be made
for argument in the morning.

State)
vs.) A & B)
James Burleson)

This day came the Soliciter General on the part of the State, and the
defendant in proper person who being arraigned and charged upon the Bill of
Indictment pleads Not Guilty of his trial, puts himself on the country & the
Soliciter General likewise and thereupon came a Jury of good and lawful men To
Wit Jacob Herrol, Wm. Todd, Alexander Aiken, Robert Thompson, Elijah Bennet,
Joseph Morman, Allen Hamblin, Joshua Hazlewood, Mohn Shepherd, Abner Pillow,
John James, & Thomas Read who being elected empannelled & sworn the truth to
Pg speak upon the issue of Traverse joined upon their oath do say they find the
303 defendant Guilty in manner and form as charged in the Bill of Indictment. It
is therefore considered by the Court that the said James Burleson be fined the
sum of three dollars, and that the state recover of him the costs in this behalf
expended and be in mercy etc.

State)
vs.) A & B)
John Warren)

This day came the Solicitor General on the part of the State & the defendant in proper person who being arraigned & charged upon the Bill of Indictment pleads Guilty and puts himself on the mercy of the Court. And thereupon it
is considered by the Court that he be fined the sum of one dollars & pay the
costs of this prosecution and that he be in custody etc.

Pg
303 State   )
       vs.) A & B   )
William Lamhum   )
         This day came the Soliciter General on the part of the State and Josiah
Dunn the prosecutor in this cause being solemnly called to come into Court
and give evidence on behalf of the state in this said suit as he is bound to
do came not. And it appearing to the satisfaction of the Court that the said
Josiah Dunn had been regularly subpoened to appear at this Court and give
evidence on behalf of the State in said suit when called. Therefore it is
Pg   considered by the Court that the State recover of the said Josiah Davis the
304 sum of one hundred & twenty five dollars unless he appear at our next term
of this Court and show cause why execution thereof should not be are exposed
against him, and that Scive Facias issue accordingly.

       State   )
         vs.) A & B   )
William Lamhum   )
         This day came the Soliciter General on the part of the state and moves
the Court to enter a Nolli Purequi in this case and which with the concurrence of the Court is done. And thereupon the said Soliciter General moves
the Court that Josiah Dunn the prosecutor in this case be taxed with the
costs. And it is thereupon considered by the Court that the said Josiah
Dunn be taxed with said costs as moved by the Soliciter General etc.

       State   )
         vs.) Peace Warrant   )
Booker Foster   )
         This day comes the Solicitor General on the part of the state, and on
motionhand with the assent of the Court this case is dismissed and thereupon
the said Booker Foster comes and assumes all costs. It is therefore considered by the Court that the State recover of the defendant her costs about
this prosecution expended etc.

Pg   An inventory of the Estate of Joseph C. Deprist was returned into
305 Court by the administrator and ordered to be recorded.

         The Grand Jury returned into open Court under the charge of their
sworn officer appointed to attend on them a Bill of Presentment the State
of Tennessee vs. Grubbs for keeping a tippling house one also, The State
for the same agt. Joseph Watson, one also the State against Allen Hill for
keeping the same severally indorsed a New Bill Alexander Kirkpatrickforeman
of the Grand Jury.

       Abner Pillow   )
         vs.   ) Petition for Certiovari   )
John Watson   )
         This day came into open Court Abner Pillow and prays the Court that
writs of Certiovari & supercedias may issue directed to Elijah Gossett Esq.
Justice of the Peace for this County and Thompson Constable for same directing the said Gossett to bring up a transcript in this case & that said
constable do stay further proceedings. And on hearing said petition it is
Pg   ordered by the Court that writs issue as prayed for on the said petitioners
306 giving bond & security as the law directs.

         A deed of relinquishment from Samuel Polk to Thomas McNeal for 66 2/3
acres was produced in open Court the death & signature of Samuel Polk which
appears signed to the same was duly proven by James K. Polk and Alexander
Kirkpatrick as to his hand writing etc.

Pg
306   An article of agreement between Thomas J. Hardeman for his son Thomas
M. Hardeman, James K. Polk for his brother Marshall T. Polk, Ezekial P.
McNeal, Rufus P. Neely and Andrew Martin was produced in open Court and the
execution thereof was duly proven by the oaths of C. C. Collier & Allen
Hill the subscribing witnesses thereto and the same was ordered to be certified
for registration.

Newell W. Crain   )
       vs.   )   Present same Justices as before.
William Bell   )
William C. Bell   )   Debt)
William S. London   )
and James Ruffin   )
Executor of William   )
N. Fleming decd.   )

        This day came the parties by their attorneys and thereupon came a Jury
of good and lawful men to wit H. C. Warren, Isaac L. Moody, James Elkins,
William Pirtle, Wm. H. Moore, John Mills, Walden Fuller, John A lsup, Daniel
Davis, Thomas Grantham, John Foster & James Marsh, who being elected impannelled & sworn the truth to speak upon the issues joined upon their oath do say
that they find the issues in favour of the plaintiff and that the defendants
Pg   have not paid the debt of one hundred dollars in the declaration mentioned
307 and assess the plaintiffs damages by reason of the detention thereof to three
dollars & fifty cents. Therefore it is considered by the Court here, that
the plaintiff recover of the defendants said debt of one hundred dollars also
the sum of three dollars fifty cents damages aforesaid by the jury aforesaid
assessed also his costs about this suit in this behalf expended, to be levied
of the proper goods and chattels lands and tenements of the said William Bell,
William C. Bell and William S. London and of the goods and chattels of the
said William N. Fleming decd. in the hands of James Ruffin executor as aforesaid to be administered etc.

        A deed of conveyance from Thomas Jefferson Green to George Anderson for
five hundred & twelve acres was produced in open Court and the execution thereof was duly proven b y the oaths of Thomas M. Rone & John Anderson two of
the subscribing witnesses thereto the same was ordered to be certified for
registration.

        A plot & certificate with the transfer thereon from Mathias Wright to
Eaton R. Newsom for 25 acres of land produced in open Court & duly acknowledged by said Wright & ordered to be so certified.

        Solomn Willoughby proved two day attendance as a juror also Jacob M.
Harrell two days, Hiram B. Willoughby twodays.

Pg   Matthew Barrow   )
308   vs.) No. 25   Debt   ) Present James Ruffin, Edward D. Tarver & West
Thomas B. Gilliam   ) Harris Esq.
        This day came the parties by their attornies and thereupon came a Jury
of good & lawful men To Wit Humphrey C ..Warren, Isaac L. Moody, Thomas Grantham Wm. Fellow, James Elkins, James Marsh, William Pirtle, William N. Moore,
John Mills, Michial Read, Newell W. Crain & Thomas Neuland who being elected
empannelled & sworn the truth to speak upon the issues joined in favor of the
plaintiff, and that the defendant has not paid the debt of one thousand
dollars in plaintiffs declaration mentioned & they assess his damages by reason
thereof to eighty dollars. It is therefore considered by the Court that the
plaintiff recover of the defendant the debt in the declaration of said plain-

Pg
308
táff mentioned and the damages aforesaid in form aforesaid assessed by
the Jury also this costs by them about his suit in this behalf expended
from which judgment the defendant prays and obtains an appeal to the
next Circuit Court for this County and gave bond with Thomas I. Vaughan as
his security.

```
Joseph Catton      )
      vs.    ) No. 38 Debt  )  Present same Justices as before.
Thomas I. Vaughan  )
```

Pg
309
This day came the parties by their attornies and thereupon came a
Jury of good and lawful men To Wit H. C. Warren, Isaac L. Moody, Thomas
Grantham, Wm. Fellow, James Elkins, James Marsh, William Pirtle, William
H. Moore, John Mills, Michial Read, Newel W. Crain & Thomas Newland who
being elected empannelled and sworn the truth to speak upon the issues joined upon their oath do say they find the issues joined upon their oath do
say they the issues joined in favor of the plaintiff, and that the defendant has not paid the debt of six hundred dollars in the Plaintiffs declaration mentioned, and they assess his damages by reason of the defention
thereof to forty eight dollars. It is therefore considered by the Court
that the Plaintiff recover of the defendant the debt in his declaration
mentioned and the damages aforesaid in form aforesaid assessed by the Jury,
also his costs by him about his suit in this behalf expended from which
said judgment the defendant prays and obtains an appeal to the next
Circuit Court for this County and gave bond with Thomas B. Gilliam as his
security.

```
Isaac Ricks
      vs.  )  No. Trespass )  Present same Justices as before.
James Burleson
```
This day came the plaintiff and says he will no further prosecute
his suit, and takes a nonsuit. And thereupon comesthe said defendant and
assumes all the costs of this Court. It is therefore considered by the
xCourt that the plaintiff recover of the defendant his costs aforesaid
about his suit in this behalf expended etc.

Pg
310
And the Court adjourned to tomorrow morning 9 O'clock.
James Ruffin
Elijah Gossett
Johnston Jones

Friday 10 th Oct. 1828

Pg
311
Court met according to adjournment present the worshipful James Ruffin,
Edmond D. Tarver & West Harris, Esquires Justices, Thomas J. Hardeman
Clerk, J. C. N. Robertson, Sheriff, V. D. Barry, Solicitor.   Proclamation
being made as the form is etc.

Ordered by the Court that William D. Lennard oversee the clearing
out and keep in the road leading from the west end of the town of Bolivar
in a direction so as to intersect the Porters Creek road by A. Cavitts,
J. C. McKeans & that he have all the hands as far south as Nicholsons
and one mile this side of Spring Creek and two miles the other side, not
otherwise appropriated work thereon under his directions, so as to include
Cavetts, Harris Wrights, Thompsons, & Blounts hand work and his directions.

Ordered that James Duff Green N. Walker Alfred Walker Thomas Thompson,
Thompson Gillespie Jonathan Crane & Carson Duff or any five them be app-
ointed a Jury of view to mark out a road from the road marked out from
Martain Taylors to the mouth of Hickory Creek to leave at a point between
Joseph Rogers & Isaac Ricks the nearest and best way to intersect the road

Pg
311   leaving from Estanaula to Summerville near the County line.

Pg   Ordered by the Court that Thomas Shaw Wm. H. Moores, David Lane,
312   Edmund D. Tarver, Wm. Pirtle, Nathl. B. Norment & Jacob Herrol or any
        five of them be a Jury of view to mark out a road, to leave the Simpsons
        ferry road at a place, near where Charles Polk formerly lived, the nearest
        and best way to the County line in a direction for Estanaula.

                Ordered that John Moore oversee the clearing out and keep in repair
        that part of the Brownsville road from near the 3 mile post as lately
        marked out to the top of the ridge near Daniel Minners and that he have
        all the hands that formerly worked on that part of the road to work under
        his directions.

                Ordered by the Court a sufficient number of Justices being present,
        that that the County Trustee pay James Ruffin & Edmund D. Tarver for ser-
        vices as Commissioners five days each for settlement with County Trustee
        for the years 1824-5-6 && ? two dollars & fifty cents pr. day and also
        to pay Edward R. Belcher for same duty for ten days services at same per
        diem allowance.

                The Commissioners appointed to settle with the County Trustee for
        the years 1824-5- 6&7 made a report to Court and the same was ordered to
        be received and filed in Clerks office.

Pg   Isaac Johnsons comes into Court and resigns as constable the same
313   ordered to be accepted.

        State   )
           vs.) Called out Motion)
        Willie I. Riddle   )
                This day came the defendant in proper person and moved the Court
        to set aside the proceedings in this case, and for cause shown. It is
        ordered by the Court that the same be set aside on his paying the costs of
        the Court etc.

        James Bougard   )
           vs.   )
        Joseph L. Rosson   )
                This day came the plaintiff by his attorney and Martin D. Ramsay a
        witness summoned to attend on behalf of said plaintiff came not but made
        default on being solemly called.

                It is therefore considered by the Court that the Plaintiff recover
        against said Martin D. Ramsay the sum of one hundred & twenty five dollars
        unless he do make his appearance at next term of this Court and show cause
        if any he has why Judgment final and execution thereof should not issue
        against him and that a Sciri Facias issue accordingly afterward the said
        Ramsay moved the Court to set aside said judgment and on cause shown. It
Pg   was ordered on his paying all costs accruing thereon.
314
                Ordered by the Court that Solomon Willoughby have license to keep
        an ordinary on his giving bond & security as required by law.

        State   )
           vs.) Pert. Tippling House)
        Allen Hill   )
                This day came the Solicitor General on the part of the state and the

Pg
314 defendant in proper person who being arraigned etc. plead guilty and submit to Court. It is therefore considered by the Court that the said Hill be fined one cent & pay the costs of this prosecution etc.

The Grand Jury returned into open Court and in the charge of their sworn officer. Bills of Presentment, The State of Tennessee Aaron Payton for petit larcency one The State vs. Joshua Thurman for keeping a Tippling House, The State vs. Green Hastings severally invased a True Bill Alexander Kirkpatrick foreman of the Grand Jury and by twelve other jurors. Also a Bill of Indictment, The State vs. Eli Sweeton & Booker Foster for an affray & a Bill of Indictment the state is therefore Hanks & others severally indorsed a True Bill Alexander Kirkpatrick foreman of the Grand Jury.

John F. Smyth   )
      vs.) Certiovari No. 13   )
William Todd   )

Pg
315 This day came the parties by their attornies and on motion of the plaintiff by his attorney, and it appearing to the satisfaction of the Court that the Plaintiff has not complied with the order of said Court that we should give new security at this term fort the prosecution of his said certiovari. It is considered by the Court that the said Certiovari be dismissed and that the Plaintiff pay all the costs as were thereBefore the Justice below as of this Court that the defendant have exedution etc.

William Lumbley   )
      vs.) Certiovari No. 14)
James Alexander   )

This day came the parties by their attornies and thereupon came a Jury of good & lawful men To Wit Humphey C. Warren, Isaac L. Moody, Thomas Grantham, William Fellow, James Elkins, James Marsh, William Pirtle, William H. Moore, John Mills, Michial Read, Newell W. Crain, & Thomas Newland, who being elected empannelled & sworn to try the matter in controversy between the parties upon their oath do find the judgment of the Justice below to be correctand they do find in favor of the defendant James Alexander the sum of thirty dollars & fifty cents. It is therefore considered by the Court that the said Alexander recover of said Lumbley and on motion of William Martindale his security the said sum of thirty dollars & 50 cents together with twelve per ct. interest on the same from the 12 Jany. 1828 to its present time & that he have execution etc.

Ordered by the Court that the County Trustee pay Wm. Chisolm fifty dollars for the maintenance of John Micham Children for twelve months commencing from the 26th July last.

Pg
316 Thomas Simmons
)
      vs.) Attachment No. 16)
Chs. H. Shuffer   )

This day came the plaintiff by his attorney and thereupon came a Jury to inquire the damages which the said Plaintiff hath sustained by reason of the assumption in the Plaintiffs declaration alleged, To Wit Humphey C. Harren, Isaac L. Moody, Thomas Grantham, William Fellow, James Elkins, James Marsh, William Pirtle, Wm. H. Moore, John Mills, Michial Read, Newll W. Crane, & Thomas Newland who being elected empannelled ans sworn well and truly to inquire the damages the Plaintiff hath sustained by reason of the defendants non performance of his said assumptions as alleged in Plaintiffs declaration in their oath do say they find his damage to be seventy five dollars. It is therefore considered by the Court that the Plaintiff recover

Pg
316his damages aforesaid in form aforesaid assessed by the Jury together with
his costs in this behalf expended etc.

David Hay   )
     vs.) Motion   ) Present James Ruffin, E. D. Tarver & West Harris
Duguid Mimms   ) Esquires.
C. C. Collier   )

     On motion and it appearing to the satisfaction of the Court that an
execution had issued against the defendants by Jos. W. McKean Esq. an
Pg acting Justices of the Peace for Hardeman County on behalf of the Plain-
317 tiff Iss'd 10th day of Oct. 1828, for the sum of sixty seven dollars &
fifty three cents debt & interest and which said execution had come to the
hands of Philip L. Kearney a Constable of said County, and by him for want
of personal property levied on forty acres of land in the 10th District
Range 2 and Section 4 the 10th day of October 1828.
     It is therefore ordered adjudged and decreed that said land be exposed
to sale as the law directs to satisfy said debt & costs, and also the
costs of this motion & that a venditiona Exponas issue accordingly.

James A. Hart   )
     vs.   ) Present same Justices as Before.
E. T. Hannis Adm.   )
D. P. Hannis Samuel)
Hannis decd.   )

     This day on motion and it appearing to the satisfaction of the Court
that an execution had issued against the defendant from Thomas James Esq.
a Justice of the Peace for this County, on behalf of the plaintiff the 10th
day of Oct. 1828 for forty three dollars & thirty seven cents debt & costs
and which said execution had come to the hand of Martin D. Ramsay a Constable of said County and by him for want of Personal Property levied on
100 acres of land being the north half of 2000 acres granted to Samuel
Hannis by grant No. 251 on both sides of Spring Creek there being no personal property of David P. Hannis or Samuel Hannis to be found. It is
therefore ordered, adjudged and decreed that said land be exposed to sale
Pg   as the law directs to satisfy said debt & costs as also the costs of this
318 motion & that a venditiona Exponas issue accordingly.

Francis McGavock   )
     vs.) Motion   )Present same Justices as Before.
E. P. Hannis Adm.   )

     This day on motion and it appearing to the satisfaction of the Court
that an execution had issued from Thomas James Esq. a Justice of the Court
that an execution had issued from Thomas James Esq. a Justice of the
County on behalf of the Plaintiff against the defendant for the sum of fifty
dollars debt & costs & which said exedution had come to the hand of Martin
D. Ramsay a Constable of said county and by him for want of personal property
levied on 100 acres of land in Hardeman County being the north half of
200 acres granted to Samuel Hannis by grant No. 250 on both sides of
Spring Creek this being no personal property of David P. Hannis or Samuel
Hannis to be found. It is therefore ordered adjudged and decreed that the
said tract of land be exposed to sale as the law directs to satisfy said
debt & costs & also the costs of this motion & that a venditiona Exponas issue
accordingly.

Gillan Pillow   )
     vs   ) Covenant)
Abner Pillow   )

Pg
318   This day came the plaintiff by his attorney and the defendant in
proper person and upon the affidavit of the Plaintiffs attorney that the
Covenant upon which this suit is founded has been mislaid by him since
Pg   the issuing of the original writ in this cause, and moved the Court for
319   time to file the declaration which motion being argued both by the Plaintiffs attorney and the defendant in proper person it is ruled and ordered
by the Court that the following imparlance be entered that the Plaintiff
have until the next term of this Court to file his declaration and if the
declaration shall be filed with the Clerk, by the first Monday in November next, the defendant to plead to the same by the next term and the cause
to stand there for trial, but if the declaration shall not be filed until
the next term then the defendant to have until the next succeeding term
then the defendant to have until the next succeeding term to reply to the
same. It is also further ordered that the plaintiff pay the costs of this
application.

Same   )
  vs.) Debt)
Same   )

     Upon the same application and for the same reasons as given in the
preceeding case, it is ordered by the Court that the same suit and imparlance be granted as in the proceeding case at the costs of the plaintiff.

Pleasant M. Miller & William A. Cook   )
              vs.   )
Jesse Ward and John N. McKinnie   )
     This day came the plaintiffs and the defendant John N. McKinney
by their attorney and thereupon came and therefore came a jury of good
and lawful men, to wit, Humphrey C. Warren, Isaac L. Moody, Thomas Grandham,
William Fellow, James Elkins, James Marsh, William Pirtle, William H.
Moon, John Mills, Michial Read, Newell W. Crane and Thomas Newland who
being elected, tried and sworn will and truly to try the issue joined between the said Plaintiffs and the defendant John N. McKinny upon their
Pg   oath do say they find the issue in favor of the plaintiffs, and that the
320   defendant does over to the plaintiffs the debt of one hundred and fifty dollars in the declaration mentioned and that the same is unpaid and they
assess the Plaintiffs damages by reason of the detention thereof to seven
dollars and fifty cents.

     It is therefore considered by the Court that the Plaintiffs recover
of the defendant John N. McKinney the debt aforesaid and the damagess
aforesaid by the jury in form aforesaid confessed and also his costs by him
about his suit in this behalf expended and the defendant in mercy do.

     A settlement with the administrator on the estate of John. E. Old
decd. returned into Court by the commissioners ordered to be recorded.

     A division of the personal estate between the heirs of Henry G. Kearney
returned into Court by commissioners is appointed to make said division
ordered to be recorded.

     John Ham produced in open Court the scalp of one woolf adjudged to
be over four months odd ordered that he have his certificate.

     A deed of conveyance from Alexander Ross to John Ham for 80 acres of
land produced in open Court & the execution thereof duly proven by the oaths
of William Sample & William H. Dewberry the subscribing witnesses thereto
the same was ordered to be certified for registration.

Pg
321   This day came into open Court Jacky Old and John C. McKean, Adm. of
the Estate of John E. Old and John C. McKean moves the Court here to be
released from the responsibility as Adm. and Jacky Old releasing her former
security gives bond with Ed D. Tarver in the sum of one thousand dollars
conditioned for her faithful performance of the duties of administratrix.
It is therefore ordered by the Court that John C. McKean, Adml and Jos. W.
McKean former security for said John C. McKean & Jacky Old stand hereafter
discharged and requitted from all responsibility for the future performance
of said Jacky in the said administration.

James Boguard   )
      vs.   ) Motion
Joseph L. Rosson   )
      This day came the parties by their attornies and it appearing to the
satisfaction of the Court that an execution which issued heretofore from
Gabriel Bumpass, Esq. a Justice of the Peace for Hardeman County, on a
Judgment in favour of said Bogard against James P. Boydston, commanding
the said defendant as constable to make the sum of forty six dollars and
ninety five cents with interest thereon from the 25th day of December 1825
until paid besides costs, of the goods and chattels lands and tenements of
the said John P. Boydston, which said execution came to the hands of the
said Rosson constables as aforesaid defendant on the 12th day of April 1828
and he having failed to pay over the moneys in said execution specified
to the said plaintiff agreeable to the direction of the said execution or
to return the same in twenty days on the money prescribed by law. It is
  therefore considered by the Court that the plaintiff recover of the said
defendant the said sum of forty dollars balance due on the said execution
also his costs about his motion in this behalf expended etc.

Pg   And the Court adjourned to tomorrow morning 9 O'clock.
322   James Ruffin J. P.
                                          T. W. McKean, J. P.
                                          E. D. Tarver, J. P.

                Saturday Octo. 11th 1828
Pg ───
323
      The Court met according to adjournment. Present the worshipful James
Ruffin, Edmund D. Tarver, & Thos. W. McKean, Esq. Justices.
Thos. J. Hardeman Clk.   J. C. N. Robertson, Shff.

State   )
   vs.) Motion for a new trial)
Edward Burleson   )
Joseph Burleson   )
      This day came the Solicitor General on the part of the state and the
defendants in proper person and the open the motion for a new trial and
being argued by Council and understood by the Court. It is the opinion of
the Court that a new trial should be granted in this case and which is
thereupon ordered.

State) Recognizance   )
   vs.)   )
Edward Burleson   )
Joseph Burleson   )
      This day came into open Court Edward Burleson and who acknowledged
himself to be indebted to the State of Tennessee in the sum of one hundred
and twenty five dollars for himself and the sum for Joseph Burleson to be
levied of his goods and chattels land and tenements but to be void on con-

Pg
323 dition that they do make their personal appearance at our next County Court
and answer the State of Tennessee on a Bill of Indictment for a riot and not
depart without leave etc.

Thomas Hazlewood)
Joshua Hazlewood&)
Wm. T. Land)   Present Justices as above.
      vs.   () Case No.   ))
Michial Read)

Pg   This day came the parties by their attornies and thereupon came a Jury
324 of good and lawful men To Wit Humphy C. Warren, Isaac L. Moody, Thos. Grantham, James Elkins, James March, Wm. Pirtle, Wm. H. Moors, John Mills,
Geo. W. Adams, Daniel W. Love John Foster & Robert Thompson who being elected
emapnnelled and sworn the truth to speak upon the issue joined upon their oath
do say they find the issue joined in favor of the defendant and that he did
not assume in manner and form as alleged in the Plaintiffs declaration. It
is therefore considered by the Court that the defendant go hence without day
and recover of the plaintiff his costs in this behalf expended etc. from which
judgment the plaintiffs pray an appeal to the next Circuit Court and gave bond
according to law.

Rhea & McCrabb)
      vs.) Debt No.)   Present same Justices as before.
William Bell)
William L. Bell)
      This day came the parties by their attornies and thereupon came a Jury
of good & lawful men To Wit Thomas Washburn, Michial Read, John C. Cherry,
John P. Darley, Joshua Hazlewood, William Ramsay, Thomas Newland, Daniel Davis
James Hardy, John N. Arnold, Thomas Hazlewood & Wm. Bogard who being elected
empannedlled and sworn the truth to speak upon the issues joined upon their
Pg   oath do say they find the issue of Infancy in favor of the defendant Wm. L.
325 Bell and they do find further that William Bell the other defendant has not
paid the debt of one hundred in the Plaintiffs declaration mentioned and they
do assess the Plaintiffs damages by reason thereof to four dollars & sixteen
cents. It is therefore considered by the Court that the Plaintiffs recover
of the defendant William Bell the said sum of one hundred dollars & the damages aforesaid in form aforesaid assessed by the Jury & also their costs about
their suit in this behalf expended etc.

State)
      vs.   ) Debt No.   )   Present the same Justices.
Thomas Washburn)
      This day camek the parties by their attornies and thereupon came a Jury
of good & lawful men To Wit John Jones, Wm. Todd, D. C. Powell, Wm. Sample,
Elijah Bennet, Thos. J. Oliver, John Hodges, Walden Fuller, Wm. Bell,
Stephen Jarmon, Hiram Williams & Newel W. Crane who being elected empannelled
& sworn the truth to speak upon the issues joined upon their oath do say they
find the issues joined in favor of them defendant. It is therefore considered
by the Court that the defendant go hence without day and recoverof the state
his costs in this behalf expended & that etc.

      The Grand Jury returned into open Court under charge of the sworn officer
Pg   a Bill of Presentment . The State agt. William Johnson as overseer of a road
326 indorsed a True Bill Alexander Kirkpatrick foreman of the Grand Jury and
signed by twelve others.

Thephlus W. Cockburn)   Present same Justices as before.
      vs.   ) No. Debt   )
Matthias Wright)

Pg
326

This day came the parties by their attornies and thereupon comes a Jury of good and lawful men To Wit John Jones, Wm. Todd, D. C. Powell, Wm. Sample, E lijah Bennett, Thos: J. Oliver, John Hodges, Walden Fuller, William Bell, Stephen Jarmon, Hiram Williams & Newel W. Crane who being elected empannelled and sworn well and truly to try the issues joined upon their oath do say they find the issues joined in favor of the plaintiff and that the defendant has not paid the debt of four hundred dollars in the Plaintiffs declaration mentioned, and they do assess his damages by reason thereof to forty two dollars. It is therefore considered by the Court that the Plaintiff recover of the defendant his debt aforesaid as also his damages aforesaid in form aforesaid assessed, as also his costs by him in his said suit expended etc. from which judgment the defendant prays and obtains an appeal to the next Circuit Court and gave bond as the law directs, etc.

Jesse Pipkin five days as constable M. D. Ramsay 4 days.

Pg
327

James Elkins   )
    vs.) No. Debt   ) Present same Justices as Before.
Walden Fuller   )

This day came the Plaintiff by his attorney and says he will no further prosecute this said suit but takes a non suit. It is therefore considered by the Court that the said defendant go hence without day and recover of the Plaintiff his costs about his suit in this behalf expended.

Littleton Johnson for the   )
use of Needham Stevens   ) Present same Justices as before.
    vs.) No. 33 Debt   )
Edmund R. Anderson   )q

This day came the parties by their attornies and thereupon came a Jury of good and lawful men To Wit Humphey O. Warren, Isaac L. Moody, Thomas Grantham, James Elkins, James Marsh, Wm. Pirtle, Wm. D. Moors, John Mills, Geo. W. Adams, D. W. Love, John Foster & Robert Thompson who being elected empannelled & sworn the truth to speak upon the issues joined upon their oath do say they find in favor of the plaintiff and that the defendant has not paid the debt of one hundred & ninety seven dollars the debt in the Plaintiffs declaration mentioned & they do assess his damages by reason of the detention thereof to nine dollars & fifty cents. It is therefore

Pg
328

considered by the Court that the Plaintiff recover of the said defendant his debt aforesaid as also his damages aforesaid in form aforesaid assessed by the Jury also his costs about his suit in this behalf expended etc.

Robert Thompson   )
    vs.   ) No. 34 Case)
Hatley & Bougard   ) Present same Justices as before.
Adm of the Estate Tho.   )
Alsup decd.

This day came the Plaintiffs & defendants by their attornies and thereupon came a Jury of good & lawful men To Wit John Jones, Wm. Todd, D. C. Powell, Wm. Sample, Elijah Bennett, Thos. J. Oliver, John Hodges, Walden Fuller, Wm. Bell, Stephen Jarmon, Hiram Williams & Newel W. Crane, who being elected empannelled and sworn the truth to speak upon the issues joined upon their oath do say they find the issues joined in favor of the Plaintiff and assess his damages to three hundred and twenty dollars. It is therefore considered by the Court that the plaintiff recover of the defendant the said sum of three hundred & twenty dollars by the jury aforesaid in form aforesaid assessed also his costs about this suit in this behalf expended to be levied of the goods & chattels of the said Thomas Alsup deceased in the hand of the said defendants to be administered etc.

James Bougard)
 vs.) Motion agst. Constable)
Joseph L. Rosson)
 This day came the defendant in proper person and prays and obtains an appeal to the next Circuit Court and gave bond with V. D. Barry as his security.

R. D. Sheppard)
 vs.) A. Attachment
Breedlove & Robertson)
 This day comes the plaintiff by his attorney and thereupon comes Arthur Gloster who is summoned all garnishee in this behalf who being sworn says that he is indebted to the defendants in the sum of seventy five dollars. It is therefore considered by the Court that the plaintiff recover against said Gloster the said sum of money and that final judgment be staid for six months in this behalf etc. Whereupon said money is by said Gloster paid into Court etc.

A. Taylor Ranger)
 vs.) No. 1 Debt) Present same Justices as before.
Michial McKennie)
 This day came the parties by their attornies and thereupon the demeaner of the plaintiff to the defendants plea coming on to be argued by counsel and here understood by the Court. It is the opinion of the Court that the said demeaner be overuled, upon which judgment the plaintiff prays and obtains an appeal in the nature of a writs of error to the next Circuit Court to be held for this County, ordered accordingly.

Thomas Middleton)
 vs.) No. 35 Debt) Present same Justices as before.
Walden Fuller)
 This day came the parties by their attornies and thereupon came a Jury of good & lawful men, Michial Read, John Cherry, John P. Darly, Thos. Washto Inlow Hazlewood, William Ramsay, Thomas Newland, Daniel Davis, James Hardy, John W. Arnold, Thomas Hazlewood, & Wm. Bogard, who being elected empannelled and sworn the truth to speak upon the issues joined upon their oath do say they find the issues joined in favor of the plaintiff and that the defendant has not paid the debt of one hundred & forty dollars in the plaintiffs declaration mentioned and they do assess his damages by reason of the detention thereof to thirteen dollars & thirty cents. It is therefore considered by the Court that the plaintiff recover of the defendant the debt aforesaid & the damages aforesaid in form aforesaid by the Jury assessed together with his costs about his suit in this behalf expended etc.

Robert Thrasher)
 vs.) No. 37 Debt) Present as before.
Mark R. Roberts)
 This day came the parties by their attornies and thereupon came a Jury of good & lawful men To Wit, Humphrey C. Warren, Isaac L. Moody, Thomas Grantham, James Elkins, James Marsh, Wm. Pirtle, Wm. H. Moors, John Mills Geo. W. Adams, D. W. Love, John Foster, Robert Thompson who being elected empannelled and sworn the truth to speak upon the issue joined upon their oath do say they find the issues joined in favor of the Plaintiff and that the said defendant has not paid the debt of one hundred & sixty three dollars & twenty five cents in the plaintiffs declaration mentioned and they do assess his damages by reason of the detention thereof to three dollars &

Pg
331 twenty six cents. Therefore it is considered by the Court that the plaintiff recover against the defendant the debt aforesaid, as also his damages aforesaid in form aforesaid assessed together with his costs about his suit in this behalf expended, etc.

Enoch B. Benson   )
    vs.) No. 39 Debt   ) Present as before.
Alfred M. Shelby   )

    This day came the parties by their attornies and thereupon came a Jury of good and lawful men To Wit, John Jones, Wm. Todd, D. C. Powell, Wm. Sample, Elijah Bennett, Thos. J. Oliver, John Hodges, Walden, Wm. Bell, Stephen Jarmon, Hiram Williams, & Newel W. Crain, who being elected empannelled and sworn the truth to speak upon the issues joined upon their oath do say they find the issues joined in favor of the plaintiff and that he has not paid the debt of ninety one dollars & fifty four cents in the plaintiffs declaration mentioned and they do assess the plaintiffs damages for the detention thereof to thirty seven dollars & fifty cents. It is therefore considered by the Court that the plaintiff recover of the defendant the debt aforesaid, together with the damages aforesaid assumed as also his costs about his suit in this behalf expended etc.

William Ramsay   )
    vs.) No. 43 Debt   ) Present as before.
William Steelman   )

Pg
332   This day came the parties by their attornies and thereupon came a Jury of good & lawful men To Wit John Jones, Wm. Todd, D. C. Powell, Wm. Sample, Elijah Bennett, Thomas J. Oliver, John Moore, Walden Fuller, Wm. Bell, Stephen Jarmon, Hiram Williams & Newel W. Crain who being elected empannelled and sworn the truth to speak upon the issues joined upon their oath do say they find the issues joined in favor of the plaintiff and that he has not paid the debt of one hundred & seventy two dollars debt in the plaintiffs declaration mentioned and they do assess his damages by reason of the detention thereof to three dollars & forty four cents. It is therefore considered by the Court that the plaintiff recover of the defendant his debt aforesaid and the damage aforesaid in form aforesaid assessed by the jury together with his costs about his suit in this behalf expended etc.

James H. Sheppard   )
    vs.) No. 44 Writ of Inquiry   ) Present as before.
Joseph Morman   )
Levy Crow   )

    This day came the parties by their attornies and thereupon came a Jury of good and lawful men To Wit Humphey C. Warren, Isaac L. Moody, Thos. Grantham, James Elkins, James March, Wm. Pirtle, Wm. S. Moore, John Mills, Geo. W. Adams, D. W. Love, John Foster & Robert Thompson who being elected empannxelled and sworn well and truly to inquire of the damages the said plaintiff
Pg
333 has sustained by reason of the breach of covenant in the plaintiffs declaration upon their oath do say that the said plaintiff hath sustained damages by reason of the breaches of said covenant to the amount of eighty five dollars.

    Therefore it is considered by the Court that the plaintiff recover of said defendants the said sum of eighty five dollars damages aforesaid by the Jury aforesaid in form assessed also his costs about his suit in this behalf expended etc.

Hiram Casey   )
    vs.) No. 45 Case   ) Present as Before.
William Sheppard   )

    This day came the parties by their attornies and thereupon came a Jury of good & lawful men, To Wit Thomas Washburn, Michial Read, John C. Cherry, John P. Durley, Joshua Hazlewood, Wm. Ramsay, Thomas Newland, Daniel Davis

Pg

333 James Hardy, John H. Arnold, Thomas Hazlewood, & Wm. L. Bogard who being
elected empannelled and sworn the truth to speak upon the issues joined upon
their oath do say they find the issues joined in favor of the plaintiff and
that he hath sustained damages by reason of the defendants not performing
his promise & undertakings to sixty three dollars & ninety three cents. It
is therefore considered by the Court that the Plaintiff recover of the defendant his damages aforesadd in form aforesaid assessed by the Jury as
also his costs about his suit in this behalf expended etc. from which judg-

Pg ment the defendant prayed and obtained an appeal to the next Circuit Court

334 and gave bond with V. D. Barry as his security.

Oney Harvey   )
    vs.) No. 46 Covenant) Present as before.
Nicholas Nail   )

    This day came the parties by their attornies and thereupon came a Jury
of good and lawful men To Wit Thomas Washburn, Michial Read, John C. Cherry
John P. Durley, Joshua Hazlewood, Wm. Ramsay, Thomas Newland? Daniel Davis,
James Hardy, John W. Arnold, Thos. Hazlewodd, & Wm. Bougard, who being
elected empannelled & sworn well & truly to try the issues joined between
the parts upon their oath do say they find in favor of the plaintiff and
that the defendant has not kept and performed his covenant as is alleged in
the plaintiffs declaration, and they assess the plaintiffs damages to four
hundred & ninety four dollars & fifty five cents.

    It is therefore considered by the Court that the plaintiff recover of
the defendant the damages aforesaid in form aforesaid assessed, by the Jury,
as also his costs by him about his suit in this behalf expended etc.

    Humphrey C. Warren, James Marsh, James Elkins, William Pirtle, Isaac
L. Moody, Wm. H. Moore, & Thomas Grantham 5 days as Jurors.

Pg   James B. Smith   )
335   Daniel D. Berry   )
    vs.) No. 47 Debt   ) Present as Before.
   Needham Stevens   )

    This day came the parties by their attorneys and thereupon came a Jury
of good and lawful men to wit Thomas Washburne, Michial Read, John C.
Cherry, John R. Durley, Joshua Hazlewood, Thomas Hazlewood, Wm. Ramsay,
Thos. Newland, Dnaiel Davis, James Hardy, John W. Arnold, & Wm. Bougard,
who being elected empannelled and sworn the truth to speak upon the issues
joined upon their oath do say they find in favor of the plaintiffs and that
the defendans have not paid the debt of one hundred dollars in the plaintiffs
declaration mentioned and they do assess their damages by reason of the detention thereof to three dollars & fifty cents. It is therefore considered
by the Court that the plaintiffs recover of the said defendants the debt
aforesaid together with the damages aforesaid in form aforesaid assesssed by
the Jury together with the costs in their behalf expended etc.

State   )
   vs.   ) Malicious Mischief)
John Foster   )

    Thomas J. Oliver who was mark as prosecutor and was turned with the
costs in this suit comes in and prays an appeal in the nature of a writ of
error to the next Circuit Court for his bill of exceptions which is granted
and enters into bond of one hundred dollars penally with P. M. McKinney
& Peter G. Rives his securities.

Pg   State
336   vs.) No. 57 Debt) Present as Before.
   Vivian B. Holmes

Pg
336
This day came the State by the Solicitor General and on motion says
he will no further prosecute his suit. And therefore the said suit with
the assent of the Court is dismissed as said Holmes paying the costs acc-
umulation thereon.

Nathaniel Steele)
      vs.) No. 52 Case) Present as before.
John H. McKennie)

This day came the parties by their attornies and thereupon came a Jury
of good and lawful men To Wit Humphey C. Warner, Isaac L. Moody, Thos. Grantham, James Elkins, James Marsh, Wm. Pirtle, Wm. H. Moors, John Mills,
Geo. W. Adams, D. W. Love, John Foster & Robert Thompson who being elected
empannelled & sworn the truth to speak upon the issues joined upon their
oath do say they find the issues joined in favor of the Plaintiff and they
assess the Plaintiff damages by reason of the non performance of the defendants assumption to one hundred & fifty dollars. It is therefore considered by the Court that the plaintiff recover of the defendant the
damages aforesaid in form aforesaid assessed by the Jury as also his costs
by him about his suit in this behalf expended etc.

The Grand Jury served five days. John Mills twoi days.

Pg
337
Nathaniel Steéle)
      vs.) No. 53 Covenant) Present as before.
John N. McKennie)

This day came the parties by their attornies and thereupon came a
Jury of good and lawful men To Wit Humphrey C. Warren, Isaac L. Moody,
Thomas Granthm, James Elkins, James Marsh, Wm. Pirtle, Wm. Moore, John
Mills, Geo. W. Adams, John Foster, Robert Thompson & Thomas Clifft, who being
elected empanneleled and sworn the truth to speak upon the issues joined
upon their oath do say they find in favor of the plaintiffs and that the defendant has not kept his said covenant as declared upon by the plaintiffs,
and they assess the plaintiffs damages by reason of the defendants non
performance thereof of six hundred dollars. Therefore it is considered by
the Court that the plaintiff recover of the defendant the damages aforesaid
in form aforesaid assessed by the Jury as also his costs by him about his
suit in this behalf expended etc. And thereupon the plaintiff by his attorney
moved the Court to grant a new trial and which after solemn argument by
counsel was overruled by the Court and the plaintiff agrees to stay execution until the 25th of Dec. next to which old several dedisions the
defendant accepts and a Bill of Exceptions is signed sealed & made a part
of the record.

The Grand Jury returned into open Court under charge of their Juror
officer a Bill of Presentment The State of Tennessee vs. Wm. Robinson as
overseer of a road, indorsed a True Bill Alec Kirkpatrick foreman of the
Grand Jury & the balance of said Jury also a Bill of Indictment the State
vs. Grie Hastings for keeping a disorderly House indorsed a True Bill
Alexander Kirkpatrick, Foreman of the Grand Jury. Also a Bill of Indictment
the State vs. Jesse Laird for Gaming indorsed not a true Bill Alec Kirkpatrick, foreman of the Grand Jury.

Pg
338
John Foster)
      vs.) Motion)
John Thompson a constable))
and Jno. M. Davis,)
Garret Fitzgerald, James Hardin,) Present Edward D. Tarver, James
Ephes Sparks, Jno. H. McKinnie) Ruffin, and Elisha W. Boyte.
as his securities.)

Pg
338

This day came the parties by their attorneys and whereupon the plaintiff moved the Court for a judgment against the said defendants, because said defendant John Thompson Constable aforesaid had not complyed with the law in paying over the money returning the following executions to wit one against A. L. Lockman and Daniel Davis for fifty dollars bearing interest from the 15th day of March 1828, one execution against John Dillingham for fifteen dollars 87 cts. one on William S. London for dollars issued by William L. Duncan Esq. a Justice of the Peace for said County and after argument be had there on. It is considered that the plaintiff tiff take nothing by his motion and that the defendants recover of the said plaintiff their costs about this motion expended etc. From which judgment the plaintiff prayed and obtained an appeal to the next Circuit

Pg
339

Court and give bond & security as the law directs.

A platt and certificate with the transfer thereon from William H. Chompson for himself and wife to Asa Roberson for fifty acres of land was produced in open Court and proved by the oath of E. O. Crisp & Mansil Crisp, the assignment thereon and it is ordered that the same be so certified.

A plat and certificate for one hundred acres of land was produced in Court and the assignment thereon from Michial McKinnie to David McKinnie was duly proven by the oath of E. C. Crisp and Mansil Crisp the subscribing witnesses thereto and it is ordered that the same be so certified.

```
State                          )
 vs. ) Pert. for a Tippling House )
Joseph Watson                  )
```

This day came the Solicitor General on the part of the State and the said defendant being arraigned plead Guilty and submits to the Court.

It is therefore considered by the Court that the said defendant be fined one dollar and pay the costs of this prosecution & that execution issue etc.

```
Hugh A. Reynold                |
     vs. ) Certiovari          )
James Hill                     )
```

This day came the Plaintiff by his attorney and the said James Hill being solemnly called to come into Court and defend the action of Hugh A. Reynolds against him came not.

It is therefore considered by the Court that the said Hugh A. Reynold

Pg
340

recover of said James Hill his costs about his certiovari in this behalf expended & have execution etc.

```
State              )
 vs ) Indictment   )
Joshua Thurman     )
```

This day came the Solicitor General on the part of the State, and the defendant in proper personwho being arraigned upon the Bill of Indictment pleads Guilty and submits it to the Court. It is therefore considered by the Court that the said Thurman be fined one cent and pay the costs of this prosecution and that he be taken etc.

```
Thomas Hazlewood, Joshua Hazlewood ,     )
& Wm.  T. Laird from Hazlewood & Laird   )
          vs) Sci Fa                     )
John C. Cherry                           )
```

Pg
340
This day came the plaintiffs by their attornies and thereupon the said John C. Cherry being solemnly called to come into Court and plead to the Sci Facias ran against him came not. Therefore it is considered by the Court that the said plaintiffs recover of said defendant the sum of one hundred & twenty five dollars and penalty as the law directs as also their costs about their Sciri Facias in this behalf expended etc. and that execution final issue accordingly.

```
Chas. McAlister et al          )
firm of Charles McAlister      )
           vs.  ) Case         )
Leony R. Smith                 )
```

Pg
341
This day came the Plaintiffs by their attorney and the defendant being solemnly called to come into Court and defend the action brought by the Plaintiffs against him came not but made default and it appearing to the satisfaction of the Court him that said action sound in damages theretofore let a Jury came at next term of this Court to inquire of the same and that the same issue etc.

This day came into open Court Jeremiah Williams who on yesterday was elected Constable of this County in the place of Isaac Johnson resigned and he having given bond as the law directs with Walden Fuller, E. W. Boyte, Wm. Fuller, Thornton Jones, Robert Taylor, Isaac Johnson, Jaden Lanbun as his securities took the oaths prescribed by law.

Ordered that the Clerk be permitted to take in lists of taxable property for the year 1828 until the 1st January next.

```
Nathaniel Steele       )
      vs.  ) Covenant   )
John N. McKennie       )
```

After the signing the Bill of Execution then came the defendant by his counsel moved the Court that he be permitted to enter into Bond and Security for the costs only of the Circuit Court not to operate as a Supesedias which said motion the Court overruled. And the Court adjourned to Court in Course.

> J. M. McKean J. P.
> Thomas James J. P.
> F. Shoemake J. P.

Monday 5 Jan. 1829

Pg
342
At a Court of pleas and Quarter sessions began and held for the County of Hardeman at the County of Hardeman at the Court House in the Town of Bolivar on the first Monday in January A. D. 1829. Present the worshipful James Ruffin, Chairman, Edmund D. Tarver, John G. Cockeram, West Harris, Thornton Jones, Francis Shoemake, Thomas James Caleb Brock, Joseph W. McKean, Thomas Deen, John Rosson, William B. Robinson, Elijah Gosset, James Bogard, Alexander McKenzie, Lazarus Stewart, Daniel Hughs, John Slaughter, Williams L. Duncan & Edward Owens, Esquires Justices Thomas J. Hardeman, Clerk, J. C. N. Robertson, Sheriff, Valentine D. Barry, Solicitor, Proclamation being made as the form is.

The Court proceeded to appoint the quorum Court for the year 1829 as follows to wit Edmund D. Tarver, James Ruffin & John Y. Cockeram, Esquires.

A deed of conveyance from Henry T. Rucker & Nancy Rucker his wife to

Pg

342 William D. Kannough for 99 acres of land was exhibited in open Court and duly acknowledged by Henry T. Rucker and Nancy Rucker having been privily examined by the Court separate & apart from her husband acknowleges the same to be done freely of her own will without the coertion or permission of her husband & the same was ordered to be certified for registration.

An inventory of the hire of negroes belonging to the heirs of E. Polk decd. for the years 1828 & 1829. Returned into Court by A. G. Neilson Guardian & ordered to be recorded.

Pg

343 A settlement with Thomas J. Hardeman & John H. Bills Executors to the will of E. Polk, decd. returned into Court by Joseph W. McKean & William Ramsay who was appointed by the Court to make said settlement or ordered to be recorded.

A deed of conveyance from Jesse D. Hall to John Matthews for 179 acres of land was produced in open Court acknowledgec by said Jesse D. Hall ordered to be certified for registration.

A deed of conveyance from Robert Thompson to John Thompson for 70 acres of land produced in open Court acknowledged by said Thompson & ordered to be certified for registration.

A plat and certificate for 89 acres of land with the transfer thereon from John L. Kimbro to Nathaniel Gordon was produced in open Court & duly acknowe ledged by said Kimbrough & it was ordered to be so certified.

A deed of conveyance from Thomas J. Hardeman & John H. Bills, Executors of the Estate of E. Polk Decd. to James K. Polk & James Walker Executors of the Estate of Samuel Polk decd. for 320 acres produced in open Court & acknowledged by said Hardeman & Bills. Ordered to be certified for registration.

A deed of conveyance from Jesse Blunt to John Blunt for 25 acres of

Pg land was produced in open Court and duly acknowledged by said Jesse Blunt &

344 ordered to be certified for registration.

A dded of conveyance from Robert Thompson to Ephram Sparks for 25 acres of land was produced in open Court and duly acknowledged by said Thompson . Ordered to be certified for registration.

A Bill of Sale for a negro boy from Ann Rivers W. Peck Marsh Rivers Sarah I. Rivers & Thomas M. Rivers to Blackstone Hardeman was produced in open Court & acknowledged by said Ann Marsh Thomas Rivers & by W. Peck the same ordered to be certified for registration.

A deed of conveyance from Miles Davis to Justice Lake for 100 acres of land was produced in open Court and duly acknowledged by said Davis & ordered to be certified for registration.

A deed of conveyance from Miles Davis to Justice Lake for 200 acres of land was produced in open Court and duly acknowledged by said Davis & ordered to be certified for registration.

A deed of conveyance from Miles Davis to Justice Lake for 200 acres of landwas produced in open Court and duly acknowledged by said Davis & ordered to be certified for registration.

A deed of conveyance from Stephen Shinault & Drtter Shinault to John

Pg
344 P. Robinson for 93 acres of land and the execution thereof was duly proven
by the oaths of Henry Webster and William Whitaker the subscribing witnesses
thereto & ordered to be certified for registration.

A deed of conveyance from Josiah G. Henry & Hugh Henry to Adam R.
Pg Alexander for 51 acres of land was produced in open Court and the execution
345 thereof was duly proven by the oaths of Henry Reagon & Andrew Taylor the
subscribing witness thereto the same was ordered to be certified for registration.

A plat and certificate with the transfer thereon from Annis Parker to
Robert for 10 acres was produced in open Court & the execution thereof was
duly proven by the oaths of Wm. Pirtle & Isaac Pirtle the subscribing witnesses thereto. Ordered to be so certified.

A deed of conveyance from John H. McKennie to Roderick Oliver for one
& half acres of land was produced in open Court and duly acknowledged by
said McKinnie & ordered to be certified for registration.

A deed of conveyance from David Whyte to Daniel & Peter Minner for 81
acres was produced in open Court and duly acknowledged by said White & ordered to be certified for registration.

A division of the personal estate of Samuel Steel deceased returned
into Court ordered to be recorded.

The Dower of the widow Steel widow of Samuel Steel deceased returned into
Court and by the Commissioners appointed for that purpose ordered to be
recorded.

An account of William H. Moores Guardianship of Amanda F. Reynolds
& May M. Reynolds, minor orphans of C. Reynold decd. returned into Court
Pg allowed & ordered to be recorded.
346
An inventory of the estate of Aaron Burlesson deceased returned into
open Court. Ordered to be recorded.

An additional inventory of the Estate of T. Polk decd. returned into
open Court. Ordered to be recorded.

The last will and testament of Hiram Casey deceased was produced in
open Court and the execution thereof was duly proven by the oaths of Jos.
Morman and Daniel McKinza two of the subscribing witnesses thereto and the
same was ordered to be recorded and thereupon came William Whitaker and
Newel D. Crain two of the executors named in said will and by consent of the
Court gave their bond of fifteen thousand dollars with William Crain & West
Harris as their securities and was qualified accordingly and received letter
testamentory.

The last will & testament of Robert Rivers deceased was produced in
open Court and the execution thereof was duly proven by the oaths of V. D.
Cossett and John Adams two of the subscribing witnesses thereto and the
same was ordered to be recorded and the executors named in said will failed
to qualify thereto thereupon came Willie Peck and with the consent of the
Court administered on said estate with the will annexed and gave bond of
sixty thousand dollars with Edmund D. Tarver A. Kirkpatrick Ann Rivers,
Thomas M. River & Wm. Ramsay & as his securities and was qualified accordingly.
Ordered that he have letter of administration.

Pg
347   Jane Campbell and John Molloy came into open Court and moved the Court
that they may administer on the estate of George S. Campbell deceased and
all matters and thing thereunto arising being properly understood ordered
that they be permitted to administer on said estate who gave bond of three
hundred dollars with Edmund D. Tarver as their securities and was qualified
accordingly received letter of administration.

This day came into open Court Rebecca Burleson and with the consent of
the Court she was appointed Guardean to her children (to wit) Elizabeth,
Johathan, Jane, Sarah Ann, John, Lucinda, Malinda Matilda, Marelda & Amanda Burlesson , minor orphans of Aaron Burleson deceased who gave bond in
the sum of four thousand dollars with Edward Burlesson & N. W. Crain as her
securities.

This day came into open Court David B . Carnes and with the consent
of the Court was appointed guardeen to Ninan S. Steel Nancy M. Steel &
Prudence E. Steel minor orphans of S amuel Steel decd. who gave bond of
six thousand dollars with Stephan Jarmon as his security.

An application of William Kensley ordered that he have licence to
keep an ordinary at his now dwelling who gave bond agreeable to law with
Thornton Jones & David Brock as his securities.

The Court proceeded & elected Jason Wilson Constable in Capt. Claytons
Pg   Company for the next two years who gave bond with Robert Robson, Joseph
348   Hickman & Thomas L. Duncor as his securities and was qualified accordingly.

The Court proceeded to elect a Register to fill the vacancy occassioned
by the death of E. W. Boyt and taking the ballots it appeared that Rufus
P. Neelly was duly elected to that office who gave bond of ten thousand
dollars with John H. Bills & J. C. N. Robertson as his securities and was
qualified.

Ordered by the Court that the County Trustee pay the costs on the
following suits To Wit State vs. Barney Chambers Green B Chambers same
Willie Chambers I. E. Mayfield, Wm. Bell, Jesse S utton Alex Brown B.
Donaldson vs. County C. H. Tar Wm. Nelson & Thomas J. Oliver vs. County
making to the clerk of the Circuit Clerk fifty dollars & thirty one cents
County Clerk ten dollars and sixty six cents Sheriff eighteen dollars and
forty eight cents to the Solicitor forty seven dollars and fifty cents and to
the witnesses three dollars eighty one & one fourth cents agreeable to the
account rendered by the Clerk of the Circuit Court.

Ordered by the Court that the Sheriff and collector of Hardeman County,
for the year 1828, be released from the payment of the tax on 44 free polls
having been run away or insolvent 8 slave polls two town lots and 2964 acres
of land the (add 300) 3264 , same having been twice listed or appears to the
Pg   satisfaction of the Court for 1828.
329
Ordered by the Court that the Sheriff and Collector of the public taxes
for the year 1827 be released from the payment of the tax on 735 acres of
land appearing to the Court that the same had been erronously reported except 10 acres which was not sold for want of a bid.

Ordered by the Court that Edmund D. Tarver, Chesley D. Kay & George
M. Firtle be appointed Commissioners to lay off and set apart one years
provisions for Jane Campbell widow of George S. Campbell decd. & make report
to next Court.

Pg
349
Abner Denson produced in open Court the scalp of one wolf over 4 months old ordered that he have his certificate.

Jonathan Willoughby produced in open Court one wolf scalp over four months old. Ordered that he have his certificate.

Lot Foster produced in open Court the scalps of two wolves over four months old. Ordered that he have his certificate.

A deed of conveyance from Daniel Cadwell to Henry Stevens for 100 acres of land was produced in open Court and proved by the oath of Joshua Cadwell one of the subscribing witnesses thereto . Ordered to be so certified.

Pg
350
Lewis Johnson excused as a juror at this term.

Isaiah Davis was elected Constable in Capt. Mohundros Company.

James Hill who was arrested under a Copias adfatisfaciendum came into open Court and rendered a scdule of his property and took the oath of insolvency etc.

Ordered that James Walden oversee the clearing out and keep in repair a road as lately laid out from Waldens Bridge on Hatchie in a direction for Legrange from the bridge to the hill on the side of Big Muddy and that he have all the hands in the fork of Muddy Hatchee work thereon under his direction.

Ordered that Boles Burner oversee the clearing out and keep in repair that part of the road leading from Waldens Bridge towards Lagrange from the Hill west of Muddy to Porters Creek and that he have the hands within 1⅛ miles of said road work under him.

Ordered that John Burnes oversee the clearing out and keep in repair that part of the road running from Waldens Bridge to Legrange from Porters Creek to Henry Goodwins on Spring Creek and all the hands within ½ miles of said road work under his directions .

Ordered that Blake Brantly oversee the clearing out & keep in repair the road from Henry Goodwins on Spring Creek to the Cotton Gin Road and he have the hands within 1½ miles of sd. road to work thereon.

Pg
351
Ordered that David Anderson oversee the clearing out and keep in repair the road from Waldens Bridge leading for Legrange from the cotton gin road to the County line and that he have the hands within 1½ miles of said road to work under his directions.

Ordered that James McMillan be appointed overseer of the road leading from bolivar to Memphis in the place of John Crain etc.

Ordered that John Gage oversee the clearing out and keep in repair that part of the road leading from Bolivar to Purdy from the East end of the part under Robert Hays to Wades Creek and that all the hands on Wades Creek N. W. of the same and the hands on Hays mCreek and all on said part of the road work thereon under his direction first class.

Ordered that Peter Rogers oversee the clearing out and keep in repair that part of the Covington road from the Branch west of Peelers field

Pg
351 to the East bank of Clear Creek and all the hands including John Stewart
W. C. Warren, John Y. Cockeram, Edmund Rivers, R. D. Cockeram Stephen
Ruddle, Harvey Kirk, Henry T. Rucker, Jacob Polk, Robert Clinton & William
Todd work under his directions 1st class.

Ordered that John Y. Cockeram, James Ruffin, John Rosson, West Harris,
R. D. Tarver, Thornton Jones & E. Gossett or any five of them be a Jury of
view to mark a road as the law directs the nearest and best way from the
town of Bolivar commencing at any street they may select to the foot of the
bridge across Hatchie in a direction to Jackson & that they report to the
present term of this Court.

Pg
352

Ordered that this Court will do County Business Tomorrow (Tuesday).

Ordered by the Court that Thos Joyner oversee and keep in repair that
part of the road leading from Bolivar to Jackson, beginning at the north
end of Loftons causeway & thence to Grays Creek and that he have all the
hands that formerly worked landed the direction of Sol Willoughby work
under him 1st class.

Ordered by the Court that the precinct Election heretofore held at
the house of Roland Roberts Calias Harpers old place be removed to William
Cranes store.

Ordered by the Court that the Clerk issue to Van Dyke Gossett a
ticket for his servides as officer at July Term 1827. The original having
been mislaid.

Ordered that Thomas Washburn have leave to turn the road round his
plantation by putting in good order as required by Laird.

Pg
353

Ordered that William Gage oversee the Memphis road from the fork near
Arthur Morrow West to Spring Creek and work all the hands south of said
road to the 1st Section line 1st Class.

Ordered that Daniel Minner oversee and keep in repair that part of the
road leading from Bolivar to Brownsville from the north bank of Short
Creek to the north bank of Clear Creek and that John Caldwell John Huddlestone,
John Wilson, Josiah Chandler, John Tiggret & Hugh A. Reynolds work under his
diredtions.

Ordered by the Court that Barkley Donnelson be appointed overseer of
that part of the road leading from Simpsons ferry to the County line,
between this & McNairy County and that all the hands two miles & perm north
& 1 per mile south of said road work under his directions from Big Hatchie
River to the County line.

Ordered by the Court that Coleman Draper be appointed overseer of the
road beginning at Piney 5 miles toward Warnersville in the place of Bennet
Highfield he have the same hand allotted to said Highfield formerly.

Pg
354

Ordered that William Wilson be added to the number of hands at present
allotted to Wm. Davis as overseer of this state Line Road and also that said
Davis have leave to turn the road around Wathum & Wilsons fields.

Ordered that Asa Bishop be appointed overseer over that part of the
Simpsons ferry road that Eli Cox was overseer of and be allowed the same
hands that said Cox had under his directions.

Ordered by the Court that the Election Precinct heretofore held at Warnersville be altered to R. C. Friars Store.

Ordered by the Court that Samuel Jones be appointed overseer of the road leading from Saml. Jones to McNairy County line, in the place of William Kennedy and work the same hand 2'd class.

Ordered that Richard Hatley be appointed overseer of the Road from Allsops prairie, west to the Bridge on the Memphis Road opposite William Whitakers and to have all the hands in that bound which was allotted William Bogard and that Hatley keep said bridge in order. It is also ordered that N. W. Payne be overseer of the Memphis Road from the Bridge opposite William Whitakers west to the County line and have all the hands in that bound which were allotted to William Bogard.

Ordered there being a majority of Justices present, that John P. Boydston have leave to establish and keep up a ferry on Hatchie River at the place where John Jones formerly kept a boat and that he be allowed the customary fees established by this Court.

Ordered that the County Trustee pay Thomas J. Hardeman one hundred and eighty one dollars the amount of claims due him from this county which are unpaid & are lost or mislaid in the office of the former Trustee.

Ordered by the Court that the rates of taxes for the ensuing year be as follows:

County Tax on each 100 acres of land	19 cents
Poor Tax	6
Jury Tax	18 3/4
River Tax	12
Court House Tax	37½
	93 3/4

County Tax on each Town Lot	25
Poor "	6
Jury "	19
Court House Tax	50½
	87½

County Tax on each Slave	25
Poor "	6
Jury "	19
Court House Tax	50
	$1.00

County Tax on each Free poll	12½
Jury	12½
Court House Tax	25
	50

County tax on each Retail Store	$7.50
" " " " 4 wheel carriage	5.00
" " " " 2 " "	2.50
" " " " stud horse of Jack the price of the season.	

A decree by the Court that Friday be set apart for the transaction of County business.

Pg
356   The Clerk of the County Court presented the following receipts
(to wit) Received of Thomas J. Hardeman Clerk of the County Court of
Pg Hardeman nine hundred and ninety five dollars & fifty three cents the
356 amount of state tax by him collected for the year ending the last day of
September 1828 Dec. 23, 1828.

                  James Carruther, T. W.

    Received of Thomas J. Hardeman Clerk of the County Court fourteen dollars
and seventy six cents it being the amount of fines and fortunes which said
Clerk is bound to account to me for the above settlement with him by the County
Commissioners Boliver Jany. 1. 1829,

                  J. W. McKean.

Pg
357

William Walden   )
    vs.) Covenant   )
Thomas M. Patrick   )
John Moore   )

    This day came the Plaintiff by his attorney and the defendants in proper
person who say they cannot gainsay the Plaintiffs action in this behalf confesses that the Plaintiff hath sustained damages by reason of the non performance of this said covenant in this behalf to the amount of two hundred
and thirty eight dollars & fifty cents and thereupon came into open Court
Thompson D. White and Green Fryor who confess judgment jointly with the said
defendants for the same. It is therefore considered by the Court that the
Plaintiff recover against the said defendants together with the said Thompson
D. White & Green Fryor the damages aforesaid in form aforesaid confessed together with his costs about his suit in this behalf expended etc. and the
plaintiff stay execution in this behalf the fifteenth day of June next.

William Whitaker   )
    vs.) Debt)   )
Daniel Smith   )

    This day came the Plaintiff and defendant in proper person and the
defendant says he cannot gainsay the Plaintiffs action in this behalf but
confesses that the defendant owes the said plaintiff the sum of one hundred
dollars and thereupon comes into open Court Newel W. Crane and confesses judgment jointly with the said defendant for said sum of one hundred dollars. It
is therefore considered by the Court that Plaintiff recover against the said
defendant together with the said Newell W. Crane the sum aforesaid in form
aforesaid confessed together with his costs about his suit in this behalf
Pg expended and Plaintiff stays execution six months.
358

Charles Ready   )
    vs.) Debt)
Ezekial Owens   )

    This day came the Plaintiff by his attorney and says he will no further
prosecute his suit, but dismisses the same. It is therefore considered by
the Court that the said defendant recover of the plaintiff his costs about
his suit in this behalf expended etc.

James Webster   )
    vs.) Trespass)
Alexander Dickson   )

    This day came the Plaintiff by his attorney and says he will no further
prosecute his suit but dismisses the same and thereupon came the defendant
and assumes all costs. It is therefore considered by the Court that the
Plaintiff recover of the defendant his costs etc. in this behalf expended.

Pg
359
Whereas it appears to the Court that Samuel W. Echols has removed from the Captains Company for which he was elected and has thereby in the opinion of this Court vacated his office as Constable for said Company in in this County. It is ordered that an election be held for the purpose of supplying the vacancy so occassioned as aforesaid.

And the Court adjourned
to Tomorrow morning, tomorrowxmorning.
9 O'clock.
James Ruffin
Edmund D. Tarver
John Y. Cockeram

Tuesday 6th January 1829

Court met according to adjournment Present the worshipful James Ruffin, Edmund D. Tarver and John Y. Cockeram, Esquires Justices, Thomas J. Hardeman Clerk, J. C. N. Robertson Sheriff, V. D . Barry, Solicitor.

Proclamation being made as the form is the Sheriff returned into open Court a Venira facias in the following words and figures (to wit) The State of Tennessee

To the Sheriff of Hardeman County Greeting You are hereby commanded to summons the following persons to attend at our next Court of Pleas and Quarter Sessions to be held for the County of Hardeman at the Court House in the town of Bolivar on the first Tuesday after the first Monday in January next to serve as Jurors at said term (to wit) Josiah Wemmack Robert Box (Major) Andrew Cain, John Fortner, Booker Foster , Eli Sweeton, Kinchen Borden Charles McDaniel, Michael Beavers, Wm. H. Dewberry, Peter G. Rives, Samuel Lambert Charles T. Howard Robert Kelly, James Elkins, James Slaughter, William Ramsey, James B. Smith, William W. Lennard, William Kelly, William Taylor, Lewis Johnson, Newel Crain, George Kirk Daniel Minner and Jacob Pirtle also Henry W. Brown to serve as constable.

Herein fail not and have you,then & there this writ witness Thomas J. Hardeman Clerk of said Court at office the first Monday in October A. D. 1828.

Thos. J. Hardeman Clerk

On the back of which was Venira facias to January Term 1829.16th Oct. 1828.

Pg
360
Came to hand October 18th 1828. Thereby certify that I have summoned all of the within named Jurors except (Josiah Dammask) and that they are all free holders or home holders over the age of twenty one years and in - habitants of Hardeman County. Given under my hand this 6th day of January 1829------J. C. N. Robertson, Sheriff.

Of whom the following persons being duly elected empaneled sworn & charged to enquire for the body of Hardeman County retired to consider of Presentments under the care of Henry W. Brown an officer sworn for that purpose to wit Newel W. Crain, Foreman appointed by the Court Michael Beavers, James B. Smith, Charles M. Daniel, Eli Sweeten, George Kirk, John Fortner, Andrew Cain, Kinchen Borden, James Elkins, Daniel Minner Booker Foster & Jacob Pirtle.

Jesse Cockeram came into open Court and with the donsent of the Court was appointed guardean to William Ware a minor orphan and gave bond of one hundred & twenty dollars with Hugh A. Reynolds as his security.

Josiah Davis who was elected constable on yesterday came into Court gave bond with William B. Robinson & Jason Wilson as his securities and was qualified.

Pg
360   A power of attorney from William Latch to Ezekial P. McNeal was produced in open Court and the execution thereof was duly proven by the oaths of Allen Hill & Samuel Leeper two of the subscribing witnesses thereto ordered to be certified for registration.

Pg
361   A Bill of sale from Jonathan Joyner to Thomas Joyner was exhibited in open Court and the Execution thereof was duly proven by the oaths of Walter Robinson & Robert D. Fort subscribing witnesses thereto the was ordered to be certified for registration.

A deed of conveyance from Jacob Burleson to John Burleson for 100 acres of land was produced in open Court and duly acknowledged by Jacob Burleson ordered to be certified for registration.

A deed of conveyance from William G. Steel to David W. Wood for 200 acres of land was produced in open Court & duly acknowledged by said Steel. Ordered to be certified for registration.

A deed of Trust from William Johnson to Roger Barton was produced in open Court & the execution thereof was duly proven by the oaths of Pitser Miller & Carter C. Collier two of the subscribing witnesses thereto the same was ordered to be certified for registration.

A deed of conveyance from Abbot Hancock by his attorney in fact David White to Hugh Caruthers for 114 acres of land was produced in open Court and duly acknowledged by said White. Ordered to be certified for registration.

Pg
362   A mortgage from Nathaniel Steel to William G. Steel was produced in open Court and the Execution thereof was duly proven by the oaths of Richard Lamb & David W. Wood the subscribing witnesses thereto the same was ordered to be certified for registration.

A deed of conveyance from Edward Burleson to John B. Justice for 125 acres of land was produced in open Court and duly acknowledged by said Burleson ordered to be certified for registration.

John P. Bardstrum who obtained an order on yesterday to keep a ferry across Hatchee River came into Court and gave bond with John G. Gage as his security.

A deed of conveyance from Nathaniel Steel to John Lea for 76 acres of land was produced in open Court and the Execution thereof was duly proven by the oaths of Wm. F. Jeffer & William G. Steel the subscribing witnesses thereto the same was ordered to be certified for registration.

Ordered that James Cody be released from being overseer on the road from Spring Creek to Middleburgh.

Ordered by the Court there being a majority of the Justices present that James Ruffin, Edmund D. Tarver, West Harris Newel W. Crain John Y. Cockeram & Jacob Pirtle be appointed a to view and lay offf a road from the north end of Main Street continuing due north to a point near the house whereon Wm.

Pg
363 T. Land now lives running thence straight to the bridge on Hatchee River and that the Jury asses what damages the owners of land may sustain by reason of the road running through their land & report to this Court also the damages that may acrue from the road running from Water Street to the Bridge

Pg
363   The Jury of view appointed yesterday to mark out a road the nearest
best way to the Bridge on Hatchee reported as follows
State of Tennessee)
Hardeman Count   )
        Pursuant to an order of this Court January term 1829 we the undersigned
after being duly sworn according to law have examined and laid out a road
from Bolivar to the New Bridge on Hatchee a majority of us have agreed that
the road start from the north end of Water Street running with the new
road a little below the Cotton Gin therein with a line of stakes and marked
tires to the west end of the Bridge given under our hand & this 6th Jan.
1828.

                          Edmund D. Tarver
                          John Rosson
                          John G. Cockeram
                          James Ruffin
                          West Harris

        Ordered by the Court that Amos G. Thompson oversee and keep in repair
that part of the road leading from Thomas Washburns on the Memphis Road to
Dobbs old cabin and that he have all the hands not otherwise appropriated
on the north and South side of said Road within one and a half miles of
said Road.

Pg   Ordered by the Court that Joseph W. McKean, A. Kirkpatrick and Francis
364 Shoemake be appointed commissioner to assist Joseph W. Talbot Esq. to
settle with the County Trustee of Madison County concerning claims dues
from said County to Hardeman County and report to next term of this Court.

        Ordered by the Court that William C. Sparks oversee and keep in repair
that part of the Summerville Road from Isaak Davis west to Arthur Morrows
and work the same hands that worked under Thos. Washburn.

        Ordered by the Court that the following jurors be appointed a Jury
of review to wit Newell W. Crain, William Bogard, William N. Coleman,
Wilkins I. Hunt and Matthew Farrar & James Ruffin to mark out a road com-
Pg mencing at J. Crains on the Memphis road thence through Middleburg to the
365 nearest point of the County line in a direction for Le Grange.

        For reasons appearing to the satisfaction of the Court. It is ordered
that the Commissioners heretofore appointed to settle Josiah Hatley adm.
of Lewis Dillahunty decd. be allowed until July term 1829 of this Court to
make such settlement and report.

        Ordered by the Court that the following Justices of the Peace be app-
ointed to take lists of the Taxable Property & Polls for the present year.
To Wit
x In Capt. Boytes Company   John Rosson Esq.
x "   " Mahundros   "   Lazerus Stewart
x "   " Rossons   "   Daniel Hughs
" "   X Carnes   "   John Slaughter
"   x Butcher   "   James Bogard
"   x Claytons   "   Elijah Gossett
"   X Chapmans   "   Alex McKenzie
"   x Hudsons   "   James Ruffin
"   x Hazlewood   "   Thomas James
"   x Bonds   "   Caleb Brock
"   x Hubbard   "   John T. Cockeram
"   x Walker   "   E. D. Tarver

Pg
385 x   x   Chism Company   Walter Scott
     "   x   Hills   "   Thornton Jones
In Capt. Boytes Company
     "   x   Rainey   "   West Harris
     "   x   Davis   "   Thomas Deen

Ordered by the Court that William Caldwell George Hanks Benjamin Nabor,
Pg Nathan Williams Richmond Carroll, Thomas Tombs, Joseph Mashborn, or any
366 five of them be appointed a Jury of view to lay off & mark a road from
where the Cotton Gin road crosses the State line toward Summerville the
nearest and best way as for on the west boundary of Hardeman County to make
report to the next term of this Court.

Ordered by the Court that Howell Mynick D. W. Hullan, John Williams,
Elisha W. Harris, William Mirick Perry G. Nabors and Joshua Moore be appointed a Jury of view to lay off a road from the north west corner of
William Rennick field to intersect the old state line road at or near William Caldwells thence the nearest and best way towards L agrange and make
report at the next term of this Court.

Ordered by the Court that John H. Arnold Daniel Dodd, Robert Kelly
Robert Bays John Jones, Richard Arnold & William Sanders be a Jury of
View to mark and lay out on road the nearest and best way from the new
Bridge near Bolivar, on towards the bridge on Johnson Creek and then to
intersect the Purdy road leading on to Hays ferry and report to next Court.

Ordered that Russell J. Crawford Charles Cook, John Brantly Samuel
Pg Howell Joseph Jones, Joseph Dobbs & James Brown be appointed a Jury of
367 view to mark out a road from Joseph Jones to Charles Cocks mill on Spring
Creek and make report to next term.

Ordered that Edward R. Belcher James Ruffin and E. D. Tarver be appointed commissioners to settle with the clerks of the Circuit & County
Court for the County and the County Trustee for the year 1829. Also that
they be appointed commissioners to settle with the Trustees of the Bolivar
Academy agreeable to the law enacted on that subject.

Ordered that William Ramsay oversee and keep in repair that part of
the Purdy Road, from the West End of Market Street to the West bank of
Spring Creek and that he have all his own hands to work under him. Recorded.

Ordered that Thomas J. Hardeman oversee and keep in repair that part
of the Summerville road from the South end of Hardeman line, to the top
of the hill west of the Branch and that he have all his own hands to work
thereon under his directions.

    Ordered by the Court a majority of Justices being present that the
Pg County Trustee pay John H. Bills Clerk of the Circuit the sum of twelve
368 dollars it being for the seal of his office & the Blank Book for Record
of said Court.

Ordered by the Court that the County Trustee pay the costs on the
following suits decided in the County Court by a majority of Justices present & when execution have been returned not satisfied To Wit

	Clerk	Sol.	Shff.	Witness
State vs. Mack Drummons	21	5.00	.60	Laird .50
" " Zackariah Chandler	4.40	5.00	2.50	L. Boy

Pg			Clerk	Sol.	Shff.	Witness
368	State vs.	Ezekial Farmer	65	5.00		L. Boyt 1.00
"	"	John Curtner	3.80	5.00	2.25	
"	"	Wm. Arnold	1.80			
"	"	Bryant Gay	2.40	5.00	.60	
"	"	John Marlin	3.40	5.00	1.10	
"	"	do	3.40	5.00	1.10	
"	"	P. S. Ramsey	3.40	5.00	1.04	Wm. Pirtle 2.75
"	"	William Murlin	2.40	5.00	1.00	
"	"	Joseph Ferris	3.40	5.10	1.25	
"	"	John Alsup	3.87½	5.00	1.41	.50
"	"	John Hays	1.80	5.00	Com. Justices	.50
"	"	Thomas L. Duncan	5.67	5.00	1.75	
"	"	do	5.67	5.00	1.91	
"	"	Benjamin Rook	1.77½	5.00	.50	
			40.06	75.00	17.29	

A. Stokes	2.00
L. Stewart	2.00
L. Stewart	1.00
A. Stewart	1.00
Wm.M. Bet	2.00
E. Right	2.00
	16.25

Ordered by the Court that the Sheriff do summon the following persons to attend at our next County Court as Jurors To Wit April Term 1829 viz Thomas Shaw, James Pirtle, John Brantley, William Richie, John

Pg 369 Cole, John Huddlestone, John Wilson, John Caldwell, Solomon Willoughby, Robert Hart, Aden Lenham, Jacob Norton, Franklin Robb, William Pirtle, Jones Robinson, Allen Hill, Charles Stewart P. Matheny, James Chisum, William Polk, Adam R. Alexander, Wilkins L. Hunt, Howell Myrick, Wm. N. Coleman, Thomas Gilliam & Williams Truett and Charles Jones to act as Constable and that Venira Facies issue accordingly.

State)
 vs.)
Eli D. Hanks)

This day came the Solicitor General on the behalf of the State and with the consent of the Court he enters a Nole presequi and thereupon came Eli D. Hanks in open Court and assumes the costs of this prosecution. Therefore it is considered by the Court that the State recover off the defendants the costs about this suit in this behalf expended etc.

State)
 vs.)
Eli Sweten)
Barker Foster)

This day came the Solicitor General on behalf of the State and with the consent of the Court enters a Nole prosequi in this case and thereupon came the defendants in proper person and assumes all costs of this prosecution therefore it is considered by the Court that the State recover off the defendant the costs about this prosecution so assumed.

State)
 vs.)
Joseph C. Teague)

This day came the Solicitor General on the part of the State and the Dept. in proper person who being charged upon the bill of Indictment pleads guilty and puts himself upon the mercy of the Court therefore it

Pg 370 is considered by the Court that the defendant be fined the sum of fifty cents and that the state recover of the said defendant his costs about

Pg
380 this suit in this behalf expended and the defendant in mercy.

State   )
   vs) Affray   )
Richard Rogers   )

This day comes the Solicitor General on the part of the State and on motion and by consent of the Court a Nolli Prosequi is entered in this case against the defendant and thereupon comes the said Richard Rogers and assumes the costs of this suit. It is therefore considered by the Court that the State recover of the said Richard Rogers her costs in this behalf expended and the defendant in mercy etc.

State   )
   vs.) Recognizance)
James M. Gunter   )

This day came into open Court James M. Gunter and John Jones who acknowledged themselves to be jointly indebted to the State of Tennessee in the sum of one hundred and twenty five dollars each, to be levied of their goods and chattels land and tenements. But to be void on condition that the said James M. Gunter do make his appearance before the Justices of this Court on the first Thursday after the 1st Monday in April next at the Court House in the Town of Bolivar then and thereto answer the

Pg   State of Tennessee on a Bill of Indictment for an Assault Battery
371 and not depart without leave first had etc.

State   )
   vs.) Indicy for a Riot)
Edward Burleson   )
Joseph Burleson   )
Alexander Aiken   )

This day came the defendant Edward Burleson into open Court and acknowledged himself to be justly indebted to the State of Tennessee in the sum of two hundred dollars to be levied of his goods and chattels land and tenements but to be void on condition that defendant do make his personal appearance before the Justices of our Court on the first Thursday after the first Monday in April next to answer the State of Tennessee on a Bill of Indictment for a Riot and not depart without leave first had etc.

Robert Robson   )
   vs) Attachment   )
John Watson   )

The plaintiff discharges all those summoned as garnishees except Wilkins I. Hunt who states that he owes John Walton eight dollars to be paid when he gets a return for his cotton, and Sand Montgomery who states that he owes John Watson three dollars and Benjamin Riddle who states that he owes John Watson and Chesterfield Bowers jointly five dollars and Thomas Whitlock who states he owes John Watson & Chesterfield Bowers five dollars jointly. But because the said Robson has not obtained judgment against the said Watson it is ordered that the Court delay rendered judgment in this case until next term of this Court.

Pg
372

Newell W. Crain   )
   vs.   )
Wm. C. Bell et ac.   )

John Reed who was summoned as a garnishee to state how much he owes William C. Bell etc. who states that he has in his hands four dollars which belongs to the said Bell therefore it is considered by the Court that the said Newel W. Crain recover of the said John Reed the sd. sum of four dollars etc.

And the Court adjourned
to tomorrow morning
9 O'clock
James Ruffin
Edmund D. Tarver.

Wednesday January 7th 1829

Court met according to adjournment Present
        The Worshipful
        James Ruffin   )
        Edmund D. Tarver) Esq. Justices.
        John Y. Cockeram)

On motion and it appearing to the satisfaction of the Court that the following executions have come to the hands of the Sheriff of this County and by him have been returned no property found. It is ordered that the costs in this behalf be paid by the County Trustee out of any monies in his hand not otherwise appropriated.

State vs. John Warren----------- Clerk 3.75
Sheriff 2.00 Solicitor 5.00 Jason Wilson-- 50¢ H. W. Brown 50¢
State vs. Thompson Edwards----Clerk 4.25
Sheriff 2.16 Solicitor 5.00 John Jones 50¢
State vs. Josiah Dunn----Clerk 3.12
Sheriff 1.25   Solicitor 5.00

William Lytle   )
    vs.   )
Thomas Simmons   )

This day came the parties by their attornies and thereupon comes a Jury of good and lawful men, To wit, William Duncan, Eli Dl Hanks, Justice Lake, Moses Force, Jesse G. Crice, Sampson Edwards, Thomas Hazlewood, James T. Scott, William R. Deberry, John P. Boydston, William W. Lennard, and John Hodges who being elected tried and sworn the truth to speak upon the issue joined on their oath to say they find the defendant indebted to the Plaintiff in the sum of fourteen hundred and eighty seven dollars and assess his damages by reason of the detention thereof to eight hundred and two dollars and forty four cents. It is therefore considered by the Court that the Plaintiff recover against the defendant the debt and damages aforesaid in form aforesaid assessed together with his costs about his suit in this behalf expended etc.

Under the care of their sworn officer the Grand Jury returned into open Court two bills of presentment one against John Reagan & Samuel Owens for an affray one against Johnson for keeping a Tippling House severally and a true bill and signed by all the Grand Jury.

Charles McAlister J R.   )
Robert Buchanan) Case No. 1   )
Edward Yorke & Edmd. McAlister   )Present James Ruffin Edmund D.
Firm of Charles McAlister J. R.   )Tarver & John Heckersons.
      vs.) Writ of Inquiry   )
Sidney F. Smith   )

This day came the Plaintiffs by their attorney and thereupon came a Jury of good and lawful men to inquire of the damages the Plaintiffs have sustained by reason of the defendants not performing his promises and undertakings To Wit Michial Beavers, James B. Smith, John Fortner

Pg
374 Andrew Cain, Daniel Minner, N. W. Crane, Booker Foster, Samuel Lambert, W. H. Duberry, Charles T. Howard, James Slaughter & Wm. W. Lannard who being elected empannelled and sworn well and truly to inquire of the damages the said plaintiffs have sustained as alleged in the Plaintiffs declaration upon their oath do say that the said Plaintiff hath sustained damages by reason of the non performance of his said promises and assumption in the Plaintiffs declaration mentioned to the sum of one hundred & sixty six dollars & forty four cents. It is therefore considered by the Court that the Plaintiffs recover of said defendant the said sum of one hundred & sixty six dollars & forty four cents damages in form aforesaid assessed by the Jury as also their costs about this suit in this behalf expended etc.

A deed of conveyance from Lenin H. Coe to Austin Miller for part of a town lot was exhibited in open Court and acknowledged by said Coe. Ordered to be certified for registration

Pg   William Banks suing   )
375 Partner firm of Mason & Banks   )
           vs.   Present same Justices
Jacky Old Adm. and John C. McKean   Adm. Estate)   as before.
Of J. E. Old deceased   )

This day came the parties by their attornies and thereupon came a Jury of good and lawful men To Wit William Duncan Eli D. Hanks, Justus Lake, Mores Floren Jesse G. Grice, Sampson Edward, Thos. Hazlewood, James T. Scott, Wm. H. Dubery, John P. Boydston, Wm. W. Lennard & John Hodges who being elected empannelled and sworn the truth to speak upon the issues joined upon their oath do say they find the issue of fully administered in favor of the defendant and that they have fully administered all the goods & chattels rights & credit of the said John E. Old decd. Thereupon they do further find the issue of payment joined in favor of the Plaintiff and that there is a balance of one hundred and forty one dollars and thirty cents due on the note declared as by the Plaintiff and they do assess his damages by reason of the detention thereof to twenty eight dollars three and per cents. It is therefore considered by the Court that the Plaintiff recover of the said defendants the said balance of one hundred and forty one dollars and thirty cents debt, and the damages aforesaid in form aforesaid assessed by the Jury to be levied of the goods & chattels of said John E. Old when they may come into the hand of the said administrator. And on motion and it appearing to the satisfaction of the Court that sufficient assets
Pg   are not in the hands of said administrators to satisfy said balance of
376 debt. Therefore it is ordered by the Court that Sciri Facias do issue to the heirs of the said John E. Old requiring them to be and appear before the Justices of the Court at the next term to show cause if any they have of can why execution should not be issued against the land and tenements of the said John E. Old at the time of his death into which legal title may have vested in said heirs by virtue of the Equity in the said John E. Old at the time of his death also his costs about his suit in this behalf expended etc.

Robert Rivers   )
        vs.) No. 7 Covenant   )
William P. Haden   )

This day came the plaintiff by his attorney and suggests the death of the Plaintiff scince the pleadings were made upoin this cause and thereupon came into Court Willie B. Peck who produce letters of administration on the estate of said Rivers, and prays to be admitted Plaintiff in said suit and that the suit aforesaid be revived and it is ordered accordingly.

Pg
376 Riddler & Howard   )
            vs.) No. 12 Certiovar)
Roderick Williams et al   )

This day came the parties by their attornies and thereupon came a
Jury of good and lawful men To Wit William Kelly, William Taylor, John
Little, James Slaughter, James Bartlett, Hansford Hanks, John F. Robertson, John Crane, Nathaniel McAfter, Nathan Fuller, Archibald Chaffin
and Jamy Rutherford who being elected empannelled and sworn well and truly
Pg to try the matter in controversy between the parties upon their oath do
377 say they find in favor of the defendants.

Therefore it is considered by the Court that the defendants go hence
without day and recover of the Plaintiffs the costs about their defense
in this behalf expended etc.

A power of attorney & Bill of Sale from Wm. H. Clifft to Enos Murphy was produced in open Court and the same duly acknowledged by said
Clifft to be his act and deed. Ordered to be certified for registration.

Samuel A. Gillespie   )
Joseph Spener firm of   )
J. A. Gillaspie   )
            vs.) Debt No. 16   )
Abner Pillow   )

This day came the parties by their attornies and thereupon came a
Jury of good and lawful men To Wit William Kelly, William Tayler, John
Little, James Slaughter, James Bartlett, Harnford Hanks, John F. Robertson, John Crane, Nathaniel McAffer, Nathan Fuller, Archibald Chaffin and
James Rutherford, who being elected empannelled and sworn the truth to
speak upon the issues joined upon their oaths do say they find the issues
joined in favor of the defendant. It is therefore considered by the
Court that the defendant go hence without day and recover of the Plaintiffs his costs in his defence expended etc. from which said Judgment
the Plaintiffs prayed and obtained an appeal to the next Circuit Court
Pg and gave bond with Roger Batton as security.
378

Gideon Pillow   )
            vs.) No. 18 Debt   )
Abner Pillow   )

This day came the parties by their attornies and thereupon came a
Jury of good and lawful men To Wit Samuel Lambert, W. H. Dubery, James
T. Scott, Moses Fuler, Wm. W. Lemnaw, William Duncan, W. R. Rogers,
Hardin S. Adams, Wm. H. Stacy, John Hodges, Thomas Hazlewood, &
William Haynes who being elected empannelled and sworn the truth to
speak upon the issues joined upon their oath do say find the issues
joined in favor of the plaintiff, and that the defendant has not paid
the debt of four hundred and niney seven dollars & forty cents debt in
the plaintiffs declaration mentioned and they assess the plaintiffs
damages by reason of the detention thereof to two hundred and three
dollars. It is therefore considered by the Court that the Plaintiffre-
cover of the said defendant the debt aforesaid and the damages aforesaid assessed by the Jury together with his costs about his suit in this
behalf expended.

A deed of conveyance from Duguid Mims to Rich'd B. Phillips for
part of a town lot was exhibited in open Court and acknowledged by said
Mims. Ordered to be certified for registration.

Pg
379 John Little   )
   vs.) No. 14 Appeal)
Thomas James   )
  This day came the parties by their attornies and thereupon came a
Jury of good and lawful men To Wit Samuel Lambert, Wm. W. Lennard,
Wm. Duncan, Wm. R. Ragon, Hardin L. Adams, Wm. H. Stacy, John Hodges,
Thomas Hazlewood & William Haynes who being elected empannelled and
sworn the truth to speak upon the matters in controversy upon their
oath do say they find in favor of the defendant. It is therefore considered by the Court that the defendant go hence without day and re-
coverof the Plaintiff his costs about his defence expended etc. from
which said Judgment the defendant prays and obtains an appeal to the next
Circuit Court and gave bond with Dan Hughes as his security.

  Goodall Caruthers   )
    vs.) Appeal No. 13)
William Whitaker   )
  This day came the Plaintiffs by their attorney and says he will no
further prosecute his appeal and takes a nonsuit. It is therefore considered by the Court that the defendant go hence without day, and recover
of the said Goodall & Caruthes and Albert G. Harper their security his
costs about his defence in this behalf expended.

  The Grand Jury discharged the 2'd day except N. W. Crain he served
3'd days.

Pg
380 Wilkins I. Hunt   )
   vs.) Debt No. 19   ) Present the same Justices as before.
Alexander McClanahan)
  This day came the parties by their attornies and thereupon came a
Jury of good and lawful men To Wit William Duncan, Eli D. Hanks, Justices
Lake, Moses Foren, Jesse G. Grice, Sampson Edward, Thomas Hazlewood,
James T. Scott, Wm. H. Duberry, John P. Boydston, Wm. W. Lennard & John
Hodges who being elected empannelled and sworn the truth to speak upon
the issues joined upon their oath do say they find the issues joined in
favor of the Plaintiff and that the defendant has not paid the debt of
one hundred and nineteen dollars and eighty three cents in the Plaintiffs
declaration mentioned And they assess his damages by reason of the detention thereof to seven dollars & twenty cents. It is therefore considered by the Court that the Plaintiff recover of the defendant the
debt aforesaid, and the damages aforesaid in form aforesaid assessed by
the Jury together with his costs about his suit in this behalf expended
etc.

  James Walker   )
  Executor etc.   )
    vs.) Covenant No. 8)
Robert Rivers   )
  This day came into open Court Willie B. Peck and produced letters
Pg of administration with the will annexed on the Estate of Robert Rivers
381 the defendant whose death was suggested at last term of this Court. And
thereupon the said Willie B. Peck administrator aforesaid acknowledges
the service of a Sciri Facias or him as administrator and pleads to
the action. And thereupon further says he has nothing to allege why
judgment should not had by the Plaintiff against him as administrator
aforesaid and in open Court confesses Judgment for the sum of two thous-
and six hundred and seventy seven dollars six sixty cents damages. It
is therefore considered by the Court that the Plaintiff recover against
the defendant the damages aforesaid, as also his costs by him about his
suit in this behalf expended to be levied of the
                goods and chattels

Pg
381 rights and credits which were of the said Robert Rivers at the time of his death, in the hands of the defendant to be administered if so much there be and if so much there be not then the costs of the proper goods and chattels land and tenements of the defendant.

Robert Rivers   )
        vs.   ) Debt   )
Martin Savage   )

     This day came the Plaintiff by his attorney and suggests the death of the Plaintiff since the Commencement of this action and thereupon came into open Court Willie B. Peck and who produces letters of administration on the Estate of said Rivers, and prays to be admitted Plaintiff on said suit and that said suit be revived which is ordered
Pg accordingly.
382

Archibald Chaffin   )
Fanny Chaffin   )
        vs.   )
Hardin S. Adams   )

     This day came the Plaintiffs by their attorney and Edward B. Hill a witness summoned on behalf of the Plaintiffs being solemnly called to come into Court and give evidence on behalf said Plaintiff came not but made default. It is therefore considered by the Court that the Plaintiff recover of said Edward B. Hill the sum of one hundred and twenty five dollars unless he appear at the next term of this Court and then cause if any he has or can why judgment final & execution thereof against him should not be had, and that a Sci Facias issue accordingly.

     A deed of conveyance from Lenin H. Coe to Levi Joy for two town lots was produced in open Court and the same acknowledged by said Coe to be his act & deed. Ordered to be certified for registration.

Nathaniel Steele   )
        vs.) Debt   ) Present James Ruffin, Edward D. Tarver and John
John H. McKinnie   ) Y. Cockeram Justices.

     This day came the parties by their attorneys and thereupon came a Jury of good and lawful men to wit, Samuel Lambert, William H. Duberry, James T. Scott, Moses Foren, William Lenard, Wm. Duncan, William R.
Pg Rogers, Hardin & Adams, Willis A. Stacy, John Hodges, Thomas Hazle-
383 wood, William Haynes who being elected empannelled and sworn the truth to speak upon the issues joined upon their oath do say they find in favour of the Plaintiff and that the defendant has not paid the debt of one thousand dollars in the plaintiffs declaration and that they assess the plaintiffs by reason of the defendants non conformance of the conditions in the covenant named to four hundred and twenty five dollars. It is therefore considered by the Court that the plaintiff recover of the defendant his debt of one thousand dollars to be discharged nevertheless by the payment of four hundred and twenty five dollars the damages aforesaid by the jury aforesaid assessed also the costs about this suit in this behalf expended etc.

                And the Court adjourned to
                Tomorrow morning 9 O'clock.
                James Ruffin J. P.
                Edmund D. Tarver J. P.
                John Y. Cockeram J. P.

Pg
384　　　　Court met according to adjournment. Present the worshipful James
Ruffin Edmund D. Tarver & John Y. Cockeram Esquires Justices, Thos. J.
Hardeman, Clerk, J. C. N. Robertson, Sheriff, V. D. Barry Solicitor.

A deed of conveyance from the commissioners of Bolivar to Allen
Hill for one town lot was produced in open Court and the execution thereof was duly proven by the oaths of Rufus P. Neilly & W. Peck the subscribing witnesses thereto. Ordered to be certified for registration.

State　　　　　　　　　)
　　vs.) A & B　　　　　)
James Gunter　　　　　　)

This day came into open Court J ames Brown and acknowledged himself
to be indebted to the State of Tennessee in the sum of one hundred and
twenty five dollars to be levied of goods and chattels land and tenements,
but to be void on condition that he the said James Brown do make his
personal appearance at the Court House in the town of Bolivar on the 1st
Thursday after the 1st Monday in April next to giveevidence on behalf
of the State against said Gunter for an assault & Battery and not depart without leave first had etc.

State　　　　　　　　　　　)
　　vs.) Overseer of Road　)
William Johnson　　　　　　)

This day came the Solicitor General on the part of the State and the
sd. William Johnson being solemnly called to come into Court and answe-
Pg　er the charge of the State on a Bill of Indictment for not keeping a
385　road of which he is overseer in order as directed by Law, came not and
Jacob Ross said defendants Bail being solemnly called to come into Court
and bring with him the body of the said William Johnson also came not
but made default. It is therefore considered by the Court and bring
with him the body of the said William Johnson also came not but made default. It is therefore considered by the Court that the State recover
of the said William Johnson and Jacob Ross the sum of one hundred and
twenty five dollars unless they do make the personal appearance before
the Justices of our Court of Pleas & Quarter Sessions on the 1st Friday
after the 1st Monday in April next and then show cause if any they have
or can why Judgment jinal and execution thereof should not be had against
them and that Sciri Facias issue accordingly.

State　　　　　　　　　)
　　vs.) A & B　　　　　)
Edward Burleson　　　　　)

This day came the Solicitor General on the part of the State and
Edward Burleson as Bail of Joseph Burleson being solemnly called to
come into Court and bring with him the body of Joseph Burleson to answer the State of Tennessee on an Indictment for an Riot came not but made
default. Therefore it is considered by the Court that the State recover of the said Edward Burleson the sum of one hundred and twenty
five dollars unless he do make his personal appearance on the 1st Thursday after the 1st Monday in April next then and there to show cause if
any he can why Judgment final and execution thereof should not be had
Pg　against him and that a Sciri Facias issue accordingly.
386
A deed of conveyance from Joseph A. Wallace to Nathaniel Stelle for
four hundred & twenty six acres in HardemanCounty was produced in open
Court and proved by the oaths of Austin Miller and Joseph Coe the subscribing witnesses thereto and was ordered to be certified for registration.

Pg
386 John Rogers)
vs.) Present James Ruffin, Edmund D. Tarver, John Y. Cock-
Duguid Mims) eram, Esq. Justices.

This day on motion and it appearing to the satisfaction of the
Court that an execution had issued against the defendant from Thomas
James Esquire Justice of the Peace for this County on behalf of the
Plaintiff the 30th day of December 1828 for eighty two dollars debt
& costs with interest from the first day of January 1828 and which
said execution had come to the hands of J. C. N. Robertson Sheriff
for said County and by him for want of personal property levied on one
and three fourth acres of land adjoining the 40 acres entered in the
name of Henderson Whitlow on the west being a part of the tract that
Majr. W m. Ramsey now lives on and including the houses where said
Mimms lately lived there being no personal property to be found. It is
therefore ordered adjudged and decreed that said land be exposed to sale
as the law directs to satisfy said debt & costs as also the costs of
their motion and that a venditiona exponas issue accordingly.

Pg
387

Francis Shoemake)
vs.) Same Justices as before.
Thomas P. Blount)

This day on motion and it appearing to the satisfaction of the
Court that an execution had issued against the defendant from Thomas
James Esquire, Justice of the peace for this County on behalf of the
plaintiff the 30th day of December 1828 for twenty dollars 81½
cents & 59 cents costs with interest from that date and which said
execution had come to the hands of Jeremiah Williams a constable for
said County and by him for want of personal property levied on one
tract of land 10 acres No. Entry 1456 in range 3 Section 3--8 acres
No. 1457 Range 3 Section 3 entered in the name of James Wilkerson levied
on the D C C in part improvement Entry No. 806 for 172 acres on which
said Blount now lives which is in range 3 Section 3 Tenth District there
being no personal property to be found. It is therefore ordered adjudged and decreed that the aforesaid lands be exposed to sale as the
law directs to satisfy said debt and costs and also the costs of this
motion and that a venditioni Exponas issue accordingly.

Walden Fuller)
vs.)Justices as before.
Thomas P. Blount)

This day on motion and it appearing to the satisfaction of the
Court that an execution had issued against the defendant from Thomas
James Esquire Justice of the Peace for this County on behalf of the
Plaintiff the 30th day of December 1828 for fifteen dollars debt and

Pg
388

50 cents costs with interest from that date and which said execution Had
come to the hands of Jeremiah Williams a Constable for said County and
by him for want of personal property levied on one tract of land 10
acres No. Entry 1456 Range 3 Section 3 ditto tract 8-113 acres Entry
No. 1457 Range 3 Section 3 levied on one occupant improvement Entry
806 for 172 acres on which said Blount now lives which is in range 3
Section 3 tenth District there being no personal property to be found.

It is therefore ordered adjudged & decreed that the aforesaid
lands be exposed to sale as the law directs to satisfy said debt and
costs as also the costs about this motion and that a Venditiona Exponas issue accordingly.

E. B McCoy)
vs.)Same Justices.
D. P. Hannis)
E. P. Hannis)

Pg
388

This day on motion and it appeating to the satisfaction of the Court
that an execution had issued against the defendants from Joseph W. Mc-
Kean Esquire Justice of the Peace for said County on behalf of the plaintiff the 22nd October 1828 for seventy seven dollars and forty cents debt
and 50 cents cost with interest from the 28 February 1827 and which said
execution had come to the hands of Martin D. Ramsey a constable for said
County and by him for want of personal property levied on seventy five
acres of land which is part of Entry No. 1975 for 200 acres made in the
name of Enoch Hannis in the tenth survey 17 District R. 3 and S. 3 there
being no person and property found. It is therefore ordered adjudged and
decreed that the aforesaid land be exposed to sale as the law diredts to
satisfy said debt & costs also the costs of this motion & that a venditioni
Exponas issue accordingly.

Pg
389

State   )
  vs.   ) Justices Assault.
Austin Miller)

This day came the Solicitor General on the part of the state and with
the assent of the Court enters a Nol Pros. in this case and thereupon came
the defendant and assumes all costs etc. Therefore it is considered by
the Court that the State recover of the defendant the costs about this
prosecution etc.

State   )
  vs.   ) Presentment overseer)
William Robertson)

This day came the Solicitor General on the part of the State and the
said William Robertson being solemnly called to come into Court and answer
the charge of the state on a Bill of Indictment for not keeping a road
of which he is overseer in order as directed by law came not and John
Shepperd said defendants bail being solemnly called to come into Court and
bring with him the body of said William Robinson also came not but made
default. It is therefore considered by the Court that the State recover
of the said William R obinson and John Shepperd the some of one hundred
and twenty five dollars unless they do make their personal appearance before
the Justices of the Court of Pleas and Quarter Session on the first Thursday after the first Monday in April next and then show cause if any why
Judgment final & execution thereof should not be had against them and that
Sciri facias issue accordingly.

Pg
390

State   )
  vs.   ) Presentment for keeping a disorderly House.
Green Hastings)

This day came the defendant in proper person as well as the Solicitor
in behalf of the state who being arrigned pleads Not Guilty and for his
trial puts himself upon his County and the Solicitor likewise. Whereupon
came a jury of good & lawful men to wit James Slaughter, Charles T. Howard,
William W. Lenard, James Bartlett, William Kearly, William Taylor, William
R. Rogers, Daniel Mimms, Hugh A. Reynold, John T . Robertson, John A. Neal
& Samuel Lambert who being elected empannelled and sworn the truth to speak
upon the issues joined. But failing to ggree in their verdict by consent
of parties it is ordered that a juror be drawn and the balance respited from
rendered their verdict and cause stand for trial at the next term etc.
Whereupon the said Green Hastings and James Barkley come into Court and acknowledged themselves to owe and be indebted to the state of Tennessee in the
sum of one hundred and twenty five dollars each to be levied of theirrespect-
ive goods and chattels lands & tenements, but to be void upon dondition that
the said Green Hastings appear at the next term of this Court to answer the

Pg
390 state on the above charge and not depart hence without leave of the
Court first had & obtained etc.

Pg
391 State   )
  vs.   )
James Scott   ) Indictment for an affray)
Woods M. Smith)

   This cause having been continued until next term the said James
T. Scott and Thomas N. Giles came into Court and acknowledged themselves
to owe and be indebted to the state of Tennessee in the sum of of one
hundred and twenty five dollars each to be levied of their respective
goods & chattels lands & tenements to severally but to be void upon the
condition that the said James T. Scott appear at the next term of this
Court and answer the state on the above charge. And the said Woods M.
Smith come into Court and acknowledged himself to owe and be indebted to
the State of Tennessee in the penal sum of one hundred and twenty five
dollars to be levied of his goods & chattles lands and tenements but
to be void upon condition that the said Wood N. Smiths appear at the next
term of this Court to answer the above charge and not depart hence without
leave of the Court first had & obtained etc.

State   )
  vs   ) Sci Fa
Charles Jones   )

   This day came the defendant in proper person and the solicitor on
the part of the state and for reasons appearing to the satisfaction of
Court it is ordered that the forfeiture in this case be remitted and that
the defendant pay the costs. Whereupon the defendant paid said costs and
Pg is discharged hence without day etc.
392

State   )
  vs.   )
Bales & Johnson) Presentment for keeping a tipling house.
  & x   )
Adam Tabler   )

   This day came the defendants in proper person as well as the Solicitor on the behalf of the state. And for reasons appearing to the
satisfaction of the Court it is ordered that a Nolli Prosequi be entered.
Whereupon the defendants came into Court assumed all the costs in this
case. It is therefore considered by the Court that the state recover
of the said the defendants her costs about this suit in this behalf expended etc.

State   )
  vs.   ) Forfeiture & Sci Fa
Thomas J. Oliver)

   This day came the defendant in proper person & showed cause why
he did not attend as a witness in the case state vs. Foster and for
reasons appearing to the satisfaction it is ordered that the forfeiture in
this case be set aside on the defendants paying the costs of the Surifacias
in this case and that the state have her execution etc.

State   )
  vs.   )
Hansford Hanks)

Pg
392
      This day came the Solicitor General on part of the State and with
the assent of the Court enters a Nole prosequi in this case and it is
ordered by the Court that the County pay the costs of this prosecution.

      The Court adjourned till tomorrow morning 9 O'clock. James Ruffin,
J. P. Edmund D. Tarver, J. P. John Y. Cockeram, J. P.

Friday 9th Jan. Term 1829

Pg
393
      Court met according to adjournment. Present the worshipful James
Ruffin, John Y. Cockeram Edward D. Tarver, Esquires Justices for Hardeman County .

      A deed of conveyance from Thomas James to Green Hastings for one
half of a town lot in Bolivar was produced in open Court and duly acknowledged by said James to be his deed and ordered to be certified for
registration.

      A deed of conveyance from Thomas N. Giles to Green Hastings for
part of a town lot was duly acknowledged by said Giles to be his deed and
ordered to be certified for registration.

Harton & Elrod   )
    vs.   )
Amos Warner et al   )

      This day on motion and it appearing to the satisfaction of the Court
that an execution had issued on the 3'd day of September 1827 from William B. Robinson a Justice of the Peace for said County in favor of the
Plaintiffs for sixty seven dollars 96 cents with interest from the 3rd
day of September 1827 & fifty cents costs which came to the hands of
Philip I. Keanney a constable for said County and for want of personal
property levied on 44 acres of land in Range 1 Section 3 10th District
on the property of Amos Warner. It is therefore ordered adjudged and
decreed that the said tract of land be exposed to sale as the law directs
to satisfy said debt & costs and also the costs of this motion & that
a venditiona exponas issue accordingly.

      An inventory of the Estate William Martindale returned in Court.
Ordered to be recorded.

      The Commissioners who was appointed to lay off & set a part one years
provisions for the widow of William Martindale decd. returned in Court
ordered to be recorded.

Pg
394
      Ordered that Gersham Mooss oversee the clearing out and keep in
repair the Summerville Road from Arthur Morrows west to Spring Creek
and that he have all the hands of Rivers Ridgeway Pearson Daniel Thomas
McClehans James Lee Joel & Alfred Rainer B. Yeasy E. Bennett H. & I.
Williams work thereon under his directions.

      Ordered that Isaih Davis oversee the clearing out and keep in re-
pair the road from said Davises to Shirly Goodwins and that all the
hands one mile north of the road and as far south as to take in Hills
& Davises also Mafields be Robinsons C agle J. C. Harris & Steders hands
work thereon under his directions 2nd class.

      This day came into open Court William Chisum and on application and
all matters and things thereunto arising being properly understood it
was ordered by the Court that said William Chisum be appointed guardean
to Jackson Meacham and Caroline Mecham minor orphans of John Mecham deceased who gave bond of two hundred dollars with J. C. N. Robertson as
his security for the performance of his guardeanship.

Pg
394
    This day came into open Court Abram May and moved the Court to have Miles Birdsong bound to him and after all things thereunto being properly understood it was considered by the Court to said Miles Birdsong be bound until his 21 years old to sd. May as follows at the time of his arriving to the age of twenty one years he is to receive from said May a horse

Pg
395
worth sixty dollars a bridle and saddle and two good suits of decent clothes he is to be caused to be taught and instructed to read write and arithmetic as faras the rule of three inclusive.

    On application of Thomas James it was ordered by the Court that he have license to keep an ordinary at his now dwelling house.

    Ordered that Thomas Shaw oversee the clearing out and keep in repair that part of the road leading from the north boundary of this county in a direction from Estinaula to where Charles Polk formerly lived that lies between said County line and David Lanes and that hh have all the hands north of said Lanes that is or maybe living within one mile and a half of said road and report to next term of this Court.

    Ordered that David Lane oversee and keep in repair that part of the Estinola road from Charles Polks old place from said lanes to where said road crosses the west fork of Clear Creek and that all the hands north of said fork that lives within a mile and a half of said road & south of said Lanes and report to next Court.

    Ordered that William Richy oversee the clearing out and keep in repair that part of the Estinola road that lies between the west fork of Clear Creek and Charles Polks old place so as to intersect the Somerville road at said Polks old place and that all the hands south of said fork of

Pg
396
Clear Creek that lives within a mile and a half of said road and north of said Polks old place work thereon under his directions & report to next Court.

    Ordered that William Ramsey oversee the clearing out and keep in repair a road of the first class from the north end of Water Street in Bolivar to the foot of the bridge on Hatchee as marked out by the Jury of view and that he have his own hands those of Capt. McNeals Col. Robertsons and all thats living on the present road to the Bridge and those living at the upper ferry and all the hands between said Road & Spring Creek work thereon under his directions.

    Wm. Kearly, James Slaughter, William D. Taylor, Charles T. Howard & William W. Lennard served four days as jurors, Samuel Lambert three jurors.

    Ordered that David C. Pouch oversee the clearing out and keep in repair that part of the road from Bolivar to Simpsons Ferry from Amos Johnsons to Elkins Bridge and that all the hands of the south side of Johnsons branch that worked under J. H. Arnold work thereon under his direction except Henry Jacobs.

    Ordered that Green B. Carter oversee the clearing out and keep in repair the road from the north end of Main Street in Bolivar to the Bridge on Hatchee so far as where it intersects the other road and that all the hands that live on the west of said Road in the distance of one half mile and the hands on the East of said road & west of a line equidistant between

Pg
397
the said road and the road leading out of Water Street except Cal Robertsons hands work thereon under his directions this road of the first class.

Present James Ruffin, Edmund D. Tarver, John Y. Cockeram, Thomas James Francis Shoemake West Hariss, Joseph W. McKean & Walter Scott, Esquires.

State of Tennessee)
Hardeman County)
Persuant to an order of the County Court at January Term 1829 we the undersigned after being duly sworn according to law have viewed and marked a road from the north end of Main Street in the town of Bolivar north withx a line of marked trees leaving the house that William Land now lives in a little distance on the right thence a little East of North with a line of marked trees to where it intersects the road leading from Water Street to the Bridge at or near a large White oak that is marked by us we also assessed the damages to Rea and Co. for the said Road going through their land to nothing as we believe the road as marked by us to be an advantage to said land given by us this 9th day of January 1829. Edmund D. Tarver, N. W. Crain, James Ruffin, John Y. Cockeram, West Harris.

The Trustees of E. T. College)
vs.)
John A. Nears)
Ordered that the parties have leave to take depositions in this case by giving thirty days notices where it is to be taken out of the state
Pg
398
agreeable to law.

William Lane)
vs.) Debt) Justices Present, James Ruffin, Edmund D. Tarver,
Martin Taylor) John Y. Cockeram.
This day came the parties by their attorneys and thereupon came a Jury of good and lawful men to wit, Hugh A. Reyholds, John F. Robertson, James Slaughter, Charles T. Howard, William W. Lennard, John A. Neal, Vincent Willoughby, William P. Haden, Solomon Willoughby, George Martin, William Kearly & William Taylor who being elected empaneled and sworn the truth to speak upon the issues joined upon their oath do say they find the issues joined in favor of the Plaintiff and that the defendant hath not paid the debt of one hundred and eleven dollars sixty six cents in the Plaintiff declaration mentioned and they do assess his damages by reason of the detention thereof to seventeen dollars and seventy six cents. It is therefore considered by the Court that the Plaintiff recover of the defend- ant the debt aforesaid, and the damages aforesaid in form aforesaid assessed by the Jury as also his costs about his suit in this behalf ex- pended etc. And the plea of Nul Ful record being here by the Court tried there is the opinion of the Court that there is such record as the plain-
Pg
399
tiff in pleading hath alleged.

Stephen Hard)
vs.) No. 25 Debt) Present same Justices as before.
Mattain Taylor)
This day came the parties by their attornies and thereupon came a Jury of good and lawful men To Wit John F. Robertson, John Crain, James Slaughter, Charles T. Howard, William W. Lennard, John A. Neal, Vincent Willoughby, George Martin William Kearly & William Taylor who being elected empannelled and sworn the truth to speak upon the issues joined upon their

Pg
399 oath do say they find the issues joined upon their oath do say they
find the issues joined in favor of the Plaintiff and that the defendant
hath not paid the debt of ninety six dollars in the Plaintiff declaration mentioned and they do assesss his damages by reason of the detention thereof to twelve dollars and fifty cents. It is therefore considered by the Court that the Plaintiff recover of the defendant the
debt aforesaid together with the damages aforesaid in form aforesaid assessed
by the Jury together with his costs by him about his suit in this behalf
expended etc.

Joseph Taylor   )
        vs.   ) No. 26 Covenant   ) Present same Justices as before.
James H. Sheppard   )

Pg   This day came the parties by their attornies and thereupon came a
400 Jury of good and lawful men To Wit John F. Robertson, James Slaughter,W. Kerley
Charles T. Howard, William W. Lennard, John A. Neal, Vincent Willoughby,
Wm. P. Haden, Solomon Willoughby, George Martin, William Taylor & John
Crain who being elected empannelled and sworn the truth to speak upon
the issues joined upon their oath do say they find the issues joined in
favor of the plaintiff and they do assess the plaintiff damages by reason
of the defendants non performance of his covenant as alleged in the
plaintiffs declaration to one hundred and six dollars and ninety cents.

It is therefore considered by the Court that the Plaintiff recover
of the defendant his damages aforesaid in form aforesaid assessed by the
Jury, as also his costs about his suit in this behalf expended etc.

Williams Truett   )
        vs.   ) No. 31 Appeal for J. P.)
John Thompson   )

This day came Williams Truett by his attorney and the defendant John
Thompson being solemnly called to come into Court and prosecute his said
Appeal came not but made default. It is therefore considered by the Court
that the Judgment of the Justices below in all things be affirmed and that
Pg   the Plaintiff recover of the default and on motion of Daniel Davis his se-
401 curity the sum of eight dollars and six cents debt with 12½ per. cent as also
his costs as well below or in this Court expended about his suit etc.

Ambrose Carter   )
     vs.) Certiovari Motion to Dismiss)
William Jacob   )

This day came the parties by their attorneys and thereupon the motion
to dismiss being argued by council and now fully understood. It is the
opinion of the Court that the said motion be sustained and that the said
William Jacobs recover of the said Ambrose Carter and Green B. Carter his
security in the certiovari the sum of three dollars the amt. of the judgment
below the Justices of the peace also the costs as well before the Justice as
in this Court etc.

John McCrabb   )
     vs.   ) Attachment
William S. Haynes   )

This day comes the plaintiff and say s he will no further prosecute his
suit and dismisses the same. It is therefore considered by the Court that
the defendant recover of the plaintiff recover of the plaintiff his costs
about this suit expended etc.

                    And the Court adjourned
                    to tomorrow morning
                        9 O'clock.
                        Edmund D. Tarver J. P.
                        J. W. McKean J. P.
                        F Shoemake J. P.

Pg
402

The Court met according to adjournment. Present the worshipful
Edmund D. Tarver, Joseph W. McKean, Francis Shoemake, Esquires Justices.
Thomas J. Hardeman Clk.   J. C. N. Robertson, Shff.

A deed of trust from R. S. T. Stone to Austin Miller was exhibited
in open Court and proven by the oaths of David F. Brown & Jos. I. Deen
two of the subscribing witnesses thereto and ordered to be certified for
registration.

The Commissioners appointed to settle with John Crane Guardian of
Sally Hopper & Jeremiah Hopper returned an account of the same into Court.
Ordered to be recorded.

Robert Robson   ) Attachment)
John Watson   )
This day came the plaintiff by his attorney and the defendant being
solemnly called to come into Court and defend this suit came not. It is
therefore considered that the plaintiff recover of the defendant but
because it is not known what damages the plaintiff has sustained it is
ordered that a jury come at the next term of this Court to inquire of the
same etc.

Ordered that the Clerk make out a list of such Guardians that have not
reported etc. The Court then adjourned until Court in course.

                                        Edmund D. Tarver J. P.
                                        J. W McKean   J. P.
                                        J. Shoemake   J. P.

Monday April 6th 1829

Pg
403

At a Court of pleas and quarter sessions begun and held for the
County of Hardeman at the Courthouse in the town of Bolivar on Monday the
sixth day of April A. D. 1829. Present the worshipful James Ruffin,
Edward D. Tarver, John Y. Cockeram, Elijah Gossett, William B. Robertson,
West Harris, Thomas James, Joseph W. McKean, T hornton Jones Alexander
McKenqie, Lazarus Stewart, Walter Scott, William L. Duncan, John Rosson--
Thomas J. Hardeman, Clerk, Julius C. N. Robertson, Sheriff, Valentine D.
Barry, Solicitor General.

Ordered that Green Carter oversee the keeping in repair of the road
leading from the north end of Main Street in the town of Bolivar to the
bridge on Hatchee and that he have the same hands that now work under him.
Also that William Ramsey oversee the keeping in repair of the road from
the north end of Water Street in said town to the bridgeon Hatchie with
the same hands that now work under him and that said Ramsey have the
direction of his own as well on said Carters land from the forks of said
road on the north of said town to said bridge.

A deed of conveyance from Ninican Steele to Nathan Smith for 50½
acres of land was exhibited in open Court and the same acknowledged by
Pg   the said Steele to be his act and deed. Ordered to be certified for
404   registration.

A deed of conveyance from Ninican Steele to William Ritchey for
50 pr. acres of land was produced in open Court and the execution thereof
acknowledged by said Steele to be his act and deed. Ordered to be
certified for registration.

Pg 404   An article of agreement between O. S. Harvey and Samuel F. Steele was produced in open Court and this execution thereof proven by the oath of Nincan Steele subscribing witness thereto. Ordered to be certified for registration.

Joseph Butchee produced in open Court one wolf scalp adjudged by the Court over 4 months old. Ordered that he have a certificate for the same.

An order from Valentine Callahan to Eli hu Crisp, was produced in open Court and prove by the oaths of John Brantley and Blake Brantley subscribing witnesses thereto1 Ordered to be certified for registration.

A deed of Trust from R. B. Phillips to V. D. Barry was produced in open Court and the execution thereof for the purposes therein contained proven by the oaths of John N. Bills & Leroy Burt subscribing witnesses. Ordered to be certified for registration.

Pg 405   A deed of conveyance from William P. Cunningham to Eli Murphy for 80 acres of land was produced in open Court and acknowledged by said Cunningham to be his act and deed. Ordered to be certified for registration.

A deed of conveyance from Chancy Davenport to Edward Osward for one town lot was produced in open Court and the execution thereof proven by the oaths of E. R. Belcher & Thos. N. Giles subscribing witnesses thereto1 Ordered to be certified for registration.

A deed of conveyance from the Commissioners of the Town of Bolivar to Milton Moore for two town lots was exhibited in open Court and acknowleded by John H. Bills, Thomas J. Hardeman & West Harris three of said Commissioners to be their act and deed. Ordered to be certified for registration.

A deed of Trust from Daniel W. Love to Edward R Belcher was produced in open Court and the execution thereof for the purposes therein expressed proven by the oaths of Adam Tabler & Allen Hill. Ordered to be certified for registration.

A deed of conveyance from Aden Langhonn to David Hannis for 22 acres of land was exhibited in open Court and acknowledged by said Langhon to be his act and deed. Ordered to be certified for registration.

Pg 406   A deed of conveyance from Hugh Carothers to William A. Moore was produced in open Court and the execution thereof duly acknowledged by said Carothers to be his act and deed. Ordered to be certified for registration1

A deed of conveyance from William D . White et al to N. R. W. Hill was exhibited in open Court and the execution thereof duly proven by the oaths of D. F. Brown and W. W. Boman subscribing witnesses as to him and ordered to be certified for registration.

A plot & certificate with the assignments thereon from Joseph Rogers to Thomas Arrigton was produced in open Court and the execution thereof duly proven by the oaths of Thomas T. Gillespie and the signature of A. L. Parrish the other subscribing witness approved by said Thomas I. Gillespie. Ordered to be certified.

Pg
406   An occupant claim with the transfer thereon from William Duncan to Robert Thompson was exhibited in open Court and proven by the oath of Wm. L. Duncan a subscribing witness thereto. Ordered to be certified for registration.

Pg
407   Two plots & certificates with the transfer thereon from Robert Ferbarh to Wilson Wade was produced in open Court and proven by the oaths of A. Miller and V. D. Berry subscribing witnesses thereto. Ordered to be certified.

        A deed of conveyance from Amerot Johnson to Caleb P. Alexander for 280 acres of land was exhibited in open Court and proven by the oaths of E. W. Hannis & John W. Jones subscribing witnesses thereto. Ordered to be certified for registration.

        A deed of conveyance from James McDowell to Peter Rogers for 80 acres of land was produced in open Court and acknowledged by said McDowell to be his act and deed. Ordered to be certified for registration.

        A deed of conveyance from Adam R. Alexander atto in fact for James Henry to John Reagan for 154 acres of land was produced in open Court and acknowledged by said Alexander to be his act and deed. Ordered to be certified for registration.

        A deed of conveyance from Thomas McNeal to West Harris for 75 acres of land was produced in open Court and the execution thereof duly acknowledged by said McNeal to be his act and deed. Ordered to be certified for registration.

        A plot & certificate with the transfer thereon from Wilie Jones to
Pg   John & Starling Knuckles was exhibited in open Court and acknowledged by
408   said Jones. Ordered to be certified.

        A deed of conveyance from John U. McKinnie to James Eastham for 200 acres of land was produced in open Court and acknowledged by the said McKinnie to be his act and deed. Ordered to be certified for registration.

        A Bill of Sale from Joseph C. Teague to William Simpson for a horse was produced in open Court and the execution thereof proven by oath of Marshal Seddens one of the subscribing witnesses. Ordered to be certified for registration.

        A Bill of Sale from Lewis B. Allen to Wm. Simpson was exhibited in open Court, and the execution thereof proven by the oath of Marshal Seddens one of the subscribing witnesses thereto. Ordered to be certified for registration.

        An inventory of the property belonging to the heirs of Samuel F. Steele deceased returned into Court by David F. Carnes then guardian and ordered to be recorded.

        The Court proceeded to the election of a constable in Capt. Walkers Company. Whereupon on balloting Charles Jones was duly elected and qualified and gave bond with U. A. Brown & Isaac Jones as his security. They then proceeded to the choosing of a constable in Cap. Boytes Company. Whereupon
Pg   on balloting it appeared that Isaac Simpson was duly elected qualified and
409   gave bond with William Simpson and Wm. L. Duncan as his security.

Pg
409   This day came into open Court John Mills, and prayed the Court to be permitted to administer on the Estate of Armstead Martin deceased and it appearing to the satisfaction of the Court that the said Martin died without making a will. It is therefore ordered by the Court that the said Mills be allowed to administer thereon, and thereupon the then said Mills came forward and qualified as administrater aforesaid, and gave bond with Wm. Ramsey & Regan B. Cockeram as his security and received letters of administration.

Ordered by the Court that Wm. F. Rawlings have leave to keep an ordinary in the County of Hardeman and who thereupon gave bond with D. W. Love & James Stephens as his securities and was qualified. Also ordered by the Court that Arthur Morrow have license to keep an ordinary at his house in said County and who gave bond with J. C. N. Robertson as his security and was qualified as the law directs.

An inventory and Account Sales of the property of Wm. N. Fleming decd. was returned into open Court by James Ruffin, Executor and ordered to be recorded.

Pg
410   An account Sales of the property of Eli Donald decd. was returned into Court by the administrater and ordered to be recorded.

An Account Sales of the Estate of Drusilla Satterwhite decd. was returned into Court by R. C. Moore administrator and ordered to be recorded.

An inventory & Acct. Sales of the property of Geo. L. Campbell decd. was returned into Court by John Mollory administrator and ordered to be recorded.

The Commissioners appointed to settle with Danl. Hughes adm. of David Tedford decd. made a report to Court. Ordered that the same be recorded.

Ordered by the Court that E. R. Belcher and James B. Smith be appointed Commissioners to settle with Green B. Carter Adm. of N. Wapkins decd. and make report.

Ordered that the County Trustee pay a majority of the Justices being present and voting for the same William Overall the sum of twenty five dollars for attending, nursing and burying Enoch Wade a pauper who died at his house in this county.

Ordered by the Court there being a majority of Justices present and voting for the same that the County Trustee pay Geo. M. Pirtle seven
Pg
411   dollars & fifty cents his services for three days in settling with clerks & County Trustee as Commissioners of the County Revenue.

Ordered by the Court there being a majority present and voting for the same that the County Trustee pay Austin Miller twelve dollars & fifty cents for five days services in settling with the clerks & Trustee of this County or County Commissioners.

Ordered by the Court, there being a majority of Justices present voting for the same that the County Trustee pay Shedrock Owens, Willis Dillard & Owen Dillard thirty dollars as additional to their former compensation for building a bridge over Spring Creek.

Pg
411   Ordered by the Court that the County Trustee pay Jasen Wilson (a majority voting of the magistrates for the same) five dollars and fifty cents for taking care of prisoner Aluce McDonald arrested on a charge of hors stealing.

Ordered that the County Trustee pay John Dunaway the sum of six dollars for parting sheep, proven away from said Dunaway (a majority of Justices being present and voting for the same). It seemed that he had wrongfully paid said sum to Trustee.

Ordered by the Court (there being a majority of Justices present and unanimously voting for the same) that the County Trustee pay Thomas J.
Pg   Hardeman Clerk of this our Court forty eight dollars and fifty cents for
412 Books purchased by him for the use of his officer agreeable to accounts exhibited the Court.

Ordered by the Court (a majority of the Justices present and voting for the same) that the County Trustee pay Julius C. N. Burton the sum of sixty dollars out of any monies in his hands not otherwise appropriated for the support of two children of said Burton which have become a county charge.

Ordered by the Court that W. R. Belcher F. Shoemake & Jos W. McKean be appointed commissioners to settle with Robt. C. Moore as administrator of the estate of Drusilla Satterwhite decd. and make report thereon.

Ordered that the Clerk of the County Court be allowed to keep his office in one of the rooms of the Court House, and that the key of the Court House be put in his possession.

On motion of Wm. Fentress. It is ordered by the Court A. Kirkpatrick and Charles Stewart be permitted to put a lock onm one of the Court House doors and that one of them keep the key thereof constantly, and be allowed to use the house for purposes of Religious Worship so as not to interfere with publick requisitions.

Pg   Ordered that Joseph W. McKean, Thomas James, Alexander Kirkpatrick,
413 & F. Shoemake, be appointed to settle with Richard Lamb Adm. of M. Pirtle & also make a division of the property and make him an allowance for the support of Pirtles heirs for the last 14 months.

Ordered by the Court that Joseph W. McKean & Francis Shoemake Esq. be appointed Commissioners to settle with Alexander G. Nielson guardian of the minor heirs of Ezekial Polk deceased and report to next Court.

Ordered by the Court that Joseph W. Talbot of Jackson, Madison County, and John W. Bills of Hardeman County or either of them be appointed commissioners to settle and adjust with the proper authorities of the County of Madison, or any commissioners appointed on their part the claim of this County, upon that County for the taxes due by act of Assembly, and make report to the next term.

Ordered by the Court that Friday next be set apart for County business.

The last will and testament of John Wright deceased was produced in open Court and offered for record and it appearing to the satisfaction of

Pg
413 the Court that there are no witnesses to said Will at the time of its execution. Thereupon came John Rosson, Anderson Street and Joseph L. Rosson who
Pg being sworn in due form of law say that they believe the said will to be in
414 the handwriting of John Wright and that they are well acquainted with his
writing and that the signature to said will is that of John Wrights to the
best of their belief. Ordered by the Court that the same be recorded.

The Commissioners of the County Revenue returned into Court a report
and settlement with the County Trustee for the year 1828 and which was
ordered to be recorded.

Ordered by the Court that Richard Lamb administrator of the estate
Michial Pirtle deceased give new security for the faithful administration of
the estate of said Pirtle deceased against the last day of this Court or
surrender the goods and chattels of said estate into the hand of Carter C.
Collins and Benjamin Gay his present securities.

Ordered that James Lane oversee the clearing out and keeping in repair
that part of the Simpsons ferry road from Elkins branch to Cub Creek and
that all the hands living between those points that have heretofore worked
on said road work under his directions 2nd class.

Ordered that David McKennie oversee the clearing out and keep in repair
Pg that part of the Simpsons ferry road from Cub Creek to Porters Creek and all
415 the hands that live between these points that worked on said road heretofore
work under his directions 2nd class.

Ordered by the Court that the Simpsons ferry road as it at present runs
round Robert Rivers field be established as the proper course.

Ordered by the Court that William Bryant, Adam R. Alexander, Caleb
Brock, Peter C. Reeves & John Polk or any three of them be appointed Commissioners to divide and lay off the proportion of Jacob Burleson & wife to
property on the estate of Aaron Burleson decd. and make report to this term.

Ordered that Amos G. Thompson, oversee and keep in repair the road
leading from Thomas Washburns to Coxes Mill as far as Dobbs Cabin, and that
all the hands, Henry Thompson, W. Lea, T. Woods, I. Lowdermilk, & G. Reed
work thereon under his direction 2nd class.

Ordered that James Baker oversee and keep in repair the road leading from
Boydstones ferry to McNairy County line, and that he have all the hands living
within two miles to the north of said road to work under his directions.

Ordered that John P. Boydstone oversee the road from his ferry to B.
B. Boydstones and that he have B. Boydstones, Saml. Barnetts, Elernelius
Hoopers hands to work under his directions.

Ordered by the Court that Charles Cock, Thomas Cox, John Brantley, Joseph
Pg Jones, Joseph Fonber and John Elliston, R. I. Crawford or any five of them be
416 a Jury of view to view and mark the road from Henry Goodwins to intersect
the old state line near the Widow Nails the nearest and best way and make
report to next Court.

Ordered that John Bradford, Shirley Tisdale, Isaac McElroy, Larkin
Hess, Benjamin Pirtle, William Pirtle, John Murray, & George Terry of any
five of them be a Jury of view to bear and mark out a road the nearest and

175

Pg
416 best way from the north end of the Coast way, through the low ground of big
Hatchie Crossing Mill Creek at Murrays Bridge so as to intersect the old
Brownsville Road on the ridge between Mill Creek and Clover Creek.

Ordered that Hugh M. Simpson oversee and keepin repair that part La
Grange road from the Widow Nails to the S. W . boundary of the County
toward La Grange for 1½ miles that he have all the hands to work under his
directiona 2nd class.

Ordered that Robert Ford, Wm. Ramsey, Jacob Moreton, Thomas James, Isaac
Brown, W. W. Maker & James B. Smith or any five of them be appointed a Jury
of view to view and mark out a road, the nearest and best way from Bolivar
to Fdds ferry on Hatchie River and report to next Court.

Ordered that Edmund Philpot have leave to turn the road leading from
Bolivar to Summerville about three hundred yards so as not to run through
Pg his field, and that he have leave to shut up the road as it now runs where
417 the one contemplated is opened.

Ordered that Thomas Joyner oversee and keep in repair that part of the
road, leading from Bolivar to Jackson from the north end of the causeway
to Vincent Willoughbys and that he have all the hands that formerly worked
under his directions.

Ordered that Hugh Pipkin oversee the clearing out and keep in repair
that part of the Larkin road, from Vincent Willoughbys to Mill Creek and
that he have the hands that worked under the direction of David Hanis To Wit
Jesse Pipkin, James Pipkin, James Pilos, Hensen Day, Milton Day, Robert D.
& A. Jackson, Geo. S. Gibson, John Henson, James McKerby, J. Henley, Greene
Robb & David Hannis and all others within his bounds.

Ordered that Joseph Jones be appointed overseer of the road from said
Jones to Coxes Mill on Spring Creek, and that he have all the hands within
1½ miles of said road to work under his directions.

Ordered that David Lane overseer the keeping in repair that part of
the Etanaula road that lies between his house and Clear Creek and that he
have James Mitchel, Robert Mitchel & John, E. D. Tarver hands Samuel Duncan
and the hand of Joseph Tayler Jr. to work under his directions.

Ordered that Nath E. Norment, Wm. Posten, John Elgin, Edw. L. Peters,
Thomas Wilkes and E. D. Tarver or any five of them be a Jury of view to
mark that part of the road leading from the mouth of Clover Creek to Summerville from the South End of Thomas Wilkes field to the County line, where
the said road from Sommerville strikes the line between said County and
report etc.

Pg   Ordered that Moses Bumpass oversee and keep in repair that part of the
418 Cotton Gin Road from the State line to Spring Creek a little north of Mullens
Store and have all the hands that workedm under D. F. Rees.

Ordered that Thomas McNeal, Rob C. Moore, Green Roper, Wm. P. Haden,
Nicholas Nail, Joshua Hazlewood & Wm. Remsay or any five of them be appointed
a Jury to assess the damages for two roads running through the land of J.
C. N. Robertson from Bolivar to the Bridge on Hatchie River and make return
to the present term of this Court.

Pg
418   Ordered that John Neely oversee and keep in repair that part of the
road, that A. Nail worked and the same hands, beginning at the Creek near the
widow Nails and work to Coxes branch.

Ordered that Alexander G. Neilson oversee that part of the Sommerville
road from the east end of his fence, west to the third range line in place
of William Johnson and that he have all the hands of E. Fitzhugh, A. Foster
and the widow Patrick and all within one half mile on the north side of said
road, and all within one mile of the south side of said road to work thereon
under his directions, with leave to cross Pleasant Run at Hardeman Mill provided its the best way 2nd class.

Ordered that Edward Philpot, Geo. M. Pirtle, Charles W. Hutcherson,
Pg   Rowley Gray, Mark Alexander, Samuel Rogers, Burley Needham and John Lea be
419   appointed a Jury of view to mark out a road leading from Bolivar in a direction
for Sommerville as far west as the County line and report to next Court.

Ordered that John Kelly be appointed overseer to keep in repair the road
from Kellys bridge on Spring Creek to where it intersects the Simpsons ferry
road and have the two Parkers Abrm. Smith, I. Bartletts, Hillen Williams,
Rainers, McClanhan, Jos. Slaughter, Jas. Kelly, Potts, Jos. Litten, John Gram
& Allen Hamlan to work under his directions.

Ordered that William Taylor oversee and keep in repair the road formerly
kept up by John Teague and have the same hands.

Ordered by the Court that Garret Moore oversee and keep in repair, the
road leading from the new bridge near Bolivar in Spring Creek on towards the
Bridge on Johnsons Creek near Robt. Kellys so as to intersect the Purdy Road
leading on to Hays ferry and have all the hands that lately worked under
Robert Kelly.

Ordered that William Todd, Henry T. Rucker, John Wilson, John Moore,
John Campbell, Levi Todd, be a Jury of view to mark and alter the road leading
from John Moores to Short Creek toward Brownsville to intersect near Capt.
Reynolds so as not to interfere with Robt. Farbush.

Ordered that John Rogers, Joseph Stewart, William P. Stewart, Eli
Pyres & Eli Crum be a Jury of view to lay out and mark a road from John Burns
by Davis Mill on Porters Creek the nearest and best way on to Bolivar and
report to next Court.

Pg   This day came into open Court Thomas P. Blount and he the said Blount
420   being delivered up by his bail. He prays the Court to be permitted to take
the benefit of the Insolvent oath of the State. And the Court being satisfied
as to the petitioners claims and he having filed a khedule of property as the
law directs. It was ordered that the oath be administered which was done accordingly by the Clerk and the said Blount discharged.

Ordered by the Court that the following persons be summoned by the
Sheriff to appear at the next Circuit Court for this County to be held en the
4th Monday in May to act as Jurors, To Wit William Ramsay, Thomas N. Giles,
Alext. G. Neilson, Thornton Jones, John Ruffin, Joseph Taylor Sr. Ebenezer
Killpatrick, William Sparks, Daniel Smith, Benjamin Bowers, Lewis Johnson,
Isaac Ricks, James Duff, Joseph Shaw, Benjamin Pirtle, William Stephens, John
P. Robertson, William A. Moore, Wm. L. Duncan, Thomas Boyt, John Rosson, John
Chisum, John Cole, Robert Moore, William Kearly & Oney S. Harvey and also

Pg
420 Anthony Bennett Philip I. Kearney as Constables and that a Veniri Facias
issue accordingly . And the Court adjourned to tomorrow morning 9 0'clcokk.
James Ruffin
Edmund D. Tarver
John Y. Cockeram

Pg
421 _____ Tuesday 7th April Term 1829 _____

Court met according to adjournment. Present the worshipful James
Ruffin, Edmund D. Tarver, John Y. Cockeram, Esquires Justices.
Thomas J. Hardeman Clerk
J. C. N. Robertson, Sheriff
V. D. Barry Solicitor.
Proclamation being made as the form is the Sheriff returned into Court
a Venira facias in the words & figures following (to wit) The State of
Tennessee to the Sheriff of Hardeman County Greeting. You are hereby com-
manded to summon the following persons to attend at our next County Court
to be held on the first Tuesday after the 1st Monday in April next to
serve as Jurors To Wit Thomas Shaw James Pirtle John Brantley William
Richie John Cole John Huddleston John Wilson John Caldwell Soloman Willoughby Robert D. Fort Aden Langhan, Jacob Norton, Franklin Robb, William
Pirtle, Jonas Robinson, Allen Hill Charles Stewart O. Matheny James Chisum
William Polk, Adam R. Alexander Wilkins I. Hunt Howel Myrick, Wm. H.
Coleman, Thomas Gilliam and Williams Trewett and Charles Jones to act as Constable and have you then there this writ witness Thomas J. Hardeman Clerk
of the Court of Pleas & Quarter Sessions for Hardeman County at office the
1st Monday in January A. D. 1829 & 53rd year of American Independence.
Thos. J. Hardeman Clerk.
On the back of which was Venira Facias to April Term 1829 issued Jan-
Pg uary 17th 1829. Came to hand same day issued. Thereby certify that I have
422 summoned all the within named Jurors and that they are all free holders or
house holders over the age of twenty one years and inhabitants of Hardeman
County given under my hand this 6th day of April 1829. J. C. N. Robertson,
Shff, out of whoom the following persons being duly elected empanaled sworn
& charged to enquire for the body of the County of Hardeman returned under
the care of their sworn officer to consider of presentments (to wit) Adam
R. Alexander foreman of the Grand Jury John Cole, Solomon Willoughby, Thomas
Shaw, John Brantley, Allen Hill, John Caldwell, John Wilson, Franklin Robb,
Aden Langhan, Wilkins I. Hunt, Robert D. Fort, Aden Langhan, Wilkins I.
Hunt, Robert D. Frost & Jenas Robertson. Charles Jones Constable sworn to
attend on the Grand Jury.

The Grand Jury returned into open Court under the charge of their
sworn officers, a Bill of Presentment. The State of Tennessee vs. John
P. Boydstone as overseer of a road. Indorsed a true bill, A. R. Alexander,
Foreman of the Grand Jury.

Robert Rivers   )
    vs.   ) Covenant No. 1)
Martin Savage   )
Henry Marsh   )
This day came the Plaintiffs by his attorney and says he will no
further prosecute his suit and thereupon came Henry Marsh one of the defendants and assumes all costs. It is therefore considered by the Court that
the Plaintiff recover of said Henry Marsh the costs aforesaid in form
aforesaid confessed and that the Plaintiff have execution etc.

Pg
422   An Account Sales of the property of Hiram Casey decd. was returned
into Court by the Executors of said estate, and ordered to be recorded.

Pg
423   An inventory and Account Sales of the Property of Robert Rivers
deceased was returned into open Court by the Executor, and the same ordered
to be recorded.

        A deed of conveyance from Duguid Mims to James Hodge for one town lot
was produced in open Court and the execution thereof acknowledged by said
Mims to be his act and deed. Ordered to be certified for registration.

        A deed of conveyance from Elijah Bass to John Williams for 100 acres
of land was produced in open Court and the same acknowledged by the said
Bass to be his act & deed. Ordered to be certified for registration.

        A deed of conveyance from Nathaniel Steele to Robert C. Friar for
224½ acres of land was exhibited in open Court and proven by the oaths of
Den M. Gwinn & C. C. Collier subscribing witnesses thereto and ordered to
be certified for registration.

        A deed of conveyance from John D. Love by his attorney A. A. King to
Nathaniel Steele for 325 acres of land was produced in open Court and the execution thereof proven by the oath of Miles Davis one of the subscribing
witnesses and ordered to be so certified.

        A deed of conveyance from Robert C. Friar to Nathaniel Steele for one
town lot was exhibited in open Court and the execution thereof proven by
the oath of Wm. Ramsay Joseph W. McKeary the subscribing witness. Ordered
to be certified for registration.

        A deed of conveyance from Grizzy Johnson to Ezekial P. McNeal for 22 3/4
Pg   acres of land was exhibited in open Court and the execution thereof proven by
424   the oaths of Jacob Moreton & Wm. Johnson subscribing witnesses thereto and
ordered to be certified for registration.

        Three plats certificates from Wm. Johnson to E P. McNeal with the
transfer thereon were produced in open Court and proved by the oaths of
C. C. Collier and Wm. R. James subscribing witnesses and ordered to be
so certified.

        A plot and certificate with the transfer thereon from John M. Davis
to Wm. E. Beavers was produced in Court and acknowledged by said Davis.
Ordered to be so certified.

        A power of attorney from Thomas M cNeal to Jesse W. Egneur was pro-
duced in open Court and the same acknowledged by said McNeal. Ordered to
be certified for registration.

David Dancey   )
     vs.) Case No. 1   ) Present James Ruffin, Edmund D. Tarver & John Y.
Abner Pillow   ) Cockeram
        This day came the parties by their attornies and thereupon came a Jury
of good and lawful men To Wit, James Chisum, Howell Mynick, Williams,Truett,
James Pirtle, Thomas Gilliam, Wm. H. Coleman, John Huddlestone, Jacob Norton,
Wm. Pirtle, Thomas Hazlewood, David Ammons, & Washington Lumbley, who being
elected empannelled nd sworn the truth to speak upon the issues joined upon
their oath do say they find the issues joined in favor of the Plaintiff

Pg
424 and they assess his damages by reason of the non performance of the defendants upon pleas in the Plaintiffs declaration mentioned to one hundred and six-
Pg
teen dollars by the Court that the Plaintiff recover of the defendant the said
425 sum of one hundred and sixteen dollars & twenty five cents damages aforesaid
in from aforesaid assessed by the jury as also his costs about his suit in this
behalf expended and the defendant in mercy etc.

Sampson Edwards   )
          vs.) No. 2 Trover   ) Present as before.
Jesse C. Grice   )
Silas Hart   )

This day came the parties by their attornies and thereupon came a Jury
of good and lawful men To Wit James Chisum, Howell Mynick, Williams Truett,
James Pirtle, Thomas Gilliam William N. Coleman, John Huddlestone, Jacob
Norton, Wm. Pirtle, Thomas Hazlewood, David Ammons, & Washington Lumbley
who being elected empannelled and sworn the truth to speak upon the issues
joined upon their oaths do say they find in favor of the Plaintiff and that
the defendants are guilty in manner and form as declared by the Plaintiff, and
they assess the Plaintiffs damages by reason thereof to fifty five dollars &
fifty cents. It is therefore considered by the Court that the Plaintiff recover of the defendants his damages aforesaid in form aforesaid assessed by
the Jury. As also his costs about his suit in this behalf expended and the
defendants in mercy etc.

Pg
426 John Lea   )
       vs.) No. 4 Case   ) Present as before.
Archibald   )

This day came the Plaintiff by his attorney and says he will no further
prosecute his suit at this time but suffers a nonsuit. It is therefore considered by the Court that the defendant go hence without day recover of the
Plaintiff his costs about his defence expended etc.

John Reagan   )
       vs.) No. 11 Case   ) Present as before.
Ethan A. Murphy   )

This day came the Plaintiff by his attorney and says he will no further
prosecute his suit and takes a non suit. It is therefore considered by the
Court that the defendant go hence without day and recover of the Plaintiff his
costs about his defence expended etc.

Martin Thomas & Wm. Phillips)
          vs.) Debt No. 12   ) Present as before.
Roebo B. Phillips   )

This day came the parties by their attornies and thereupon came a Jury
of good and lawful men To Wit Leray Burt Alexander McClanahan, Richard Hatley,
William Todd, James Panky, Wm. N. Webster, Joshua Hazlewood, Alexander Norden,
Jesse C. Grice, John P. Boydston, Elihu Cornelius & Hugh P. Read who being
elected empannelled and sworn the truth to speak upon the issues joined upon
their oath do say they find the issues joined in favor of the plaintiffs and
that the defendant has not paid the debt of one hundred & twenty dollars &
Pg   seventy six ¼ cents the debt in the Plaintiffs declaration mentioned and they
427 do assess the plaintiffs damages by reason of the detention thereof to sixteen
dollars and sixty cents. It is there fore considered by the Court thatthe
Plaintiffs recover of the defendants the debt aforesaid together with the
damages aforesaid in form aforesaid by the Jury as also their costs in this
behalf expended etc. And that they have execution.

427 Alexander McClanahan   )
           vs.   ) No. 15 Certiorari   )
Lazarus Stewart   )
     This day came by his attorney and the said Lazarus Stewart being solemnly
called to come into Court and plead to the certiovari against him came not but
made default. It is therefore considered by the Court that the Plaintiff
recover of him his costs about his suit in this behalf expended etc.

Commissioners of Bolivar   )
           vs.   )
Elizabeth Barnett Ex   )   Present as before.
Robt. W. Burnett   )
Samuel Lambert Ex.   )
     This day came the parties by their attornies and thereupon came a Jury
of good and lawful men To Wit James Chisum, Howell Mynick, William Truett,
James Pirtle, Thomas Gilliam, Wm. H. Coleman, John Huddlestone, Jacob Norton,
William Pirtle, Thomas Hazlewood, David Ammons & Washington Lumbley who being
xelected empannelled and sworn the truth to speak upon the issues joined upon
Pg theit oath do say they find the issues joined in favor of the Plaintiffs and
428 that the defendants have not paid the whole of the debt issue the Plaintiffs
declaration mentioned, but there remains a balance due of one hundred and
thirteen dollars & ninety two cents debt, and they do assess the plaintiffs
damages by reason of the detention thereof to eleven dollars & twenty six
cents. It is therefore considered by the Court that the Plaintiffs recover of
the defendants the balance of debt aforesaid, and the damages aforesaid in
form aforesaid assessed by the Jury together with their costs about their
suit in this behalf expended, to be levied of the goods and chattels rights
and credits of the said William Barnett decd.

William Fall   )
           vs.) Debt No. 19) Present same Justices as Before.
Adam R. Alexander   )
     This day came the parties by their attorneys and thereupon came a Jury
of good and lawful men To Wit Chauncy Davenport, Leroy Burt, John Kelly,
Howel Myrick, John B. Gilliam Jacob Norton, Thomas Hazlewood, Williams Truett,
James Chisum , William Pirtle, Joseph Pirtle,   & John Huddlestone who being
elected empannelled and sworn the truth to speak upon the issues joined upon
their oath do say they find the issues joined in favor of the Plaintiff and
that the defendant hath not paid the debt of three hundred and twenty dollars
in the Plaintiffs declaration mentioned and they do assess the Plaintiffs damages
by reason of the detention thereof to twenty dollars. Therefore it is
Pg considered by the Court that the Plaintiff recover of the defendant the debt
429 aforesaid together with the damages aforesaid in form aforesaid assessed by
the Jury as also his costs about his suit in this behalf expended and that he
have his execution etc.

William Polk   )
Thomas P. Devereux   )
           vs.) No. 20 Debt   )   Present same Justices as before.
Martin Lawrence   )
James Winters   )
     This day came the defendants in proper person, and say they cannot gainsay
the Plaintiffs right of action and confess Judgment for three hundred and
sixty five dollars and forty nine cents debt and eighty eight dollars and
sixty three cents damages.
     It is therefore considered by the Court that the Plaintiffs recover of
the defendants the said sum of three hundred and sixty five dollars 49 cts,
debt and the damages aforesaid as confessed as also their costs about their

Pg
429 suit for this behalf expended and it is agreed by the Plaintiffs to stay
execution for 6 months from the 1st of Jany. last. This Judgment was to
have been entered of last term, but being ommitted is now entered Nune
protem etc.

Thomas Keencrut & Robert Steele   )   .
            vs.   ) Debt No. 21   )   Present as before
Thornton W. Pinkard   )
      This day came the Parties by their attornies and thereupon came a Jury
of good and lawful men To Wit Chancy Davenport, Leroy Burt, John Kelly,
Howell Myrick, John B. Gilliam, Jacob Norton, Thomas Hazlewood, William s
Truett, James Chisum, William Pirtle, Joseph Pirtle & John Huddlestone who
Pg being elected empannelled and sworn the truth to speak upon the issues joined
430 upon their oath do say they find the issues joined in favor of the Plaintiff
and that the defendant has not paid the debt of ninety three dollars in the
Plaintiffs declaration mentioned and they do assess the Plaintiffs damages
by reason of the detention thereof to six dollars & ninety one cents. It
is therefore considered by the Court that the Plaintiffs recover of the
defendant the said sum of ninety three dollars, together with the damages
aforesaid assessed together with his costs about his suit expended & that
he have his execution etc.

Joseph W. McKean   )
        vs.   ) Debt No. 23   )   Present same Justices as before.
Richard Sanders   )
      This day came the parties by their attornies and thereupon came a
Jury of good and lawful men To Wit Chancy Davenport, Leroy Burt, John Kelly,
Howell Myrick, Thomas B. Gilliam, Jacob Norton, Thomas Hazlewood, Williams
Truett, James Chisum, William P irtle, James Pirtle & John Huddlestone who
being elected empannelled and sworn the truth to speak upon the issues joined
upon their oath do say they find the issues joined in favor of the Plaintiff
and that the defendant has not paid the debt of four hundred dollars in the
Plaintiffs declaration mentioned and they assess his damages by reason of
the detention thereof to seven dollars & fifty cents. It is therefore considered by the Court that the Plaintiff recover of the defendant the debt
aforesaid, together with the damages aforesaid in form aforesaid assessed
by the Jury together with his costs about his suit in this behalf expended
Pg etc., and that he have his execution etc.
431

The Trustees of the   )
University of North Carolina   )   Present as before.
        vs.) Debt No. 24   )
Mark Alexander   )
      This day came the parties by their attornies and thereupon came a Jury
of good and lawful men To Wit Chancey Davenport, Leroy Burt, John Kelly,
Howell Myrick, Thomas B. Gilliam, Jacob Norton, Thomas Hazlewood, William
Truett, James Chisum, William Pirtle, James Pirtle, & John Huddlestone who
being elected empannelled and sworn the truth to speak upon the issues joined
upon their oaths do say they find the issues joined in favor of the plaintiff,
and that the defendant has not paid the debt of seven hundred and fifty
dollars in the plaintiffs declaration mentioned and they do assess his
damages by reason of the detention thereof to one hundred and thirty nine
dollars. It is therefore considered by the Court that the Plaintiff recover
of the defendant his debt aforesaid together with the damages aforesaid
in form aforesaid assessed by the Jury and he have his execution etc.

Pg
431   The Trustees of the University of   )
North Carolina   )   Present as before.
            vs.) Debt No. 25   )
Mark Alexander   )

     This day came the parties by their attornies and thereupon came a
Jury of good and lawful men To Wit Chancey Davenport, Leroy Burt, John
Kelly, Howell Myrick, Thomas B. Gilliam, Jacob Norton, Thomas Hazlewood,
William Truett, James Chisum, William Pirtle, James Pirtle & John Huddlestone
who being elected empannelled and sworn the truth to speak upon the issues
joined upon their oaths do say they find the issues joined in favor of the
plaintiff, and that the defendant has not paid the debt of seven hundred
and fifty dollars in the plaintiffs declaration mentioned and they do
assess his damages by reason of the detention thereof to one hundred and
thirty nine dollars. It is therefore considered by the Court that the
Plaintiff recover of the defendant his debt aforesaid together with the
damages aforesaid in form aforesaid assessed by the Jury and he have his
execution etc.

The Trustees of the University   )
of North Carolina   )   Present as before.
         vs.   ) Debt No. 25   )
Mark Alexander   )

     This day came the parties by their attornies and thereupon came a
Jury of good and lawful men To Wit Chancey Davenport, Leroy Burt, John
Kelly, Howell Myrick, Thomas B. Gilliam, Jacob Norton, Thomas Hazlewood,
Williams Truett, James Chisum, William Pirtle, James Pirtle & John
Huddlestone who being elected empannelled and sworn the truth to speak upon
Pg   the issues joined upon their oath do say they find the issues joined in
432   favor of the Plaintiff and that the defendant has not paid the debt of
seven hundred and fifty dollars in the Plaintiffs declaration mentioned, and
they do assess his damage by reason of the detention thereof to one hundred
and thirty nine dollars.
     It is therefore considered by the Court that the Plaintiff recover of
the defendant the debt aforesaid together with the damages aforesaid in form
aforesaid assessed by the Jury, as also his costs about his suit in this
behalf expended etc. and that he have his execution etc.

Richard Hatley   )
     vs.) Covenant   )
Daniel Davis   )

     This day comes into open Court Daniel Davis the defendant and says he
cannot gainsay the Plaintiffs right of action and confesses judgment for
one hundred and one dollars & fifty cents damages. It is therefore considered by the Court that the Plaintiff recover of the defendant the said sum
of one hundred and one dollars and fifty cents as also his costs about his
suit in this behalf expended etc

Joseph Taylor   )
     vs.) Covenant   )
Duguid Mims   )
Thomas James   )

     This day came into Court Thomas James one of the defendants and says
he cannot gainsay the Plaintiffs right of action and confesses judgment
for two hundred and three dollars and fifty cents damages. It is therefore
considered by the Court that the Plaintiff recover of the defendant the said

Pg
432 sum of two hundred and three dollars and fifty cents, as also his costs about
Pg his suit expended etd. and the Plaintiff stays exedution till next Court.
433

Daniel Davis)
    vs.) Motion)
Stephen Harvey)
Oney Harvey)

On motion and it appearing to the satisfaction of the Court that an
execution had issued against the defendants from Caleb Brock Esq. a Justice
of the Peace for the County in favor of the Plaintiff Iss'd 1st April 1829
for thirty two dollars debt with interest from the 1st day of Sept. 1826
and one dollar costs and which said execution had come to the hands of
Anthony Bennett a Constable for said County and by him for want of personal
property levied on a tract of land in the name of Oney Harvey 10th District
3'd Range and 3'd Section lyin in said County of Hardeman. It is therefore
ordered adjudged and decreed that the aforesaid land be exposed to sale as
the law directs to satisfy said debt & costs and also the costs of this
motion & that a Venditioni Exponas issue accordingly.

John Kelly)
    vs.) Motion)
Thomas P. Blount & M. L. Kimbrough)

On motion and it appearing to the satisfaction of the Court that
an execution had issued against the defendants at the instance of John Kelly
by Francis Shoemake Esq. a Justice of the Peace for this County the 21st day
of January 1829 for fifty seven dollars debt with interest from the 1st Jany.
1829 and one dollars costs and which said execution had come to the hands of
J. C. N. Robertson Sheriff of said County and by him for want of personal
property on eighty acres of land in the 10th Dist. 3'd Range & 3'd Section
Entry No. 2412 in the name of John L. Kimborough. It is therefore ordered
adjudged and decreed that the aforesaid land be exposed for sale as the law
directs to satisfy said debt & costs & also the costs of this motion and
Pg that Vendi Exponas issue accordingly.
434

The Sheriff returned into Court the following report of lands liable for
double taxes for the year 1828.
I Julius C. N. Robertson Sheriff and Collector of the Publick taxes for
the County of Hardeman do hereby report to Court the following tracts of
land as having been ommitted to be given in for the taxes for the year 1828
that the same are liable to double taxes, that the double taxes remain thereon remain due and unpaid and that the respective owners or claimants thereof
have no goods or chattels within my county on which I can distrain for said
double taxes To Wit

Owners	Entry	Acres	District	Range	Sect.	Shffs. fee
Baker, William heirso of	982	320	10	4	1	1.00
Brown Porter	466	1000		2	5.6	1.00
Benson, Gabriel	966	44		1	3	1.00
Burleson, John	1944	150		4	6	1.00
Claiborne, Thomas	953	533 1/3		1	2	1.00
Crawford, Raiford	1214	100		3	4	1.00
Same	1644	10		3	4	1.00
Dougherty, Geo.	924	317 2/3	"	4	3	1.00
Cobbs Rob L.	887	22½	"	1	3	1.00
" " "	876	26	"	2	5	1.00
Dougherty George	877	260	"	1	2	1.00

Pg   (cont. from Pg. 183)

434 Clerks Fee	Receipts for Double Taxes		Total	
1.40	1.50	6.40	10.30	
1.40	1.50	20.00	23.90	
1.40	1.50	.88	4.78	
1.40	1.50	3.00	6.90	
1.00	1.50	10.66½	14.56 2/3	
1.40	1.50	2.00	5.90	
1.40	1.50	20	4.10	
1.40	1.50	635 1/3	10.25 1/3	
1.40	1.50	45	4.35	
1.40	1.50	.52	4.42	
1.40	1.50	5.20	9.10	

Owners Name	Entry	Acres	District	Range	Section	Shffs Fee	Clks fee		Rects for double taxes	Total
Fogg, Godfrey										
M. F. McGavock										
	969	65	10	1	3	1.00	1.40	1.50	.5930	5.20
Garth										
Thos. C.	2420	25	"	3	3	1 00	1 40	1 50	.50	4.40
"	2421	25	"	3	3	1 00	1 40	1 50	.50	4.40
Hopkins										
Thomas	1421	100	"	5	2	100	1 40	1.50	2.00	5.90
Haynes										
John	1896	50	"	4	3	1. 00	1 40	1 50	1 00	4 90
Johnson										
Randall	740	224	"	4	23	1 00	1 40	1 50	4 48	8.38
"	357	320	"	4	3	1 00	1 40	1 50	6 40	10.3

Pg 434 Owners	Entry	Acres	District	Range	Section	Clerks fees
Brt. forward						
Love, Robt & Thomas	296	5 00	10	3	4	100
Same pt. of	487	1700	"	4	1	100
Lewis Samuel	2239	50	"	2	6	100
McGavock Francis	970	70	"	2	3	100
Same	894	99 112/160	"	3	4	100
Moore Michial & Robert Searcy pt. of	253	800		3.4	3	100
Murphy Archibald	466	500		3	5.6	100
Mallery Berl	762	200		5	5	100
McMenstry Sm. C.	2198	50	"	4	5	100
Mims, Duguid	1301	100	"	4	4	100
Same	2265	50	"	4	4	100
McColliston John	2298	50		2	6	100
Peterson John	2240	50	"	3	5	100
Parker John	2299	25	"	3	5	100
Smith Richard	1153	640	"	4	6	100
Sullivan Jesse	1470	39	"	4	3	100
Same	1477	11	"	4	3	100
Same	1478	20	"	4	3	100
Sullivan Oney P.	895	200	"	4	3	100
Wilson Lewis D.	518	640	"	5	1	100
Warner Jos. M.	875	26 100/160		1	3	100
Williams Thomas G.	2332	25	"	3	5	100
Williams Thomas N.	2382	2100x		2	4	100
		100				
		9544½				

J. C. Robertson Shff. Collector

Shffs. fees	Printers fees	Double Taxes	Total
140	150	10.00	13.90
140	150	34.00	37.90
140	150	1.00	4.90
140	150	1.52	5.42
140	150	1.99	5.89
140	150	16.00	19.90
140	150	10.00	13.90
140	150	4.00	7.90
140	150	1.00	4.90
140	150	2.00	5.90
140	150	1.00	4.90
140	150	1.00	4.90
140	150	1.00	4.90
140	150	.50	4.40
140	150	12.80	16.70
140	150	.78	4.68
140	150	22	4.12
140	150	40	4.30
140	150	4.00	7.90
140	150	12.80	16.70
140	150	53	4.43
140	150	50	4.40
140	150	200	5.90

Pg
435   Whereupon it is considered by the Court that Judgment be and it is
hereby rentered against the aforesaid tracts of land and acres thereof
in the name of the state for the sum annexed to each it being the amount
of taxes costs and charges due severally thereon for double taxes for the
year 1828 and it is further ordered that the said several tracts of land
or so much thereof as shall be sufficient to satisfy taxes costs and
charges annexed to them be sold as the law directs .

Sheriffs Report

The Sheriff returned into Court the following report of lands liable
for single taxes for the year 1828 on which the taxes under unpaid,

I Julius C. N. Robertson, Sheriff and Collector of the Pulick taxes
for the County of Hardeman do hereby report to Court the following tracts
Pg of land as having been given in for the taxes for the year 1828, that the
436 same be liable for single taxes that the single taxes remain due and unpaid, and that the respective owners or claimants thereof have no goods
or chattels within my county on which I can distrain for said single
taxes, to wit:

Owners	Entry	Acres	District	Range	Section	Shff's fee
Boden, Alexander, heirs of	935	640	10	4	5	100
Cherry Daniel	395	640		2	4	100
Cherry Jesse	422	640	"	2	4	100
Cobbs, Rob L.	1148	640	"	1	1	100
Dougherty, Geo.	1084	236¼		4.5	3.4	100
Davidson Ephal E.	809	600		1.2	1	100
Goodlet Adam G. Wm. Campbell	665	1000		2	5	100
Gray Rowley	2365	100		3.4	4	100
Griffin William	2443	84		2	1.2	100
Greer James	1704	150	"	4	3.4	100
Hays Robert	1122	182	"	4	3	
Jenkins, John pt. of	1015	480	"	1	1	100
Same	995	480	"	2	4	100
Javis Mores	466	700	"	3	5	100
Key Jefferson heirs of	1532	112½		4	4	100
Love Charles I.	492	500		45	1	100
McConnel, James	1388	23		2	6	100
McLemore, Sugars pt. of	1112	94		4	2	100
Same	1049	40½	"	4	5	100
Taylor Thomas H.	466	250	"	3	5	100

Pg
436

Owner	Entry	Acres	District	Range	Section	Shff's fee
Williams, James C.	1976	100	10	3	3	1 00
Young Genoa C.	1392	65	"	2	3	1 00
McLemore Sugars pt.	of 924	105 1/5	"	4	3	1 00

Clerks fee	Printers fee	Single Taxes	
140	150	6.40	10.30
140	150	6.40	10.30
140	150	6.40	10.30
140	150	6.40	10.40
140	150	2.36½	6.26
140	150	6.00	9.90
140	150	10.00	13.90
140	150	1.00	4.90
140	150	.84	4.74
140	150	1.50	5.40
140	150	1.82	5.72
140	150	4.80	8.70
140	150	4.80	8.70
140	150	7.00	10.90
140	150	1.12½	5.02½
140	150	5.00	8.90
140	150	.73	4.73
140	150	.94	4.84
140	150	.40	4.25
140	150	2.50	4.30
140	150	1100	6.40
140	150	.65	4.90
140	150	1.05	4.55
			4.95

Pg
437
    Whereupon it is considered by the Court that Judgment be and it is hereby entered against the aforesaid tracts of land and the owners thereof in the name of the State for the sums annexed to each tract   it being the amount of taxes, costs, and charges due severally thereon for single taxes for the term 1828. And it is further ordered deemed and adjudged that the said several tracts of land or so much thereof as shall be sufficent to satisfy the taxes costs and charges annexed, to them be sold as the law directs.

John Kelly   )
   vs.   )
Thomas P. Blount   )
John L. Kimbrough   )   the court
    On motion and it appearing to the satisfaction of /the execution has issued on behalf of the Plaintiff against the defendants from Francis Shoemake Esq. an acting Justice of the Peace for this County the 21st day of January 1829 for twenty dollars debt with interest from the 3'd day of January 1829 and one dollar and fifty cents costs, which said execution had come to the hands of J. C. N. Robertson Sheriff of said County. and by him for want of personal property to be found levied on 80 acres of land
Pg 438 10th District 3 Range 3 Section Entry No. 2412 in the name of John L.

Pg
438 Kimbrough. It is therefore ordered adjudged and decreed that the aforesaid land be exposed for sale as the law directs to satisfy said debt and costs & also the costs of this motion and that a venditiona Exponas issue accordingly.

J. B. Wood   )
    vs.) Motion   )
Samuel Foster   )

On motion and it appearing to the satisfaction of the Court that an execution had issued on behalf of the Plaintiff against the defendant from Alexander McKenzie Esq. a Justice of the Peace for said County the 25th day of March 1829 for the sum of six dollars and seventy five cnets debt and fifty cents costs which said execution had come to the hand of Samuel Nabers a Constable of said County and by him for want of personal property levied on 25 acres of land Entry No. 2102 Range 4 Section One. It is therefore ordered adjudged and decreed that the aforesaid land be exposed for sale as the law directs to satisfy said debt and costs & also the costs of this motion and that a venditions Exponas issue accordingly etc.

Joseph Shinpock   )
    vs.) Motion)
Samuel Foster   )

On motion and it appearing to the satisfaction of the Court that an execution had issued on behalf of the plaintiff against the defendant from
Pg Alexander McKenzie Esq. a Justice of the Peace for said County the 24th
439 day of March 1829 for the sum of thirteen dollars and seventy five cents with interest from the 21st of Feby. 1829 and fifty cents costs which said execution had come to the hands of Samuel Nabers a Constable of said County and by him for want of personal property levied on 25 acres of land No. of Entry 2102 range 4 Section One.

It is therefore considered ordered adjudged and decreed that the aforesaid land be exposed for sale as the law directs to satisfy said debt and x costs & also the costs of this motion and that a Venditiona exponas issue accordingly etc.

Edward Heningdon)
    vs.   ) Certiovari
Gabriel Bumpass   )

This day came the parties by their attorneys and thereupon came a Jury of good and lawful men to wit James Chisum, Rowell Myrick, Williams Truett James Pirtle, Thomas Gilliam, Wm. H. Coleman, John Huddleston, Jacob Norton, William Firtle, Thomas Hazlewood, David Amons & Washington Lumly, who being elected empannelled & sworn the truth to speak upon the issues joined on motion of the plaintiff a jury is withdrawn and the plaintiff suffers a non suit. It is therefore considered that defendant go hence & recover his costs about this defence expended etc.

And the Court adjourned to tomorrow morning 9 O'clock.

James Ruffin
Edmund D. Tarver
John G. Cockeram

Pg
440

Wednesday 8th April 1829

Court met according to adjournment. Present the worshipful James Ruffin, Edward D. Tarver, John Y. Cockeram, Esquires Justices.

Pg
440 Egbert H. Sheppard)
vs.) Writ of E n quiry
Bedford Breedlove & Roberson)

This day comes the plaintiff by his attorney and thereupon came a Jury of good & lawful men, to wit, Leroy Burt, Alexander McClenahan, Richard Hatley, Wm. Todd, James Panky, Wm. N. Webster, Joshua Hazlewood, Alec Norden, Jesse G. Grice, John P. Birdstone, Elihu Cornelius, Huh P. Read who being elected empannelled and sworn the truth to speak upon the measure of the damages the plaintiff has sustained by reason of the defendants non performance of his several undertakings and assumptions, upon their oath do say that the Plaintiff has sustained damages to the amount of two hundred and sixty three dollars and thirty nine cents. It is therefore considered by the Court that the Plaintiff recover of the defendants the said sum of two hundred and sixty three dollars and thirty nine cents damages aforesaid in form aforesaid assessed by the Jury as also his costs about his suit in this behalf expended etc. and that he have execution etc.

Martin Crawley)
vs.) Debt No. 22) Present same Justices as before.
Thornton W. Pinckard)

This day came the parties by their attornies and thereupon came a Jury
Pg of good and lawful men to wit, Leroy Burt, Alexander McClanahan, Richard
441 Hatley, William Todd, James Panky, Wm. N. Webster, Josaiah Hazlewood, Alexander Norden, Jesse Grice, John P. Boydstone, Elihu Cornelius & Hugh P. Read who being elected empannelled and sworn the truth to speak upon the issues joined upon their oath do say they find the issues joined in favor of the plaintiff, and that the defendant has not paid the debt of ninety nine dollars and forty two 3/4 cents in the Plaintiffs declaration mentioned and they assess his damages by reason of the detention thereof to eight dollars and ninety one cents. It is therefore considered by the Court that the Plaintiff recover of the defendant the debt aforesaid and the damages aforesaid in form aforesaid by the Jury as also his costs about his suit in this behalf expended etc. and that he have execution etc.

William T. Laird)
vs.) Case No. 31) Present same Justices as Before
Joshua & Thomas Hazlewood)

This day came the parties by their attornies and thereupon came a Jury of good and lawful men To Wit Chancey Davenport, Leroy Burt, John Kelly, Howell Myrick, Thomas B. Gilliam, Jacob Norton, Alex Kirkpatrick, Williams Truett, James Chisum, William Pirtle, James Pirtle, & John Huddlestone who being elected empannelled and sworn the truth to speak upon the issues joined in favor of the Plaintiff and they do assess his damages by reason of the non-
Pg performance of defendants promises and undertakings to one hundred and forty
442 four dollars and twenty five cents. It is therefore considered by the Court that the Plaintiff recover of the defendants his damages aforesaid in form aforesaid assessed by the Jury as also his costs about his suit in this behalf expended and that he have execution etc.

Walter Shinault)
vs.) Debt No. 32) Present as before.
Zachariah Davis- Daniel Davis)
Davis Dunlap & Wahington Lumbley)

This day came the parties by their attornies and thereupon came a Jury of good and lawful men To Wit Chancey Davenport, Leroy Burt, John Kelly, Howell Myrick, Thomas B. Gilliam, Jacob Norten, Thomas Hazlewood, Williams Truett, James Chisum, William Pirtle, James Pirtle & John Huddlestone who being elected empannelled and sworn the truth to speak upon the issues joined upon

Pg
442 their oath do say they find the issues joined in favor of the Plaintiff and that the defendants have not paid the debt of five hundred and eighty two dollars and fifty cents in the Plaintiffs declaration mentioned, and they do assess his damages by reason of the detention thereof to fourteen dollars and fifty cents. It is therefore considered by the Court that the Plaintiff recover of the defendants the debt aforesaid, and the damages aforesaid in form aforesaid assessed by the Jury, as also his costs about his suit in this behalf expended etc. and that he have his execution.

Seth Lewis   )
    vs.   ) Trespass No. 33   )   Present same Justices as before.
John N. Neal   )

Pg
443   This day came the parties by their attornies and thereupon came a Jury of good and lawful men To Wit, James Chisum, Howell Myrick, Williams Truett, James Pirtle, Thomas E. Gilliam, Wm. N. C oleman, John Huddlestone Norton, William Pirtle, Thomas Hazlewood, Mansel Crisp & James M. Scott who being elected empannelled and sworn the truth to speak upon the issues joined upon their oath do say they cannot agree and thereupon a quen_ being withdrawn there is a mistrial the said cause by arrangement of parties is transferred to the Circuit Court.

Sampson Edward   )
    vs.) Sci Fa)
Elihu Cornelius   )
    This day came the plaintiff by his attorney and says he will no further prosecute his Sci Facias and dismisses the same. It is therefore considered by the Court that the defendant go hence without day and recover of the plaintiff his costs about his defense in this behalf expended etc.

State   )
  vs.) Recognizance   )
William Mitchell   )
    This day came into open Court John Jack and acknowledged himself to be justly indebted to the State of Tennessee in the sum of one hundred and twenty five dollars to be levied of his good and chattels land and tenements but to be void on condition that the said Wm. Mittchel do make his personal appearance before our Court of pleas & quarter sessions on Thursday the 9th day of this month and from day to day until discharged to answer the State of Tennessee on a charge of hog stealing and not to report without leave of the Court first
Pg had.
444
    The Grand Jury returned into open Court under the charge of their sworn officer and presented a Bill of Indictment. The State vs. Robert Box for an assault & Battery. The State vs. William Mitchell indictment for hog stealing severally indorsed a True Bill Adam R. Alexander foreman of the Grand Jury.

E. P. Hannis adm. of   )
D. P. Hannis decd. and of W.)
Hardeman   )   Present as before.
    vs.) Appeal   )
Thomas Hazlewood   )
Joshua Hazlewood
    This day came the parties by their attornies and thereupon came a Jury of good and lawful men To Wit Shadrock Owens, Thos. Read, William I. Riddle, John Dunawey, John Mills, William Read, A llen Hamlin, Charles Cox, Wm. P.

Pg
444 Boydstone John Nuckolls, Edward B. Hill & Alec Norden who being elected empannelled and sworn the truth to speak upon the matter in controversy upon
their oath do say they find in favor of the Plaintiff and that the defendant
is indebted the Plaintiff in the sum of six dollars and twenty five cents.
It is therefore considered by the Court that the Plaintiff recover of the
defendants the aforesaid sum of six dollars and twenty five cents and on
motion twenty five cents damages it being at the rate of 12½ pct.interest
in the same ask also his costs about his suit in this behalf expended etc.

A deed of conveyance from Isaac Jones, Sarah Jones, Abraham Smith and
John Huddlestone to Charles Jones for forty acres of land was produced in
open Court and the execution of same acknowledged by the said Isaac Jones,
Abraham Smith & John Huddlestone to their act and deed, and the execution
thereof by Sarah Jones proven by the oath of William Pirtle and James Pirtle
Pg
445 subscribing witnesses thereto. Ordered to be certified for registration.

A deed of conveyance from James Rogers to Benjamin F. Lyon for 100
acres of land was produced in open Court and the execution thereof acknowledged by the said Rogers to be his act and deed. Ordered to be certified
for registration.

A deed of conveyance from Sashel Woods to Littleberry Mason for fifty
acres of land was produced in open Court and the execution thereof proven
by the oaths of H. C. Warren & John C. Warren subscribing witnesses thereto.
Ordered to be certified for registration.

```
Robert Robson  )
      vs.      )    Writ of inquiry.
John Watson    )
```
This day came the plaintiff his attorney whereupon came a Jury of good
& lawful men to wit, A. Kirkpatrick, Green Pryor, Shadarock Owens, Thomas Reed,
Chancy Davenport, Willy J. Riddle, John Dunaway, William Reed, Allen Hamlin,
Charles Cox & William Boydston who being elected empannelled & sworn to enquire
of the damages the plaintiff has sustained in his declaration mentioned upon
their oath do say they find for the plaintiff eighty one dollars and seventy
two cents it is therefore considered by the Court that the plaintiff recover
of said defendant eighty one dollars and seventy two cents damages aforesaid
also his costs about his suit in this behalf expended etc. Whereupon the
said plaintiff by his attorney moved the Court for a judgment against Wilkins
I. Hunt as a garnishe in this case and it appearing to the Court that said
Hunt had stated at the lastterm of this Court that he owed the said Watsons
Pg   eight eight dollars it is therefore considered that the sd. Robson recoverof
446 the Hunt that amount and whereas Samuel Montgomery who was garnished in this
case discovered at the last term of this Court that he was indebted to said
John Watson three dollars. It is therefore considered that Judgment be
entered against him for that amount.

And whereas Benjamin Riddle at the last term of this Court stated that
on a garnishment in this case that he owed John Watson & Chesterfield Bowers
jointly five dollars, it is therefore considered by the Court that judgment
be rendered against the said Riddle in favour of said Watson for two dollars
& fifty cents one half of said amt.

And whereas Thomas Whitlock who was sommoned as a garnishee in this case
at the last term of this Court stated that he owed said Watson and Chesterfield
Bowers five dollars jointly. It is therefore considered that the said Robson
recover of the sd. Whitlock two dollars & fifty cents it being one half of that
amount.

Pg
446   A quit claim deed from Andrew L. Martin, E. P. McNeal, Thomas M. Hardeman, J. J. Hardeman and Rufus P. Neely to Marshall T. Polk was proven in open Court and the execution thereof acknowledged by the said Martin McNeal, Hardeman and Neely to be their act and deed for the purposes therein expressed. Ordered to be certified for registration.

A Quit claim deed from Marshall T. Polk, E. P. McNeal, Thomas M.
Pg Hardeman and A. L. Martin to Rufus P. Neely was produced in open Court and
447 the execution thereof acknowledged by the said Polk McNeal Hardeman & A. L. Martin to be their act and deed. Ordered to be certified for registration.

A Quit claim deed from Marshall T. Polk, Andrew L. Martin, Thomas M. Hardeman & Rufus P. Neely to Ezekial P. McNeal was produced in open Court and the execution thereof acknowledged by said Polk Hardeman, Martin & Neely to be their act and deed. Ordered to be certified for registration.

A Quit claim deed from Andrew L. Martin, E. P. McNeal Marshal T. Polk & Rufus P. Neely to Thos. M. Hardeman was produced in open Court and the execution thereof acknowledged by said Martin McNeal Polk & Neely to be their act and deed. Ordered to be certified for registration.

A Quit claim deed from E. P. McNeal Marshall T. Polk, Thomas M. Hardeman & Rufus P. Neely to Andrew L. Martin was produced in open Court and acknowledged by the said McNeal Polk Hardeman & Neely to be their act and deed. Ordered to be certified for registration.

Nathaniel Steele   )
    vs.) Debt   )
Richard Saunders   )

    This day came into open Court Wilkins L. Hunt who being sworn as garnishee in this case states that he is indebted to Richard Saunders in the sum of eighteen dollars or thereabouts. It is therefore considered by the Court that the said sum of eighteen dollars aforesaid and Matthew Flavor being sworn says he owes nothing and is discharged and knows of no other person owing except W. L. Hunt.

Pg William S. London   )
448 John M. Davis   )
    vs.) Debt   )
John Hemphill   )

    Whereas at July term last of this Court John Foster by the consideration of the Court recovered of the Plaintiffs William L. London & John M. Davis the sum of forty one dollars and fifty cents debt & costs. And it appearing to the satisfaction of the Court that the said London & Davis were securities of the defendant John Hemphill. It is moved by the said Plaintiffs for Judgment against the defendant John Hemphill and the Court being satisfied. It is considered that the plaintiffs recover against the said John Hemphill the said sum of forty one dollars and fifty cents the amount of the Judgment of the said John Foster against said Wm. L. London & John M. Davis aforesaid also the costs of said suit & also their costs about this motion expended etc.

Michial Read   )
    vs.   )
Enoch Latham   )

    James Panky summoned as garnisher in this case comes into Court and states that he justly owes the defendant fifteen dollars. But because the said Read has not obtained Judgment against the said Latham it is ordered that the Court delay rendering Judgment in this case until the same shall be decided and in the meantime the said Panky pays the said money into the

Pg.
448 Clerks office. And the Court adjourned to tomorrow morning 9 O'clock.

James Ruffin
Edmund D. Tarver
John Y. Cockeram

Thursday April 9th 1829

Pg
449   The Court met according to adjournment. Present the worshipful
James Ruffin
Edmund D. Tarver
John Y. Cockeram Esq.Justices.

Thomas J. Hardeman, Clk, V. D. Barry, Sol. Genl., J. C. N. Robertson, Shff.

Edwd. Herndon   )
        vs.) Motion   )
Gabriel Pumpass Justice   )
of the Peace   )

In this case Edward Herndon by attorney moves the Court for a writ of
Mandamus directed to Gabrial B umpass Esq. a Justice of the Peace for this
County commanding him by next Court to show cause why proceedings have not
been further prosessed in a case wherein he was stay for a debt rendered by
him against one C. S. Cains, and further why execution has not been issued
aforesaid. After argument and consideration by the Court it is ordered that
said Writ do issue accordingly.

State   )
    vs.) Indict Hog Stealing   ) Present as above.
Wm. Mitchell   )

This day came the defendant in proper person, and the Soliciter General
on the behalf of the State, and the said defendant being arraigned on the
Bill of Indictment plead Not Guilty and for his trial puts himself on the
country, and the Soliciter General likewise and thereupon came a Jury of
good and lawful men to wit, James Chisum, Howell Myrick, Williams Truett,
Thomas B. Gilliam, James Pirtle, William N. Coleman, Jacob Norton, William
Pirtle, James T. Scott, James T. Ewing, John L. Atkinson & Thomas P. Boidston,
who being elected empannelled and sworn the truth to speak upon the issue
Pg joined upon their oath do say they find the defendant Not Guilty in manner
450 and form as charged in the Bill of Indictment. It is therefore considered
by the Court that the defendant go hence without day and recover his costs
etc. and it is further adjudged that the County pay the costs.

E. P. Harris Adm.   )
of David Harris decd.   )
        vs.) Debt Appeal   )
Thomas Hazlewood   )

This day came the defendant by his attorney and prays and obtains an
appeal to the next Court, and thereupon came forward and gave bond with
Wilkins I. Hunt as his security.

University of North Carolina   )
        vs.) Debt   )
Mark Alexander   )

This day came the defendant by his attorney and prays and obtains an
appeal to the next Circuit Court and thereupon came the said defendant
and gave bond with John S. Dancy,Lemuel Rogers & Alexander C. Blair as his
securities.

Pg
450 The University of North Carolina)
                    vs.) Debt   )
Mark Alexander   )

This day came the defendant by his attorney and prays and obtains an appeal to the next Circuit Court and thereupon came the said defendant and gave bond with John S. Doxey, Lemuel Rogers & Alexander C. Blair as his securities.

State   )
    vs.) A & B.   )
James Allison   )

This day came the defendant in proper person and being charged on the Bill of Indictment submits himself to the mercy of the Court. It is there-
Pg fore considered by the Court that the defendant be fined the sum of six
451 and per cents and pay the costs of this prosecution & that he be in mercy etc.

State   )
    vs.) A & B   ) Present as before.
James Gunter   )

This day came the Solicitor General on the part of the state and the defendant in proper person & who being arraigned on the Bill of Indictment plead Not Guilty and for his trial puts himself on the Country and thereupon came a Jury of good and lawful men To Wit James Chisum, Howell Myrick, Williams Truett, Thomas B. Gilliam, James Pirtle, Jacob Norton, William Pirtle, Thomas Hazlewood, Leroy Burt, Joshua Hazlewood, Henry Kirkland and Samuel Barnett who being elected empannelled and sworn the truth to say upon the issue of Traverse joined upon their oath do say they find the defendant Guilty in manner and form as charged in the Bill of Indictment. It is there-fore considered by the Court that the said James Gunter be fined the sum of five dollars and that the state recover against him her costs in this expended etc. and the defendant in mercy etc.

State   )
    vs.   ) Affray   ) Present as Before.
James T. Scott   )

This day came the Solicitor General on the part of the State and with the assent of the Court enters a Nolli Prorequi in this case, and thereupon came the defendant in proper person and assumes all costs. It is therefore considered by the Court that the Plaintiff recover of the defendant her costs about her suit in this behalf expended etc.

Pg   William Fall   )
452   vs.) Debt Appeal   )
       Adam R. Alexander   )

This day came the defendant and prays and obtains an appeal to the next Circuit Court for this County and who thereupon came forward and gave bond with J. C. N. Robertson as his security.

A plot & certificate with the assignment thereon from James Crooms to to Julius Driver was produced in open Court and proven by the oaths of E. P. Neal and John McCrabb two subscribing witnesses. Ordered to be certified.

A deed of conveyance from Tho. J. Hardeman atto. in fact for Wm. D. McKay to Wm. C. Collier was produced in open Court and the execution thereof acknowledged by said Hardeman to be his act and deed. Ordered to be certified for registration.

Pg
452   A plat & certificate with the transfer thereon from Geo. T. Adams to
Daniel W. Love was exhibited in open Court and the execution thereof
proven by the oath of G. C. Crisp oneof the subscribing witnesses.

A plat and certificate with the transfer thereon from Grizzy Johnson
to E. P. McNeal was exhibited in open Court and proven by the oaths of
James G. Ewing & Jacob Norton. Ordered to be certified.

A deed of conveyance from Littleton Henderson to Thomas J. Hardeman
& E. R. Belcher for two town lots was produced in open Court and proven
by the oaths of Rufus F. Neely & Wm. Ramsay subscribing witnesses. Ordered
to be certified for registration.

Pg
453   A power of attorney from Sam. C. Hagan to Thos. J. Hardeman was exhibited in Court and proven by the oath of John W. Bills & R C. McAlpin
subscribing witness, ordered to be certified for registration.

A deed of conveyance from the Commissioners of the town of Bolivar to
David Fentress for one town lot was produced in open Court and acknowledged
by said Commissioners to be their act & deed. Ordered to be certified for
registration.

A deed of conveyance from Duguid Mims to David Fentress for one town lot
was exhibited in open Court and proven by the oaths of E. R. Belcher & Thos.
J. Hardeman subscribing witnesses. Ordered to be certified for registration.

The Grand Jury returned into open Court under charge of their sworn
officer a Bill of Indictment against Robert Eanes Alexander Eanes, William
Taylor. Pendleton Gillespie, John Garrett for an Escape Indorsed a True
Bill A. R. Alexander Foreman of the Grand Jury.

State   )
  vs.) Affray   )
Waddell Smith   )
     This day came the Solicitor General on the part of the State and the
defendant being solemnly called to come into Court and answer the State on a
Bill of Indictment for an affray came not but made default. It is therefore
considered by the Court that the State recover of the said Smith the sum
of one hundred and twenty five dollars unless he do make his personal
appearance on the 1st Thursday after the 1st Monday in July next then and
there to show cause if any he has or can why Judgment final and execution
thereof should not be awarded against him and that a Sciri Facias issue
Pg accordingly.
454

State   )
  vs.) Affray   )
Waddell Smith   )
     This day came the Solicitor General on the part of the State and Thomas
Barber the defendants bail being solemnly called to come into Court and being
with him the body of Woddsel Smith to answer the State on a Bill of Indictment for an affray came not but made default. It is therefore considered by
the Court that the State recover of the defendant the sum of one hundred and
twenty five dollars unless he do make his personal before the Court of Pleas
& Quarter Sessions on the first Thursday after the 1st Monday in July next
then and there to show cause if any be has or can why Judgment final and
execution thereof should not be awarded against him and that a Soi Facias issue
accordingly.

Pg
454 State   )
    vs) Ind. Tippling House   ) Present Edward D. Tarver, James Ruffin & John
Green Hastlen   ) Y. Cockeram Esq.

    This day came the Solicitor General on the part of the State and the
defendant in proper person who being arrigned upon the Bill of Indictment
pleads Not Guilty and for his trial puts himself in the Country and the Solicitor General likewise and thereupon came a Jury of good and lawful men To
Wit A. R. Alexander, John Caldwell, John Wilson, John Cole, Thomas Shaw,
Aden Langhorn, Franklin Robb, Robert D. Fort, John Brantley, Solomon Willoughby, Wilkins I Hunt Jonas Robertson who being elected empannelled and
sworn the truth to speak upon the issue of Traverse joined upon their oath do
Pg say they find the defendant Guilty in manner and form as charged in the Bill
455 of Indictment. It is therefore considered by the Court that the defendant be
fined the sum of six dollars and that the State recover against him the costs
about this prosedution expended etc. and that the said defendant remain in
custody of the Sheriff until said fine & costs are paid or secured.

State   )
  vs.   )
Green Hasten   )

    This day came the Solicitor General on the part of the State and the
defendant in proper person who being arraigned upon the Bill of Indictment
pleads Not Guilty and for his trial puts himself on the Country and the Solicitor General likewise and thereupon came a Jury of good and lawful men To
Wit James Chisum Howell Myrick, Williams Truett, James Pirtle, Wm. H.
Coleman, Jacob Norton, William Pirtle, Thomas Hazlewood, Mansel Crisp, Garret
Moore, Samuel Dedmond and John P. Boidstone who being elected empannelled
and sworn the truth to say upon the issue of traverse joined upon their oath
do say they find the defendant Guilty in manner and form as charged in the
Bill of Indictment. It is therefore considered by the Court that the said
State recover against him the costs about this prosecution expended etc. and
that the said defendant remain in custody of the Sheriff until said fine and
costs are paid or secured.

    Grand Jury discharged third day. John Huddlestone 2 days.

Pg State   )
456   vs.) Overseer Road   )
William Johnson   )

    This day came the Solicitor General on the part of the State and the
defendant in proper person and who being arraigned on the Bill of Presentment
pleads Not Guilty and for his trial puts himself on the Country and the
Solicitor General likewise and thereupon came a Jury of good and lawful men To
Wit James Chisum, Wm. H. Coleman, Jacob Norton, William Pirtle, Thomas
Hazlewood, Mansel Crisp, Joshua Hazlewood, William R. Cockrum, Leroy Burt
Alexander, Aiken, Abrum Pillow, & William Langhorn, who being elected empannelled and sworn the truth to speak upon the issue of Traverse joined upon their
oath do say they find the defendant Guilty in manner and form as charged in
the Bill of Presentment. It is therefore considered by the Court thatthe
defendant be paid the sum of fifty cents and that the State recovers of said
defendant his costs about this prosecution expended etc.

State   )
  vs.) Affray   )
Samuel Owens   )

    This day came the Solicitor General on the part of the State and the
defendant in proper person who being arraigned upon the Bill of Presentment

Pg
456 pleads Not Guilty and for his trial puts himself upon the Couhtry, and the
Solicitor General likewise. Thereupon came a Jury of good and lawful men
To Wit James Chism William U. Coleman, Jacob Norton, William Pirtle, Thomas
Hazlewood, Mansel Crisp, John P. Boidstone, Leroy Burt, Alexander Aiken,
Pg
457 Abner Pillow, Wm. Langhorn & Joshua Hazlewood who being elected empannelled and
sworn the truth to speak upon the issue of Traverse joined upon their oath
do say they find the defendant Not Guilty in manner and form as charged in
the Bill of Presentment. It is therefore considered by the Court that the
defendant go hence without day and that the County pay the costs of this
prosecution.

State)
  vs.) Sci Fa)
William Johnson)
Jacob Ross)

    This day came the Solicitor General on the part of the State and on
motion and by consent of the Court the forfeiture in there case is set aside
on the defendants paying all costs. It is therefore considered that the
State recover against the defendant s her costs on said Sci Fa expended etc.
and the defendants in mercy.

State)
  vs.) Sci Fa)
William Robinson)
John Sheppard)

    This day came the Solicitor General on the part of the State and the
defendants being solemnly called to come into Court and plead to the Sciri
Facias run against and it appearing to the satisfaction of the Court that
said Sci Facias has been made known to said defendants. It is thereupon on
Pg
458 motion considered by the Court that the State recover against the defendants
the sum of one hundred & twenty five dollars each but which may be discharged
by the payment of all costs which have accrued on said Sci Fa & the defendants in mercy.

State)
  vs.) Sci Fa)
Edward Burleson)

    This day came the defendant in propery person and the Solicitor on the
part of the State and for reasons appearing to the satisfaction of the Court.
It is ordered that the forfeiture in the case be set aside and that the defendant pay the costs. Whereupon came the defendant and assumes costs &
discharged etc.

State)
  vs.) Larceney)
Aaron Payton)

    This day came the Solicitor General on the part of the State and on
motion and by assent of the Court a Nolli Prosequi is entered in this
case. And it is ordered by the Court that the County pay the costs etc.

State)
  vs.) Sci Fa)
Josiah Dunn)

    This day came the Solicitor General on the part of the State and moved
the Court for Judgment final against the defendant and it appearing to the
satisfaction of the Court that there has been two returns of Nihil.
    It is therefore considered by the Court that the State recover against
the defendant the sum of one hundred & twenty five dollars penalty and also

Pg
458 the costs of this Sci Fa by the State expended etc. and that he have execution etc.

```
State              )
  vs.) Tippling House    )
Grubbs              )
```
Pg   This day came the Solicitor General on the part of the State and on
459 motion and by assent of the Court a Nolli P rorequi is entered in this case,
and it is considered by the Court that the County pay costs.

```
State              )
  vs. ) Sci Fa     )
James Bond          )
```
This day came the Solicitor General on the part of the State and moved
the Court for final judgment against the defendant and it appearing to the
satisfaction of the Court that there has been two return of Nihil on said
Sci Fa. It is therefore considered by the Court that the State recover of
the defendant the sum of one hundred & twenty five dollars penalty as also
the costs of this Sci Fa by the state expended etc. and that she have execution, etc.

```
State              )
  vs.) Bastardy    )
Martin Elrod        )
```
This day came the Solicitor General on the part of the State and the
said Martin Elrod being solemnly called to come into Court and answer the
State on a charge of Bastardy came not but made default. It is therefore
considered by the Court that the State recover against the said Elrod the
sum of five hundred dollars unless he do make his personal appearance before
the County Court on the 1st Monday after the 1st Monday in July next at
the Court House in the Town of Bolivar and show cause if any he has or
can why judgment final and execution thereof should not be awarded against
him and that a Sciri Facias issue accordingly, etc.

```
State              )
  vs. ) Bail       )
John Dunaway        )
```
This day came the Solicitor General on the part of the State and John
Pg Dunaway Martin Elrod Bail being solemnly called to come into Court and bring
460 with him the body of Martin Elrod to answer the charge of the State for
Bastardy came not but made default. It is therefore considered by the Court
that the state recover against said Dunaway the sum of five hundred dollars
unless he do make his personal appearance before the next County Court on
the 1st Thursday after the 1st Monday in July next then and there to show
cause if any that he has or can why judgment final and execution thereof
should not be awarded against him and that a Sci Facias issue accordingly.

```
State              )
  vs.              )
Robert Hays Jr.    )
Robert Hays         )
```
This day came the Solicitor General on the part of the State and
Robert Hays Jr. being solemnly called to come into Court and answer the
State of Tennessee on a charge for an assault & Battery came not but made
default and Robert Hays Sr. being also solemnly called to come into Court
and bring with him the body of Robert Hays Jr. to answer the State on a
charge for an assault & Battery came not but made default. It is therefore
considered by the Court that the State recover against the said Robert Hays

Pg
460 Jr. and said Robert Hays Sr. the sum of two hundred dollars which unless they
do make their personal appearance before the next County Court on the 1st
Thursday after the 1st Monday in July next then and there to show cause if any
they have or can why Judgment final and execution thereof should not be awarded
against him and that Sciri facias issue accordingly.

Pg   State   )
461   vs.   )
      John Reagan)

This day cames the Solicitor General on the part of the State and it
appearing to the satisfaction of the Court that at the last term of this
Court Judgement was rendered against the said defendant for the sum of six
& one fourth cents fine and costs of the prosecution. It is now considered by
the Court that said Judgment be entered as of last term for the fine and costs
aforesaid.

Lewis S. Giles)
      vs.   )
R. B. Phillips)

On motion and it appearing to the satisfaction of the Court that an
execution had been issued by Joseph W. McKean Esq. a Justice of the Peace for
this County on behalf of Lewis L. Giles against the said R. B. Phillips for
the sum of one hundred dollars debt with interest from the 20 day of March 1829
and 50 cents cost Issd 6th April 1829 and which said execution had come to the
hands of Martin D. Ramsay a Constable of said County and by him for want of
personal property levied on two acres of land lying adjoining Bolivar which
land said R. B. Phillips bought of Thomas James 6th April 1829. It is therefore ordered adjudged and decreed that said land be exposed for sale as the
law directs to satisfy said debt and costs & also the costs of this motion and
that a Venditioni exponas issue accordingly.

Thomas James   )
    vs.) Motion   )
Richie B. Phillips)

On motion and it appearing of the Court that an execution had issued from
Pg Joseph W. McKean a Justice of the Peace for the County on behalf of Thomas James
462 against Richd. B. Phillips for the sum of fifteen dollars debt with interest
from the 20th March 1829, and 50 cents costs Issd. 6th April 1829, and which
said execution had come to the hands of Martin D. Ramsay a Constable of said
County and by him for want of personal property to levy on levied on two acres
of land lying adjoining the town of Bolivar and which land said R. B. Phillips
bought of Thomas James. It is therefore ordered adjudged and decreed that
said land be exposed for sale as the law directs to satisfy said debt and costs
as also the costs of this motion that a venditiona exponas issue accordingly.

Thomas James   )
    vs.) Motion   )
Thomas Evans   )

On motion and it appearing to the satisfaction of the Court that an execution had issued from Joseph W. McKean Esq. a Justice of the Peace for said
County on behalf of Thomas James against Thomas Evans for the sum of four
dollars and 37 cents. Iss'd 6th of April 1829 and 50 cents costs with Interest
from 7th day of Feby. 1829 and which said execution had come to the hands of
Martin D. Ramsay a Constable of said County and by him in default of personal
property levied on one acre of land lying near Bolivar where the said Evans
now lives and bought of D. B. Fuine. It is therefore ordered decreed and adjudged by the Court that said land be exposed for sale as the law directs to

satisfy said debt of four dollars and costs as also the costs of this motion
and that a venditiona Exponas issue accordingly.

Gideonn Pillow   )
    vs. Covenent)Present James Ruffin, Edmund D. Tarver & John Y. Cockeram
Abner Pillow   )   Esq. Justices.

This day came the parties by their attorney and thereupon came the
parties by their attorney and thereupon came a Jury of good and lawful men
To Wit James Chisum, Wm. H. Coleman, Jacob Norton, William Pirtle, Thomas
Hazlewood, Manael Crisp, Wm. R. & Cockeram, Leroy Burt Alexander Aiken,
Wm. R. Webster William Langhorn and Joshua Hazlewood who being elected empannelled and sworn the truth to speak upon the issues joined upon their
oath do say they cannot agree and thereupon a Juror is withdrawn and there
is a mistrial.

                     And the Court adjourned
                     to tomorrow morning
                     9 O'clock
                     James Ruffin
                     Edmund D. Tarver
                     John G. Cockeram

Friday April 10th 1829

The Court met according to adjournment. Present James Ruffin, Edmund
B. Tarver, John Y. Cockeram Esq. Justices] Thos. J. Hardeman Clk., V. D.
Barry Sol. Gen. J. C N. Robertson Shff.

Ordered by the Court that John Mullin be appointed overseer of the
Cotton Gin Road in the place of Reed.

Ordered by the Court that the Commissioners that were appointed at the
January Term of this Court to view the ground for a road from I. Counces
by the way of Middleburg in the direction to La Grange have leave to report
to the July Term of this Court.

Ordered by the Court that Robert A. Dandridge be appointed overseer
in the place of Benjamin Bowers and have all the hands to work under him
that worked under said Bowers.

Ordered by the Court that Robert Hays be appointed overseer of the
road in the place of John P. Boidstone and that have all the hands that formerly worked under said Boidstone.

Ordered by the Court that the following persons to be summoned to
attend at our next County Court July Term to serve as Jurors, To Wit
Edmund Rivers, Chesly D. Key, Daniel C. Hull, James Wood, Josiah Hatley,
Peter Minter, William Sheppard, Egbert C. Sheppard, George D. Cain, Robert
M. Shelton, James Lippett, William Porten, James S. Ewing, Littleton John-
son, Joseph P. Attwood, Anthony Foster, Elijah Rudolph, Edward Philpot,
Alexander C. Blair, John Polk, Benjamin Nabers, Joshua Horne, Richmond
Carwoll, V. D. Gossett, Benjamin Riddle & Bailey Needham, and also Henry
W. Brown & Miles Birdsong to serve as constables and that a Venira Facias
issue accordingly.

Gideon Pillow   )
    vs.) Motion   )
Abner Pillow   )

Pg
465   In this case on motion of the plaintiffs counsel the Plaintiff has leave
to take the depositions of John C aruthers, William Pillow, Isaac Ferrill &
others and Gideon I. Pillow on giving legal notice.

Willis I. Riddle   )
        vs.) Certiovari   )
John L. Goodman   )
Daniel Davis   )

This day came the Plaintiff by his attorney and thereupon moved the Court
here to dismiss the Certiovari of the said defendants. Whereupon all matters
arising on said motion being heard and by the Court here fully understood. It
is considered by the Court that the said Certiovari be dismissed and that the
Plaintiff recover against the defendants and on motion against William A. Mohundro their security the sum of sixty five dollars debt with interest at the
rate of 12½ per cent per annum from the 3'd day of Feby.1829 to this term etc.

Pg John Thurman   )
466   vs.) Motion   )
Martain Taylor   )

In this case the Plaintiff on motion has leave to take depositions in and
out of the State on giving the opposite party on his attorney the legal notice.

State   )
    vs.   ) Dis. House   )
Orice Haaten   )

This day came the defendant by his attorney and moved the Court to arrest
the Judgment in this cause and solem argument had thereon. It is considered
by the Court that the said motion be overruled & that the defendant pay the
costs of this motion.

Mansfield Ware   )
        vs.) use of D. Fentress   )
W. B. Peck Adm.   )
of R. Rivers decd.

This day comes the Plaintiff by his attorney and the Deft. in proper
person who says he cannot gainsay the Plaintiffs action in this behalf and
confesses Judgment for the sum of three hundred and seventeen dollars nineteen
cents debt together with twelve dollars sixty eight cents damages. It is
therefore considered by the Court that the Plaintiff recover against the defendant the debt and damages aforesaid in form aforesaid confessed together
with his costs about his suit in this behalf expended to be levied of the
Pg goods & chattels land etc. of said deceased in his hands to be administered.
467
Ordered that Edward R. Belcher Thomas J. Hardeman and John H. Bills be
Commissioners to settle with Samuel B. Herper, John Martin, Thomas Clift,
True Rebecca Johnson, Joseph Dobbs, Sterling Nuckles, George Martin, Joseph
Hickman, Jane Henry Johnson, John H. Arnols, James Hubbard and other relatives
to their guardean ship according to law & report to next term & that they
notify said guardean of the time & place of said settlement.

Ordered that John H. Arnold be released as Overseer of Road etc.

Ordered by the Court that William R. Cockeram have leave to keep an
ordinary at his now dwelling house, and thereupon came forward and gave bond
with Jacob Martin as his security.

On the petition of William Fulghum praying the Court that Commissioners
be appointed to lay off in leveralty   his portion of a 200 acre tract of land

Pg
467 in the name of Claiborn Lewis & Loddy and it appearing to the satisfaction
of the Court that publication of his intention of presenting said petition
has been made in the Western Statesman a paper printed in the Town of
Bolivar then several times previous to this his petition and six months
preceding said application. It is ordered that John Rosson, Robert Bow,
William B. Robinson, William Simpson and Moore Bishop be appointed Com-
Pg missioners to divide said tract if land and to lay off each claimants part
468 in severality and report to next term.

Vincent Willoughby   )
            vs.) Ca, Sa   )
Walden Fuller   )
Thomas James   )

    This day came the Plaintiff by his attorney and the said Walden Fuller
being solemnly called to come into Court and surrender himself according to
the time and condition of a bond which he the said Fuller had entered into
with the said Willoughby at the time of the survey of the writ of Copus
ad Satis faciendan on him that he would make his appearance before the Court
at this term and make payment of a debt of fifty seven dollars and fity cents
and costs of suit be adjudged before J. B . McDean Esq. a Justice of the
Peace for this County, in order on oath a fair schedule of his property in
order that the same may be sold to satisfy said debt or take the oath of
Insolvency came not but made default. And the said Thomas James his security being solemnly called to come into Court and bring with him the body of
the said Walden Fuller came not but made default.
    Therefore it is considered by the Court that the said Vincent Willoughby
do recover against the said Walden Fuller and Thomas James the said sum of
fifty seven dollars and fifty cents debt with Interest thereon from the
9th day of January 1829 as also the costs on said Judgment as well as the
Pg costs of this motion & that he have execution etc.
469

Edmund Titzhugh use of)
Thos. J. Hardeman   )
        vs.   )
John F. Robertson   )
Almen Dickerson   )

    This day came the Plaintiff by his attorney and the said John H.
Robertson being solemnly called to come into Court and surrender himself
according to the tenor and effect & conditions of a hand which he the
said Robertson had entered into with the said Almen Dickerson as his security at the time of the serving of the writ of Copias ad Satis faciendum
on him which said hands recited that he would make his appearance before the
Court at this term and make payment of a debt of fifty dollars & costs with
interest from the 1st of January 1829 and cost of suit, adjudged before
Francis Shoemake Esq. a Justice of the Peace for said County, or under an
oath a form schedule of his property in order that the same may be sold to
satisfy said debt or take the oath of Insolvency, came not but made
default. And the said Almeron Dickerson his security being solemnly called
to come into Court and bring with him the body of the said Robertson, came
not but made default. Therefore it is considered by the Court that the
said Edward Fitzhugh for the use of etc. do recover against the said John
F. Robertson and Almen Dickerson the said sum of fifty dollars and interest
thereon as also the costs on said Judgment below as well as the costs of this
motion & that he have execution etc.

Walden Fuller   )
Pg   vs.   for Certiovi)
470 Joseph P. Stockton   ))

Pg
470

On motion of Plaintiff counsel and the Petition of Plaintiff being read . It is ordered that Writs of Certiovari and Supercedies issue on the Petition giving bond and security as required by law.

The Jury appointed to assess the damages in the case of the roads running through Col. J. C. N. Robertsons land returned the following report. We of the within named Jury have agreed to assess the damages to said land as to both roads, to forty dollars. R. C. Moore Wm. P. Haden , Green Roper Wm. Ramsay, Nocholas Nail, Joshua Hazlewood.

This day came into open Court Samuel A. Read a minor of fifteen years old and by consent of the Court and his own wish is bound to Henry Kirkland in the art and mastery of brick laying and plastering business had who entered into articles of Indention with the Chairman of the Court of the Adm. for the term of four years.

Obadiah Mathewy   )
    vs.) Certiovari   )
J. F. & W. W. Attwood   )

This day came into Court the said defendants by their atterney and dismiss the said suit from Court. It is therefore considered by the Court that the Plaintiff in the Certiovai do pay the costs of said Certiova etc.

Pg
471

Ordered that William Champion have the following hands to work under his direction from Bunker Hill to the County line (to wit) O. L. Harvy, Hans, Humpheys, Alexander Needham, Saml. Bonds, Blair, Dr. Doxy, Roger, Kilpatrick and Farris with their hands and all their bounds work under his directions.

Ordered that William Ritchey oversee the keeping in repair that part of the Estanaula road that lies between Clear Creek and Charlie Polks odd place and that he have the following hands, Kincan Steele, F. B. Cockeram, Edward Rivers, David Lee, Henry Lee, Wm. Lee Edmund Kirkland, William Woodward, Allen Sumnens, M. New, John Lee Lurey Lee Wm. Wells Joseph Taylor M. Matthews and John Brantly with their hands and all in those bounds to work under him.

George M. Pirtle and Chesley D. Key appointed Commissioners to lay off the widows portion of provisions allowed by law for the Widow Campbell relic of George L. Campbell decd. made a report. Ordered to be recorded.

And the Court adjourned to Court in Course.

Edmund D. Tarver
J. W. McKean
John G. Cockeram

(Written on inside back of book)

Recd. of L. Johnson three dollars this 9th day of Jany. 1829 for tax on 12 pack of cards playing.

www.ingramcontent.com/pod-product-compliance
Lightning Source LLC
Chambersburg PA
CBHW080418270326
41929CB00018B/3071